Presented To:

_____

From:

_____

Date:

_____

PRINCESS WARRIORS

ANOTHER DESTINY IMAGE BOOK BY ROBIN KIRBY-GATTO

Glory to Glory Sisterhood: God's Sorority

AVAILABLE FROM DESTINY IMAGE PUBLISHERS

PRINCESS WARRIORS

ENGAGING SPIRITUAL WARFARE

Robin Kirby-Gatto

DESTINY IMAGE₀ PUBLISHERS, INC.

P.O. Box 310, Shippensburg, PA 17257-0310

"Promoting Inspired Lives."

This book and all other Destiny Image, Revival Press, MercyPlace, Fresh Bread, Destiny Image Fiction, and Treasure House books are available at Christian bookstores and distributors worldwide.

For a U.S. bookstore nearest you, call 1-800-722-6774.

For more information on foreign distributors, call 717-532-3040.

Reach us on the Internet: www.destinyimage.com.

ISBN 13 TP: 978-0-7684-3739-3

ISBN 13 Ebook: 978-0-7684-9010-7

For Worldwide Distribution, Printed in the U.S.A.

1 2 3 4 5 6 7 8 / 15 14 13 12 11

Dedications

To all God's Daughters who choose to not give up on the fight of faith, Princess Warriors for Jesus Christ. Also, I would like to dedicate this book to Camilla, whose name means warrior maiden.

Acknowledgments

I would like to acknowledge God the Father, Jesus Christ, and the Holy Spirit for guiding me in the writing of this book. I want to thank my awesome husband, Rich Gatto, for continually encouraging me through the writing and editing of *Princess Warriors*. Rich, you are the most awesome husband a wife could ever have on earth. I could never do what I do without you in my life and know that the rewards you will have in heaven will be greatly added to with every endeavor God gives me as well as you! I love you My Italian Man! I want to thank all the Princess Warriors who have met with me, prayed with me, and continued to war for the Kingdom of Heaven. I want to thank my sons, Christopher and Matthew, again for being a joy in my life and pressing into the great fight of faith to never give up through all the warfare, the trials and the tribulations we have all gone through as a family! I love you Christopher and Matthew and am so proud of you! In addition, I would like to thank Amy Kay for being a notorious warrior of God to fight alongside me in battle! I love you Amy! I want thank Carla Tsisk and Theresa Harben for your prayers. I want to thank Suzi Whisenant and Dena Lowry for being awesome Princess Warriors with me and the ministries God has given me. I love you, sisters! Finally, I want to thank the entire Destiny Image team, especially Marti Statler, Joyce Forrester and Tracy Shuman for your exhortations, in the publication of the *Princess Warriors* book.

> *The Lord gives the word [of power]; the women who bear and publish [the news] are a great host. The kings of the enemies' armies, they flee, they flee! She who tarries at home divides the spoil [left behind]* (Psalm 68:11-12 AMP).

Endorsements

As a senior adult woman minister of the Gospel for over 30 years, I have never come in contact with anyone male or female with a prophetic voice as my friend Robin Kirby-Gatto. The first time I met her she spoke things to me that only my Lord God in Heaven and I knew. The Lord had spoken to me years ago that I was called to pioneer an end-time restoration revival, and then here comes this young lady prophetess saying just exactly what the Holy Spirit spoke to me. The anointing on Robin is what so many in the Body of Christ covet and are praying for. Jesus Christ told us in John 16:13 that the Holy Spirit would show us things to come. This is that prophetic utterance of things to come. It is a double portion Elijah mantle spoke of in the very last verse of Malachi 4:5-6 and then spoken about John the Baptist in Matthew 11:14. Not only does Robin have the double-portion prophetic mantle, but she also has the double-portion mantle for healing and preaching/teaching a word for these last days. I want you to be sure to read her words in her first book *Glory to God Sisterhood,* as well as this second book, *Princess Warriors.* I want to give another word to pastors and church leaders. Your church will never be the same after seeing and hearing this end-time gift to the Body of Christ.

Dimple McInvale
Pastor Miracle Healing Center
Founder of Millbrook Prayer Room

The Christian life is all about freedom. Robin takes us on a journey giving us the proper tools to break free and find our destiny in God. Beginning with the fear of the Lord, she explains with extreme transparency and with great clarity how we are guilty of closing our heart to God and then reveals the keys of entering into freedom and enjoying a life of walking with the Lord. Robin teaches us how to break free of any bondages and strongholds in our lives that sadly many never confront. Her explanation of various issues of the heart, such as hidden sins, submitting to authority, spiritual warfare, and living a life of praise and victory make this a life-changing book.

Steve Sampson
Evangelist
Author of *Confronting Jezebel* and
Discerning and Defeating the Ahab Spirit

Robin Kirby-Gatto will encourage you to strive to live in your God-given place as a woman in her new book, *Princess Warriors*. Writing out of her own journey to victory, she will tell you how to rise above the tricks and traps of the enemy and show you how God takes you into transformation from glory to glory through Him. You'll enjoy this book as a personal study or a group study.

Cyndi Draughon
Women's Ministries Director
Alabama Assemblies of God

Princess Warriors is a fore-runner for women in this season. It draws us into a true examination of our hearts and gives us a passion to war for Jesus.

Sherry Henderson
The Esther Banquet

Contents

SECTION III: SYMBOLS TO PRINCESS WARRIORS

Foreword

My first invitation to Princess Warriors came in 2004. At that time, the meetings were held in Robin's humble-size living room; therefore, attendance was by invitation only. Holy Ghost instructed Robin who to invite. Then Holy Ghost proceeded to hold the meeting—ministering to all who were there.

Princess Warriors began as an equipping ministry for women, and it still is to this day. The meetings begin with fellowship. Robin provides coffee and muffins/pastries. As each person arrives, the excitement of what is about to occur builds and builds. Each meeting of Princess Warriors takes on a life of its own, led by Holy Ghost. He has free access—it is His meeting. Days, sometimes weeks, before Princess Warriors, the Holy Ghost gives Robin a Word and direction on how He wants the meeting to flow. The Word is always one that touches the lives of each one there. Sometimes worship comes first, sometimes in the middle, and sometimes just before prophetic ministry.

I remember the day that Holy Ghost gave each of us the Sword of the Lord and taught us how to fight. Of course, promptly after this meeting, each of us received the opportunity to swing that sword. The warfare increased, but as Holy Ghost told us, the battle is His and the victory is ours. In a meeting during Purim, He gave us a crown of peace. Prior to the meeting, He showed Robin pears—pears everywhere she looked. He led her to a drawer in her home showing her pears that she had saved for decorating. He instructed Robin to make each of us a crown, each with one of the pears attached. This symbolized His peace and fruitfulness.

Holy Ghost is the host at every meeting and flows through each and every one of us. Those new to the gifts learn and operate in them. Seasoned warriors encourage and coach the babies. This is as the Lord instructs in Ephesians 4:11-12,

And He Himself gave some to be apostles, some prophets, some evangelists, and some pastors and teachers, for the equipping of the saints for the work of the ministry, for the edifying of the body of Christ.

In those early days of Princess Warriors, I was a baby in the Lord. Now I am a seasoned warrior. What I learned at Princess Warriors, I now apply it everyday wherever the Holy Ghost leads me.

Suzy Whisenant
Servant of the Lord Most High

Introduction

The first book of the Glory to Glory Sisterhood series, *Glory to Glory Sisterhood: God's Sorority*, introduced the female gender to the Glory to Glory Sisterhood, which is God's Sorority. The first book addresses areas of how sisters are to treat each other and not to treat each other in the sisterhood. Moreover, it gives us a look at Jesus, the lover of our souls. The first book is the beginning of each sister forming her testimony. The Word of God says that they overcame by the blood of the lamb and the word of their testimony (see Rev. 12:11).

This, the second book, allows sisters to begin a purification process whereby they can be delivered from the enemy's bondage and strongholds. This book will introduce the sisterhood to the fear of the Lord and spiritual warfare. Before we can move to spiritual warfare, we have to look at the fear of the Lord first. Our God is bigger than satan. In order to do effective spiritual warfare, we have to know how big and awesome our God, Jesus, and the Holy Spirit are inside of us.

Enter into this book continuing to yield yourself to the Lord, and allow Him to cut out offensive things that would hinder your spiritual walk. Then be prepared to be equipped with weapons of warfare that will exponentially increase your authority and understanding about your purpose on this earth. In addition, learn the symbols of Princess Warriors, which carry great revelation and meaning as to the call of God on His daughters. God bless you as you walk through the understanding of being a Princess Warrior for Jesus Christ. I wanted to start the book off by giving the reader a picture of what I believe Holy Spirit wants the reader to have a revelation of in regards to being a Princess Warrior. Understand this is not a vision, only a prompting by Holy Spirit to compel women into their position.

God sits in Heaven on His throne. In front of Him are seven spirits burning and thundering and lightening. He beckons forth the council of angels who watch over God's Dreaded Champions; for it is the Dreaded Champions who cause the demons of hell to tremble. The scene shifts to a war room where generals are called; the generals are head angels over the troops of the Lord of Hosts. There has been a war waging since the fall of lucifer, and this war has not ceased. Lucifer, who is now satan, wages war against God's saints night and day without a moment of rest.

Throughout many centuries on earth, God has brought forth great warriors who would fight the fight of faith, not giving up on the Commander of the Lord of Hosts. It is now the 21st century and God is calling forth a new battalion of champions. These champions are composed of men, women, boys, and girls who were predestined before the foundations of the earth to come forth in this time. In the war room, God's head angels are summoned and given orders to prepare the new league of warriors, the Dreaded Champions, for the end-time battle.

Jehovah's Head angel over battle, Michael, is there and gives orders to the head generals: "Devoted hosts of Jehovah it is time to gather the chosen ones for the battle. Many of these chosen ones will fight with a love for Jehovah because of where they came from. Many have been pulled out of satan's horrid darkness and brought into God's marvelous light, knowing the depth of their redemption to the Most High God through Jesus Christ." Michael's call from Jehovah goes forth from God's war room, thrusting forth from the third Heaven, where God's throne is, to the first heaven, where earth is established. Angels descend upon many people who seem ordinary enough; however, they are men, women, and children who have committed their lives, not loving their life unto death, to Jehovah God.

God's Holy Spirit wanted me to put into picture a story, although fictitious in nature, portraying to the reader, the supernatural occurrences that take place outside of our own reality. This again is not an actual occurrence in every detail. But with some of the conversations between the angel and myself, it portrays the conversations I have actually had with the Lord in our intimate communions together. However, out of obedience God wanted me to put it into a picture so that the reader, His Princess Warrior, would have a vision of being commissioned as well by the Lord.

Robin was in her prayer room at home, worshiping the Lord and bathing in the beauty of Holiness. An angel, Hieremias, who was summoned by one of God's head angels, entered the room and greeted Robin. "Blessed are you daughter of Jehovah. I have been sent to you for a special assignment by the Most High," Hieremias stated.

Robin, startled and amazed, was left speechless and sitting on the floor unable to move. Hieremias continued, "Jehovah is summoning all His Dreaded Champions forth, and you were selected for this assignment."

Robin was still astonished, being captivated by the beauty of this ornate angel, who wore a necklace carrying the gold seal of God. Robin had never seen anything like this. Hieremias was suited with armor over a deep blue robe that looked, she thought, as the waters in Greece. The armor was a brilliant fiery color, and the fire moved throughout the armor as if the armor was alive while Hieremias wore it. His hair was long and blonde, and he wore a thin gold crown around his head, similar to the crown of holiness depicted for the priests in the day of Moses. Hieremias feet were shod with beautiful burnished sandals that had the same captivating color as his armor.

"Why me?!" Robin gasped. "I am no one, just an ordinary middle aged woman. Why would Jehovah want me for His special Dreaded Forces?"

Hieremias responded by playing a scene that Robin knew all too well only because she never wanted to forget it as long as she lived. The scene was from 1998, when Robin had fallen in a drunken stupor yet again (as she had many times that year).

"God, I hate this alcohol! How did I get here, God?! I used to serve You faithfully! I was always a good girl growing up, and I served You and was rejected over and over because I chose You! I know I should not have rebelled in my anger against You, God, blaming You for everything. I'm sorry God! Help me, Jesus! I cannot stand to live like this anymore. God, please take my life; I hate living. The pain, the agony, of living anymore is beyond what I can bare! I'm worthless; everyone is so mean to me, calling me a drunkard

and whore. God please remove me from living. I'm not a life worth sparing anymore, God! My boys deserve better! It would be better if I were dead...please, God...Please!"

Hieremias looked at Robin while she was weeping deeply from a place only Jehovah God knew. As she sobbed, she cried out, **"Thank You, God! Thank You, Jesus! Thank You! Thank You! Thank You!"**

Hieremias watched Robin in great awe, wondering how humans can push through so much darkness and cry out and love a Jehovah God whom they've never seen, love Jesus whom they've never met, and believe in Jehovah God's Holy Spirit only by faith. Hieremias loved watching the faith of humankind continuously because so much of God's glory in those moments gave him such great revelation.

Hieremias then went to Robin and lifted her bowed down head. "Robin what happened after that? Do you remember?"

Robin, still undone and unable to speak, kept gasping over and over again as she prepared to open her mouth. Hieremias restated patiently, "Robin you remember....You remember what happened after that."

"Yes, I promised God that if He ever brought me out of that moment, I would die for Him! **God!! Thank You!! Thank You!!** *That I would serve Him all the days of my life."*

Hieremias then spoke, "Jehovah God at that time wrote your name down in the book of Dreaded Champions and started commissioning angels to prepare you for the day of battle when He would call His Dreaded Champions forth."

"Me! Why Me!" Robin exclaimed.

Hieremias slowly smiled and responded "Why Robin, have you not known....You are one of the great lovers of Jehovah, one of His mighty worshipers! The Dreaded Champions are the ones who love Jehovah God and their King, Jesus, more than all the other saints."

Slowly Hieremias drew somethings from underneath his blue robe, from the fiery armor—a sword, a crown, and a ball filled with fire. "Robin, today Jehovah commissions you into your call as a Dreaded Champion, and it is time to go to battle with the other chosen ones. Here is the sword that you will use as you battle the enemy. This crown is the crown of victory and gives you the same victory that Jesus Christ walked in while He was on the earth. This fire ball is filled with the fire of Jehovah and will give you strength continuously throughout the battle. Use these weapons well. Delight yourself in the fear of the Lord as Jesus did when He walked the earth and your judgments will be the righteous judgments of Jehovah Himself."

You Princess Warriors are some of God's *greatest Dreaded Champions!* You have been pulled out of deep pits, in which the enemy tried to keep you bound. Jesus reached down with His hand of redemption and pulled you out and called you and appointed you and washed you clean with His blood that cleanses sin. You are a *Dreaded Champion!*

SECTION 1

Fear of the Lord

The Beginning of
Walking in Wisdom

In this first section, we will be studying the fear of the Lord. This is what will propel all women into living a life of purification and holiness unto the Lord. This book will introduce you to a Holy God and prepare you for spiritual warfare. In book three, *At His Feet*, you will receive deliverance from bondages and strongholds. Therefore, read this book prior to going on to book three, and you will walk in a great freedom from bondages. God is doing things suddenly. When He brought Moses to deliver his people from Pharaoh, it was a "sudden" deliverance. Likewise, after you read this book and go into book three, you will experience a sudden deliverance from your bondage. A *bondage* is sin you have trouble letting go of or being set free from. You find yourself doing the very thing you hate, as the apostle Paul puts so well (see Rom. 7:15). Strongholds are contrary beliefs against the Word of God that exalt themselves above the Word of God in your mind (see 2 Cor. 10:3-5). To overcome strongholds, you have to have a transformed mind. Romans 12:2 states, *"Do not be conformed to this world but be transformed by the renewal of your mind ..."* (RSV).

When I came to understand that I am accepted in Christ, my eyes were opened to my sins. I realized that the love of God turned me to repent of my sins and to come to a loving Savior. Initially, when I returned to the Lord, I was still in bondage to sin and needed help walking through purification. At this time, I was then introduced to the fear of the Lord. I studied the fear of the Lord at great length and felt the anointing of God through John Bevere's teachings.

As I wrote this book, I felt a leading of the Holy Spirit to put a teaching in this book on the fear of the Lord to which I yield myself. This teaching is not in detail or length, as many other authors expand upon it, so I encourage you to do a further study. This is an introduction to my experience in the fear of the Lord and gives you a foretaste of how radically it can change your life. The fear of the Lord can be seen in the way you approach God, sin, complaining, dealing with authority, and submission.

And Moses said to the people, Fear not; for God has come to prove you, so that the [reverential] fear of Him may be before you, that you may not sin" (Exodus 20:20AMP).

1

Introduction to the Spirit of the Fear of the Lord

Before we begin, please pray this prayer aloud:

Dear Lord, I ask You to open the eyes of my understanding. Lord, give me wisdom and revelation regarding the fear of the Lord. I welcome You, Holy Spirit of God, and ask You to teach me regarding the fear of the Lord. In Jesus' name, amen.

WHEN GOD MADE HUMANITY

When God created humans in the beginning, He said let "*Us*" make people in *"Our image, in Our likeness"* (Gen. 1:26 NIV). The Us and Our that God refers to in this Scripture is the Holy Trinity. The Holy Trinity is made up of the Father God, God's Son Jesus, and God's Holy Spirit. Therefore, when

God spoke the first person, Adam, into being, He made him in the image of Him, the Son (Jesus), and His Holy Spirit. It is necessary to understand this before we proceed with the fear of the Lord because we are going to see that the fear of the Lord is actually one of the dimensions of God's Holy Spirit.

We are made up of body, soul, and spirit. All three of these components make up all of us. However, our souls are still a part of us, whether or not they are present with the body. The soul is separate from the body, but while we are alive, it is also a part of the body. This is the best way I've heard it explained in understanding the Trinity, which is the Godhead. Jesus has many components. First and foremost, Jesus is the Word. (see John 1:1) Moreover, Jesus is God manifested in flesh because He came as son of man and Son of God (see Luke 4:41; Luke 12:8). He left His place in glory and humbled Himself to come into earth as son of man, but He is also Son of God (see Phil. 2:7-9). He is both separate, but a part of God (see John 14:10-11). He has characteristics that manifest God to us, such as mercy, compassion, patience, forbearance, boldness, and much more (see John 14:9). Jesus even states that He and the Father are one (see John 14:11).

The Spirit of God is first seen in Genesis after God created the heavens and the earth. *"Now the earth was formless and empty, darkness was over the surface of the deep, and the Spirit of God was hovering over the waters"* (Gen. 1:2 NIV). God is in Heaven, and He sent forth His Spirit to the earth to hover over the waters. Therefore, although His Spirit was hovering over the earth while God was in Heaven, the Spirit is part of God.

God's Spirit has many dimensions. We as women have many dimensions to us, such as mother, wife, daughter, friend, worker, and so forth. In the same manner, God's spirit has many dimensions. The fear of the Lord is part of the Spirit of God, which exists in front of His throne room. This is mentioned in Revelation when John the Revelator records from the Word of God,

From the throne came flashes of lightning and the rumble of thunder. And in front of the throne were seven torches with burning flames. This is the sevenfold Spirit of God (Revelation 4:5 NLT).

God's Spirit is sevenfold, which is what the seven torches represent. This is seen in the Jewish tradition of the Menorah, which is a lamp stand bearing seven holders for candles or flames.

There are seven dimensions to the Spirit of God. The prophet Isaiah identifies the seven spirits of God when he prophesies of the coming Christ who will walk in the fullness of God by His Spirit while on the earth.

The Spirit of the LORD will rest on Him—the Spirit of wisdom and of understanding, the Spirit of counsel and of power [might], *the spirit of knowledge and of the fear of the LORD—and He will delight in the fear of the LORD...* (Isaiah 11:2-3 NIV).

The first dimension to God's Spirit is what is called **the Spirit of the Lord.** This is the actual Spirit of the Lord, which is the essence of God. This is seen in Isaiah 61:1, *"The Spirit of the Lord God is upon me...."* The next dimension is **the Spirit of Wisdom,** which is seen in Proverbs 8. Next, there is **the Spirit of Understanding** seen in Proverbs 3 and 4. *"Wisdom is supreme; therefore get wisdom. Though it cost all you have, get understanding"* (Prov. 4:7 NIV). Then there is **the Spirit of Counsel,** which is seen in Proverbs 8 and 27.

Next, is **the Spirit of Power (Might):** This is seen in the demonstrations of miracles as well as in strength. He is demonstrated in the life of Samson (see Judg. 14:6), where the Spirit of God came upon him in power, and He is abundantly displayed in the life of Jesus when He healed people and performed miracles. The next dimension of God's Spirit is *the Spirit of Knowledge,* which is seen all throughout the Scripture, especially in Proverbs. Finally, *the Spirit of the Fear of the Lord* is seen in the Proverbs, as well. *"The fear of the LORD is the beginning of knowledge, but fools despise wisdom and discipline"* (Prov. 1:7 NIV).

All of the fullness of God's Spirit is seen throughout the Word of God. He is abundantly displayed in the Proverbs.

Jesus Delighted in the Fear of the Lord

Jesus delighted in the fear of the Lord, as written by the prophet Isaiah. In Him, the fullness of the Spirit of God, for the first time, rested upon a man—Jesus, who was both fully God and fully man. When the Spirit of God rests on a person, He takes residence in and inhabits the person; thus, He possesses us throughout our journey on earth.

God is purposeful, and everything He does is with purpose that is higher than our thinking. *"For as the heavens are higher than the earth, so are My ways higher than your ways, and My thoughts than your thoughts"* (Isa. 55:9 KJV). Therefore, the dimensions of the Spirit of God have a purpose. For example, the Spirit of Wisdom is to offer us godly wisdom that is not of this world. The wisdom of the Lord is foolish to the world (see 1 Cor. 1:20). Solomon had godly wisdom when he first took the throne as king. Solomon had such wisdom that the wealth given him was beyond any measure imaginable (see 2 Chron. 1:9-11).

The Spirit of Understanding has the purpose of helping us take in the knowledge of a matter and comprehend it, thereby giving us a revelation. For example, God's Spirit of Understanding has helped me in obtaining my law degree. I can testify that when I first entered law school I did not understand the law of contracts. I had knowledge of the matter and studied it for hours upon hours. However, later my understanding opened up to where I could comprehend it. Whereas before I only had knowledge of the law, because God gave me understanding, I then actually had a revelation of the law of contracts. I had a map in my head of how the entire law of contracts was created and applied. This is only a God thing and cannot be explained away. This is seen many times in young children who are brilliant beyond comprehension.

I have laid this foundation in order to build up to this point. The whole purpose of the relationship (dimension) of the Spirit of God, which encapsulates the fear of the Lord, is to keep us from sin, lead us in lives of holiness, and bring us into places where wisdom and understanding can begin in our lives. Therefore, if Jesus, being fully God and fully man, delighted in the fear of the Lord, then shouldn't we, too?

Jesus had to have the fullness of the Spirit of God rest upon Him while He was walking the earth in order to live a perfect life and offer Himself as a spotless sacrifice, perfect and holy, in order to redeem humankind from death and hell. With this information, do you think it might be advantageous to find out what the fear of the Lord is and delight in it as Jesus did?

QUESTIONS:

1. Do you have trouble keeping the Word of God (commandments and instructions of the Bible)?

2. Are there any strongholds (mindsets) that make you feel rejected, abandoned, forsaken, or unaccepted by God? Identify your strongholds that exalt themselves

in your mind. (i.e. You think that you are not smart enough or that others do not respect you).

3. Can you commit to reading the Word of God and asking Him to give you the fear of the Lord? Can you yield yourself completely to God and allow Him to deliver you from these strongholds?

4. Do you have bondage(s) in any area of your life where you continually sin? Do you have struggles keeping the Word of God? If so, identify here what bondage(s) you want to be set free from. If you do not confront the bondage(s), then you cannot deal with them.

2

Looking at God
and Dealing With Sin

*In your anger do not sin; when you are on your beds, search
your hearts and be silent. Selah* (Psalm 4:4 NIV).

DO NOT SIN

If you read book one, *The Glory to Glory Sisterhood: God's Sorority,* you are already aware of the many bondages and strongholds I acquired due to rejection in my life. The strongholds in my mind said that I was not accepted, but instead that I was forsaken by God and was too bad of a person to come to Him. Some of the things that I was in bondage to were alcoholism and promiscuity, as well as rebellion toward authority.

Before I became in bondage to sin, I feared God and was submissive to God's Word. I had a great love for God in my youth and would have never considered committing these sins. However, after being beaten up by the enemy and listening to his lies, I lost something that I had in my youth, which was the fear of the Lord.

GRANDMA JESSIE

I remember living across the street from a Baptist church when I was 6 years old. My late grandmother, Jessie McCoy, made me dresses that reached down to the ground, which I loved because I felt like a princess. I would wear these to church each Sunday. I couldn't wait to get to church on Sundays when I was a little girl because I felt so alive there, so at peace. Many times, I sat in worship service really listening to the pastor's message. I was not a perfect child, but I knew that I loved Jesus with all that was within me. I had such a strong passion for Jesus, so much so that I felt as though I would explode.

As I grew up in the Baptist church, I encountered a reverence for God. My reverence for God was not only head knowledge, but had become an experience. I cannot explain how it began; all I remember was that I could feel God's holiness and was reverent toward His sanctuary and His ways. I did not want to be irreverent toward Him. At this same time that I had a holy fear of God, I was not afraid of Him because I loved Him. It almost felt as though I was on holy ground each time that I stepped into the church. I kept this practice for most of my adolescent years; it was in my junior year of high school that things changed.

In my junior year, I had a relationship with a senior boy at school who left me for "greener pastures." Something happened in my soul that changed me. I had a wound that I did not take to the Lord, but instead tried fixing myself. As a result, I treated this wound by looking outside to others for acceptance. I began doing things that were considered rebellious toward God and His holy temple, my body. I began experimenting with alcohol and started dating boys I would not have even considered before. The enemy had deceived me into believing that I should fear man, not referring to a specific gender, simply fearing others, (I really prefer the "fear of man in all instances here rather than the "fear of people" since it relates to a particular demonic spirit that I am referring to here), and consequently, my fear of the Lord grew cold.

Looking back over my life, the Holy Spirit revealed to me that it was at that time, when I came to have fear of man, that I lost the fear of the Lord. I had replaced the Spirit of God's fear of the Lord with the fear of man. No longer did the Spirit of God's fear of the Lord rest on me; it lifted. Because I broke relationship with God by quenching His Spirit in my life, the fear of the Lord lifted off of me. Therefore, I ended up falling into sin, because it is the fear of the Lord that keeps us out of sin.

I Did Not Love Jesus

At the time that I was in bondage, I believed and felt as though I loved God, although I did not fear Him. However, the Word says that Jesus knows who loves Him because it is those who keep His commandments (see John 14:15). Therefore, although I believed that I loved Jesus, I did not, because I did not keep His commandments. I was in flat-out rebellion and in bondage to everything. The enemy had me deceived into thinking that I loved Jesus, but according to God's Word, He cannot lie (see Num. 23:19). Therefore, if God is not lying, then I am. I professed that I loved Jesus, but my actions demonstrated that in reality I did not love Jesus while I was in rebellion. Instead, I began to make people in my life my idols. I loved people and the world and put those up as god in my life.

My desire to be accepted by people could be compared to a woman committing adultery against her husband. Similar to the adulterous woman, I was breaking my commitment to my God, and I had lost the fear of Him. I lost fear of Him finding me doing anything that would hurt Him. I was not concerned about receiving consequences for my adulterous relationship, because all I wanted was to have a good time and please myself by seeking to have people accept me.

The devil instigates these adulterous relationships through many of his devices, such as making people feel as though God let them down, that the dreams He promised them will not come to pass, and that they are a failure for the Kingdom, and so forth. When people believe these lies, they begin to desire the support and affirmation of the world and other people. However, what these people are really doing is putting their fists in God's face and saying, "What I have with You is not good enough for me. Moreover, because my heart feels broken, I think that I'll just go have another lover until our flame is renewed."

They leave an open door to return to Jesus and by their actions say, "By the way Jesus, don't divorce me; just wait till I'm through being in bed with another lover" (the world, people, lust, and so forth). How preposterous on our part, how arrogant and presumptuous for us to think that relationship with the world is not enmity with God.

> *You adulterous people, don't you know that friendship with the world is hatred toward God? Anyone who chooses to be a friend of the world becomes an enemy of God* (James 4:4 NIV).

QUENCHING THE SPIRIT OF GOD

I had a difficult time staying in relationship with the Spirit of God. I had no concern with our relationship, but rather focused on how I was feeling with my relationships with people.

My relationships in the natural interfered with and distorted my relationship with God. I allowed that distortion to severe my relationship with God, thereby quenching the Spirit of God, which removed the fear of the Lord out of my life (see 1 Thess. 5:19).

The only thing that I could see while I was feeling the pain of my hurt was my past devotion to God and how I was now being let down. I had been consecrated unto God and as a result lost my boyfriend in my sophomore year because I would not be intimate with him. I was not intimate with that young man whom I had been in relationship with for nearly two years because I loved and feared God. In fact, my ex-boyfriend went to church with me, and as a result, I felt I had a hand in him growing spiritually. Moreover when he left me, it was for another girl who would be intimate with him, unlike me. To put insult to injury, he brought the girl to my church when I was singing a solo that night, and they had the nerve to sit there in front of me while I was singing to the whole church. I asked God, "How much more do *I* have to suffer?" (Of course, that is no huge amount of suffering because many people go through much more than that in their adolescence).

I had felt as though *I* was serving God, being a "good girl," and the thanks that *I* got for that was getting dumped by my boyfriend because I wanted to be a virgin. All I knew was that I was suffering for my conviction to be "pure" for my God.

I got through that, and then in my junior year of high school, the senior whom I dated left me for "greener pastures." I had come to the point where I basically told God that I had kept myself for Him and was a "good girl," and as a result of being pure, I was getting my heart broken. I felt as though many girls my age were not being pure, but were drinking, being promiscuous, and the like, whereas I was being devoted to God.

I wasn't going to jump into everything at one time in regard to being like the world, but after being angry, I decided to start out drinking one drink. After the drink, I didn't feel the pain of my wounded heart. Then the next time I drank a couple more drinks, and I felt even better than before. Before I knew it, I had made it a habit and was drinking full-blown going into college. I had totally lost the fear of the Lord by the time that I arrived at college for my freshman year.

The only word in my life at that time was *I*. Life was all about *me*. I did not concern myself with how my Savior, Jesus Christ, left His Throne of Glory and stepped out of Heaven, came to earth as a child, and went through rejection, shame, and being despised and mutilated so that I could be redeemed to God fully. He went through more than I could ever imagine. But I had become so distorted by the fear of man that I then removed myself from relationship with God because all I could see was *I* and not God, who is I AM.

OTHER REBELS

The Bible demonstrates a similar rebellion among the people of Israel in their Exodus from Egypt. They saw Egypt (the world) and how they had lived with luxury and enjoyment. Although the Israelites were slaves, being whipped into obedience by hard taskmasters and building the Egyptian empire, they still observed how the Egyptians lived, and as a result, they desired the same lifestyle.

Similarly, I felt as though I was being spiritually beaten by the world when I would not give into temptation and protect my chastity. The young ladies who would give into promiscuity were benefiting because they were getting my boyfriends. I was watching how other young people were committing sin and appeared to be getting away without having consequences to their sin. They were living in a way that pleased their flesh and emotions. Eventually, as I observed the behaviors of the young ladies who were living like this, I begin to desire their lifestyle. I wanted to please my flesh and emotions. My flesh had been screaming, "love me, desire me, and give me attention." My emotions were saying, "I want to feel loved, I want to feel desired, and I want to feel important." However, the only one who could make me feel loved, desired, and important was Jesus. Since I turned to the world to fulfill these desires, I would remain unfulfilled until I returned to Jesus.

When the Israelites were freed from the Pharaoh of Egypt, by Moses, and went into the desert, they left with much of the Egyptian treasures and were no longer subject to being treated brutally by hard task masters. Moreover, they saw the hand of God move on their behalf to not only make a safe escape for them through the Red Sea, but also to destroy their enemies by the very waters that were parted for them. God had made Israel His chosen nation to bless them and to spread the knowledge of His Glory in the earth. They were to be a people who were set apart (see Ps. 4:3).

However, they felt as though their commitment to the Lord was not enough to satisfy them. They had witnessed the Egyptians living lives of luxury and wealth, and the fact that they were not serving God was an insult to the cruelty that had been bestowed upon God's people during their slavery. The Egyptians acted on the desires and lusts of their flesh, and the Israelites found themselves acting like the Egyptians (see. Num. 11:5).

This was exactly how I felt about my committing to be chaste before God and undefiled by people. I was hurt at the very fact that I had chosen to remain set apart from the rest of the world and keep my purity as "unto the Lord." Like the Israelites, I began to complain and eventually started drinking.

The Israelites were out in the desert and celebrating the joyful miracles of the Lord when He delivered them. After seeing the great miracle of the parting of the Red Sea, they had the audacity to complain when they had no food. They stated that it was Moses' desire to bring them to their death. The Lord heard their grumbling and did bring forth food, but He was not pleased with their grumbling (see. Num. 11:1). God told the Israelites to take the Promised Land, promising to help them, but they even grumbled about that, doubting God's word (see Num. 14:1).

GOD HATES COMPLAINING

Likewise the decision to turn away from the Spirit of God's fear of the Lord begins when you start grumbling or complaining (which is discussed in detail in the next chapter). God *hates* complaining! It is as though you are saying, "God, Your miracles, Your love, and Your goodness stink." If you had done something special for your children, and instead of them appreciating your gift or love, they turned to your face and said, "I hate this gift and could care less about you," what would you do? More than likely, you would not grab them and love them and say, "Oh, that's alright! I understand." No! You would rebuke them and send them to their rooms. You would distance yourself from them.

Complaining is distinguishable from pouring out your soul as we see Hannah do in First Samuel 1:12-15. Hannah in First Samuel one pours out her soul, her heart, to God to unveil the anguish that was already resident within her soul. She did not complain to the Lord, but simply bared her soul and was doing it in a respectful, reverent manner. Complaining is when you have no respect or reverence, it is the absence of reverence and being centered on yourself. Pouring out your soul recognizes that it is not about us but that if we are going to serve God's call in our lives we empty ourselves of anything that would be a tear or wound in our soul, something that would be a stumbling block.

Likewise, we quench the Spirit of God when we complain and gripe about our life circumstances. God is a good God, and He will not allow us to be tempted more than we can bear (see 1 Cor. 10:13). It is the fear of the Lord that keeps us from committing sin period, and complaining and griping are sin because they go against the Word of God that says:

> *I will tell of the kindnesses of the LORD, the deeds for which He is to be praised, according to all the LORD has done for us—yes, the many good things He has done for the house of Israel, according to His compassion and many kindnesses* (Isaiah 63:7 NIV).

When we complain or gripe, we are essentially stating that God is not compassionate or kind.

The Word of God says that in our anger we should not sin (see Eph. 4:26). I had become angry about my circumstances when my boyfriends left me for "greener grass" due to my being chaste and pure before God. I had not searched my heart in the midst of these circumstances, but rather closed the door to my heart and instead began to complain and gripe about how my life was compared to the young ladies who were stealing my boyfriends. As a result, my anger turned to sin.

The Word of God says that sin is lawlessness (see 1 John 3:4). Therefore, if we break the law of God, the Word, then we are in sin. Cain experienced anger when he became displeased because God did not receive his offering, though He received his brother Abel's offering.

Then the LORD said to Cain, "Why are you angry? Why is your face downcast? If you do what is right, will you not be accepted? But if you do not do what is right, sin is crouching at your door; it desires to have you, but you must master it" (Genesis 4:6-7 NIV).

Cain was angry, but instead of turning to God and doing what was right, he sinned. The Word of God demonstrates that sin, which opposes holiness, is an entity that "crouches" at the door of our hearts and desires to have us if we allow sin to come in. Moreover, God told Cain to master sin. *Master,* according to *Webster's,* means that "one has authority of another." Therefore, God is telling us, as children of God, to have authority over sin. How do we do that? We can only master sin through the Spirit of God's fear of the Lord.

CHANGE MY HEART GOD

The Lord wanted to change the hearts of the Israelites, and the way to do that was to bring them to a holy encounter with Almighty God. Moses came to the people to prepare them to meet with God. They were told to consecrate themselves for three days and to prepare to meet with the Lord. However, when the time came, the people were full of fear because they saw the thunder and lightning and heard the trumpet and saw smoke on the mountain. They told Moses to go speak to God himself because they thought that they would die if they drew near. However, Moses said something so paradoxical *"And Moses said unto the people, fear not: for God is come to prove you, and that His fear may be before your faces, that ye sin not"* (Exod. 20:20 KJV).

You might say to yourself, *"What a paradox."* God was saying that the Israelites were not to be afraid, and He was also saying that He was coming to test them so that the fear of God would be with them so that they might not sin. He didn't want them to be afraid, yet He did—what does it mean?

When we go through a process of purification, we are not even sure of what all is inside of our hearts. Only God is aware of the iniquities (sins) in our hearts. What is inside of our hearts is what motivates our speech toward and about everything (see Luke 6:45). Jesus stated that people have either evil treasure (sin nature) or good treasure (godly nature) in their hearts.

David cries in the Psalms, *"Search me, O God, and know my heart; test me and know my anxious thoughts"* (Ps. 139:23 NIV). David asked God to test him. That is what God was doing to the Israelites. He was bringing them to Himself (although in His holiness and majesty, it is fearful) in order that the fear of God would be placed in them to keep them from sinning. It is clear that the Israelites did not know the fear of the Lord because of all the sins that they committed while in the desert. They had cut off relationship with the Spirit of God's fear of the Lord. It was God's position to introduce them to the Spirit of the fear of the Lord so that they would not sin.

Webster's Dictionary defines *test* as "an examination, experiment or trial as to prove the value or ascertain the nature of something." It also is identified as "to refine metal, as in cupel." *Cupel* is defined as a hearth for refining metals. The cupellation process is a means at which impurities in metals are separated. It is an examination of what contents are in the metal. The metals are tried (tested) to establish their value or ascertain their nature. Just as the metals are tested through a process of cupellation, God was testing the people of Israel in order to establish the fear of the Lord in His people. He needed to bring them through a process whereby any fear outside of the fear of the Lord would be gleaned away from them so that His fear in them would be established.

Without the fear of the Lord, the people of Israel would remain in a sinful lifestyle. It was the fear of the Lord that would keep them from sinning. *Keep* is defined as "to maintain or cause to stay or continue in a specified condition, position." God wanted His people to maintain a position whereby they would not sin. He wanted them in essence to *master sin!* Therefore, the way Israel would master sin is by the fear of the Lord. You can see this distinguished in Moses and the Israelites.

PLEASE SEND SOMEONE ELSE

Moses, who had the fear of the Lord, had gone back to a place where he would surely face the fear of man and be an outcast from the world. He had a pleasant life in the desert, living a life of peace before returning to Egypt as the deliverer. It was not only the love of God that motivated Moses to fulfill his destiny in God's Kingdom; it was also the fear of God that put action to his plan. When Moses came to the burning bush and God told him that he was to be the deliver, initially he didn't want to go. The Lord showed him miracles that he was to perform in front of Pharaoh, which included a staff that would turn into a snake and power to bring about and heal leprosy.

Still Moses response was, *"Oh Lord, I have never been eloquent, neither in the past nor since you have spoken to your servant. I am slow of speech and tongue"* (Exod. 4:10 NIV). God's response was:

> *"Who gave man his mouth? Who makes him deaf or mute? Who gives him sight or makes him blind? Is it not I, the LORD?" But Moses said "O Lord, please send someone else to do it"* (Exodus 4:11-13 NIV).

Then we see at this response the Lord's anger burned against Moses and informed him how Moses would speak through his brother Aaron and sent him away. This is when Moses left to go on his assignment from the Lord. From this began a great relationship between man and God stemming from the encounter Moses had with the Spirit of God's fear of the Lord. Moses had come to know God's ways, and he never desired to leave the presence of God.

The reason why I do what I do for God, the ministries (God's Firewall, 22 IS 22, Princess Warriors, and Glory to Glory Sisterhood) is a combination of my love for Him and my relationship with the Spirit of the Fear of the Lord. Holy Spirit has made me an undone lover of my King Jesus! I'm compelled to do work for Him out of love, and am pleased to because I do not want to disobey Him. I love to obey Him, and it is what I live for. Remember, Jesus states, *"He who has My commandments and keeps them, it is he who loves Me."* (John 14:21). Therefore my obedience displays my love and affection for Him.

On the other hand, the Israelites, who had been in slavery for generations and who were treated with contempt by the Egyptians, were an ungrateful people. They had grown up generation after generation only to watch each other grow weak under the rule of the Egyptians. God had brought deliverance to them, and the only thing the Israelites did was gripe and complain about everything that they had need of. Moreover, they treated God with contempt by stating that they should have stayed in Egypt because things were better for them there. God told Moses:

> *How long will these people treat Me with contempt? How long will they refuse to believe in Me, in spite of all the miraculous signs I have performed among them?* (Numbers 14:11 NIV).

They only worshipped God when He did things to meet their desires. God's anger toward them was stirred, and as a result of their irreverence, they received the consequences, which were plagues and other judgments (see. Num. 11:33). God is not to be mocked.

> *Do not be deceived: God cannot be mocked. A man reaps what he sows. The one who sows to please his sinful nature, from that nature will reap destruction; the one who sows to please the Spirit, from the Spirit will reap eternal life* (Galatians 6:7-8 NIV).

The fear of the Lord cleanses us from our sin and brings us to a position of becoming holy (see Num. 15:40). The best analogy I can think of to compare this paradigm to that of deadly radiation. In some movies, we see a place where there is such a large amount of radiation that if it comes into contact with human flesh or air passage it will bring about sudden death. The radiation is present, regardless of the fact that people are unable to see it. If people walk into that area unprotected, regardless of how they feel about it, they will die.

Likewise, God's holiness is with Him. He cannot help that He is Holy; it is a fact and it cannot be changed. He is what He is. What He can do is help protect us so that when we come into contact with His holiness we will not fall over dead. Sin cannot stand in the presence of God's holiness. It's analogous to us coming into a deadly room of radiation without a proper suit that will withstand the harmful effects of it. Likewise, when we come into contact with God, we have to wear the righteousness of Jesus Christ. We do not walk in our own righteousness, but that of Jesus Christ. The Spirit of God's fear of the Lord influences us to walk in the righteousness of Jesus Christ, keeping us from ungodliness and thereby creating holiness in us. God tells us to *"be holy, because I am holy"* (1 Pet. 1:16 NIV).

The level of God's presence at Mount Sinai where He wanted to meet with His people was so heavy that purification was required. There are different levels of His presence, and when we encounter the heavy, weighty presence of God's glory, we have to make sure that we are seeking Him with pure hearts.

The Spirit of the fear of the Lord tells us that we need to put on holiness, which is the righteousness of Jesus and which allows the sin that is in us to be exposed by Holy Spirit and removed. Returning to the radiation analogy, if we have knowledge, by some measuring instrument, that there is deadly radiation in a specific location and that there is a suit that will allow us to go into the room without being harmed in any way, then we would wear it. The fear of the Lord is the measuring instrument whereby we know what God's holiness is and how to come near Him. It is an indicator that tells us, "Wait a minute; if you walk into God's presence as it was at Mount Sinai without reverence of Him (fear of the Lord) and with sin in your life, you are going to be ill-prepared to meet Him, and you will face terrible consequences." That is why the Israelites had to prepare to meet with God at the base of Mount Sinai. This kind of fear is what we need to return to. It is the very fear that God is testing us to see if it is in us.

PROTECTION FOR GODLY COMMUNION

This relationship or dimension of the Spirit of God actually protects us; it helps us in order that we master sin and come near to commune with God like Moses. God desired for the Israelites to worship Him when He brought them out of Egypt. He wanted communion with them. If we fully yield ourselves to God's Spirit, He will allow the relationship with the Spirit of the fear of the Lord to work all sin out of our lives and keep us from sin. As a result, this leads us into a deeper walk with God, whereby He brings us into the heavenly realm. We are seated in heavenly places with Christ Jesus (see Eph. 2:6). Here we truly begin to walk in our heavenly authority.

Princess Warriors, God does not want you to walk in an ungodly fear of Him, but a godly fear. Sometimes the spirit of religion can put a flogger in our hand and flog us to death; that is not God. Instead, God wants us to go from glory to glory in Him, and as we do go higher, we will desire to walk in a higher level of holiness. Here there is no flogger put in your hand, only a deeper love, whereby you become a love-wrecked daughter seeking to get closer to God.

If you want to begin the process of allowing God to work sin out of your life, pray the following prayer:

Dear Lord, I come to you right now and repent of any thoughts that I have held on to that are contrary to Your Word. I ask that You give me a fresh anointing of the Spirit of the fear of the Lord. I ask You to impart the grace I need in order to receive the fullness of the Fear of the Lord. Right now, Holy Spirit, direct my prayers and my spiritual walk so that I will be well-pleasing to the Father. God, I desire to please You above all, and I know that without Your grace and faith it is impossible. I thank You right now for the receiving of the fear of the Lord and ask that You would grow me in a deeper understanding of a Holy God. I thank You for giving me this gift so that I will delight in You, Lord. I declare that You set my feet on that pathway of holiness and accelerate my walk in You. I thank You God that I do not come to You in my own righteousness, but in the righteousness of Christ Jesus. In Jesus' name I pray. Amen.

QUESTIONS:

1. Do you have problems being reverent toward God and His sanctuary? If yes, identify whether you are embarrassed, lack boldness, are intimidated, or are pressured into serving God reverently in His sanctuary.

2. Do you find yourself having more fear of man than of God? If yes, identify the onset of the fear of man. Ask God's Holy Spirit to show you where the fear of man (again here I am talking about a specific demon called the fear of man not the demon of the fear of people) came in.

3. What is interfering with your fearing of God instead of man? Could it be the magazines you read, the shows you watch, or the people you hang out with each week? What can you do to help change the matter?

4. Can you pray the prayer on the previous page each day for two months? Date here your beginning date and then come back in two months and write the changes you have seen in your life regarding the fear of the Lord.

3

Complain or Comply

For it is God who works in you to will and to act according to His good purpose. Do everything without complaining or arguing, so that you may become blameless and pure, children of God without fault in a crooked and depraved generation, in which you shine like stars in the universe (Philippians 2:13-15 NIV).

WHO ARE WE HIRED FOR? IT MEANS WHO ARE YOU WORKING FOR, SATAN OR GOD. YOU ARE GOING TO WORK FOR ONE OR THE OTHER; THERE ARE NOT TWO MASTERS, ONLY ONE. THIS IS DISCUSSED FURTHER IN THIS SECTION IF YOU READ ON.

We in America are spoiled, spoiled, spoiled, and I do not have concern as to whether or not people are offended, because that is the sin nature that tries to work inside of us.

For in my inner being I delight in God's law; but I see an-
other law at work in the members of my body, waging war
against the law of my mind and making me a prisoner of the
law of sin at work within my members. What a wretched
man I am! Who will rescue me from this body of death?
(Romans 7:22-24 NIV)

The Holy Ghost often reminds me of areas in which I am
spoiled and where I give in to either my flesh or my old sin nature.
When people are spoiled it means that their character is impaired
by overindulgence. Our character is our main or essential nature.
Therefore, if we have been born into the Kingdom of Heaven by
Jesus Christ our Savior, our main or essential nature is to be like
Christ. If we are spoiled, that means that the nature of Christ in
us is impaired by our overindulgence in something, which is usually caused by the flesh or our old sin nature trying to rise back up
against our minds. It is important to hear God clearly, because
if we are doing the will of God, putting to death the members of
our flesh and denying the right of our old sin nature to wage war
then we will grow in the spirit, not walking in our flesh but in the
spirit (see Luke 1:80 and Luke 2:40).

For example, if I get a testimony in my spirit (a knowing inside of my inner person by Holy Spirit) that I am not to spend
money on a certain item, and I do it anyway, then I commit sin.
Remember, as stated earlier, sin is lawlessness. Lawlessness is defined by Webster's as "to not be restrained or controlled by law."
What is the law? God's Word and His will. Many people believe
that sin is only breaking the written Word of God. However, it is
more than that. Lawlessness is not doing the will of God. Jesus,
while on earth, only did the will of the Father (see John 5:30).
This included more than actions written in the Law.

Jesus even states that only the people who do the will of God have entrance into the Kingdom of Heaven:

Wherefore by their fruits ye shall know them. Not every one that saith unto Me, Lord, Lord, shall enter into the kingdom of heaven; but he that doeth the will of My Father which is in heaven. Many will say to Me in that day, Lord, Lord, have we not prophesied in Thy name? and in Thy name have cast out devils? and in Thy name done many wonderful works?" (Matthew 7:20-22 KJV)

You will know people by their fruit. The fruit Jesus is referring to here is the fruit of people's character.

But the Holy Spirit produces this kind of fruit in our lives: love, joy, peace, patience, kindness, goodness, faithfulness, gentleness, and self-control. There is no law against these things! (Galatians 5:22-23 NLT)

We do not break God's law when we walk in the Spirit, which exhibits doing His will and is evidenced by us walking in the fruits of the Spirit. This is our gift to God—demonstrating the manifestation of the presence of Jesus Christ in us, the hope of glory in our daily lives (see Col. 1:27).

If we continue to remain spoiled, giving into our flesh and sin nature, it impairs the character of Christ in us.

When you follow the desires of your sinful nature, the results are very clear: sexual immorality, impurity, lustful pleasures, idolatry, sorcery, hostility, quarreling, jealousy, outbursts of anger, selfish ambition, dissension, division, envy, drunkenness, wild parties, and other sins like these. Let me tell you again, as I have before, that anyone living that sort of life will not inherit the Kingdom of God (Galatians 5:19-21 NLT).

All these fruits of our sinful nature lead to complaining and griping. Therefore, if we are complaining and griping that should be an indicator that one if not many of these desires of our sinful nature need to be worked out of us.

If we are doing nothing other than complaining and griping, we might as well pull up a door post that states we are for hire for the kingdom of darkness. God's Kingdom does not have complaining, griping, or whining. We need to see *who* we are serving while on earth. If we are complaining and griping, we are not serving God, but instead serving satan and the kingdom of darkness. Actually, the Holy Spirit revealed to me in the spirit realm what happens when we gripe or complain. He showed me that when we start complaining an ugly mustard color scent comes out of us and up into the air. Then, when this scent is given out, demons can smell it, and they gather around and attack the person even more because that person has opened a door up to the enemy through their complaining.

The acts that we find that are not of God's Kingdom are acts of the sinful nature. The way to keep from living in a sinful nature is to operate in the Spirit, because it is by the Spirit that we operate in the Kingdom of God. If we are not operating in the realm of the Kingdom of God, we operate out of our flesh or out of satan's kingdom, which is where strongholds are set up. (This will be discussed in detail in the next section on spiritual warfare).

No, It is Mine

The best illustration of operating in the flesh is seen through the toddler age group. Remember, we are born in a fallen state because of Adam and Eve's disobedience, and we have a sin nature in us. What are toddlers famous for saying? "No" and "mine." They do not have much thought for others, because they have been operating on a self-seeking mindset since birth. When they were hungry as newborn babies, they cried. When they were uncomfortable, they cried. They do not have the capacity to think outside of their own needs. The feelings of others are irrelevant to the thought processes they have in getting their basic needs met because they are immature and selfish. (In saying all of this, I want you to understand that I absolutely adore children and am merely using this example for a point God wants to make here.)

It is very difficult teaching toddlers to share because the only concept that they have understood since birth is, "I need this"; "I need that"; and "me, me, me." When they get to the age of 2 or 3 and find out that other children their age are wanting to play with their toys, they usually tell them "no" or "mine." They only understand that they are comfortable with having their needs (flesh) met, and when there is the slightest degree of discomfort to their flesh (for example, sharing), they pout and cry. We are no different in pleasing our flesh. We have grown accustomed to feeding it whenever it says "buy this"; "give him a piece of your mind"; "tell her your opinion"; "you need a vacation"; and so forth. However, that is selfish. It is feeding the flesh, and it is not coming from God.

I'm so use to hearing Americans talk about the fact that they haven't had a vacation in a year or two. It is alright to take a rest and go on a vacation. However, for to too many Americans, vacation means spending money they do not have to go somewhere so they can relax when they want to. Moreover, if they don't get a vacation, they actually pout about it and throw a little temper tantrum, just like a 2-year-old. I have actually seen people act like this when they do not go on their regular beach vacation. Our pouting and temper tantrums look like this: "You know, I haven't done anything for me. I'm always doing things for others. I haven't been to the beach since last year, and I go every year, and I'm going."

We are so pitiful, me included. We think that if we cannot get what we want then we are being mistreated. Maybe instead we should look at it as though God is doing a work in us to bring us to a position of growing in the fruit of the Spirit. Instead of us going on vacation, God might want us to learn patience. As a result, if we looked at our schedules, we might see that we would be more rested if we were not including our children in every little league sport or dance program. God might be teaching us to go against our flesh and instead pay down our debt, thereby exhibiting the fruit of patience and self-control.

SEND ME TO ITALY; GOD PAID IN FULL

My husband, Rich, and I haven't gone on a vacation in over four years. I used to say, "You know, we haven't been on a vacation, and we deserve one." However, since I've been walking in the Spirit, I'm happy with my life, and the Lord has informed me that, when it is time for us to travel elsewhere and spend time soaking up the surroundings of another place without doing anything other than relaxing, He will let me know, and it will be already paid in full.

Rich and I so desperately want to go on vacation to Italy. Italy is one of our most desired vacations, as well as Israel and Colorado. We confess with our mouth that one-day we are going to go and vacation to those spots. However, if we were to get a huge loan in order to take one of those vacations or even a little vacation to the beach, we would be going against the will of God. The Word says that He wants us to be the lender, not the borrower (see Prov. 22:7). Moreover, we know that it is not His will for us to get outside of His timing. There will be a right time, and until then we enjoy the thought of when that day will come for us to go to those places.

FATHER, MAY I?

Most Americans look to immediate gratification of the flesh and are in debt. I myself have been guilty of this. I used to go shopping and buy my family whatever I wanted whenever I wanted. I never gave any thought as to whether or not God even cared. However, the Holy Spirit showed me, as I've grown closer to God, that He wants us to ask Him before we do things. Whenever our children go to another neighborhood child's home regularly, do we really care most of the time if they go to enjoy themselves and have fun? Usually we do not care. However, as parents, we want the courtesy of having our children get our permission. Likewise, in many things that we do, God still wants us to ask for His permission. I have learned this lesson in buying clothes, food, paying debt, and so forth. My desire is to do nothing without asking God. Moreover, when I do ask Him, He blesses it.

I asked God one week if I could buy my husband a shirt because, in my opinion, I felt he could use one for business. We had the money. However, let me show what happens when we ask God permission to do something and He blesses it. The Holy Spirit showed me which store and department to go shopping for the shirt that I was to get my husband in Birmingham, Alabama, which has great shopping. The shirt that I found was out of its normal place in the store, and moreover, it was originally priced at $130. I, getting God's blessing for the shirt, had found it on a different table, and when I went to the register to pay for it, the lady told me that it was already on sale, and on top of the sale, she said she would take an additional percentage off of it. It cost only $37. This is a designer shirt that fits him to a tee and looks as though it was made for him.

That might not impress most of you, but when you live with the blessings of God, it thrills you that He thought of such detail to make something so incredible happen. That is one of many great things that we've had happen. Over a five month period during that time, we had a total of $5,200 cash come into our hands from other people doing things. We saved over $2,900 on home repairs that were supposed to be done and instead only paid $100, and it was because we didn't move until God said move. When He told us to move, we received money and saved nearly $3,000. I mention all of this only to demonstrate that when you walk in the fear of the Lord, nothing shakes you outside of God.

I HATE MY LIFE!

God is not pleased when we grumble or complain about the life that God has given us. There are some people who find complaining an art form, and as a result, they make it their goal to deliver the best argument for why they are displeased with their life circumstances. When we are displeased with our life circumstances, what we are saying to Almighty God is, "God, I could have done a better job with my life. Why haven't You pleased my flesh?" We are no different than the Israelites who complained time after time in the desert and wanted to return to Egypt. What we should be doing instead of griping and complaining (this includes whining) is thanking God. Thank God that we are alive, that we have health, that we live in a free country, that we have food to eat today, that we have shelter over our heads, and that we have a church to attend. Most of the time people are cursing their church instead of being grateful for it, which is an apostasy to God. However, that in itself is another book and is actually addressed very well by Francis Frangipane in *The Three Battlegrounds*.[1]

QUESTIONS:

1. Do you complain or gripe about anything? If yes, do you hang around other people who do the same? Do you watch television shows or read magazines that have people complaining and griping?

2. Are there areas in which you can be more thankful to God?

3. List the areas that you can thank God daily for blessing you. Do you have your health, life, shelter, food, employment, and so forth?

Endnote

1. Francis Frangipane, *The Three Battlegrounds* (Cedar Rapids, IA: Arrow Publications, Inc., 1989).

chapter

4

Authority

Everyone must submit himself to the governing authorities, for there is no authority except that which God has established. The authorities that exist have been established by God. Consequently, he who rebels against the authority is rebelling against what God has instituted, and those who do so will bring judgment on themselves. For rulers hold no terror for those who do right, but for those who do wrong. Do you want to be free from fear of the one in authority? Then do what is right and he will commend you (Romans 13:1-3 NIV).

DON'T STRIKE ME DEAD, GOD

In order to give adequate teaching on the fear of the Lord, it is necessary to address the area of authority. Before I truly had an understanding of the fear of the Lord, I was one of those

Christians who felt it my duty to state all the wrongs present in the leadership in every arena I could think of. Moreover, I felt it my place to correct an unfair employer. I did not have much respect for anyone because I knew what their errors were. I was intolerant toward the sins of those who were in a position of authority. Praise God He has delivered me and allowed me to continue to breathe without striking me dead while I was being self-righteous and arrogant. After studying the fear of the Lord, I have come to the knowledge that that sort of behavior was sinful and a tactical device of satan to get a foothold in my life.

God has established every authority that has been since the beginning of time. This includes all of the horrible men and women who have gotten into an office of authority and as a result blood was shed. The Bible states clearly that there is no authority except what God has established (see Rom. 13:1). Therefore, we can be confident that people did not get into office without God knowing it and allowing them to take that office. Remember, His ways are higher than our ways. Thus, we should not expect ourselves to understand why certain people have gotten into a political position and abused the people under them. However, what I do know is that *all things work together for good to those who love God, to those whoe are the called according to His purpose* (Rom. 8:28). We must cast our confidence in God, who is over all, and trust that He has a plan at work of which we have no comprehension. What we can do is take Him at his Word and hold on to the Word, not our circumstances.

Authority is defined by *Webster's* as "the power or right to give commands, enforce obedience, take action, or make final decisions; jurisdiction." It is a position, not a person. The position stays constant, but the person may not. For example, we have elections here in the United States for president, and we have had numerous presidents. However, we have one office of president which has remained since the beginning of the creation of the executive branch for the United States. We have justices for the judicial branch and legislators for the legislative branch. All of those offices remain the same, but the people who hold them change.

In addition, we have families where there are parents, children, husbands, and wives. There are many people across the world in those positions. Therefore, the authority that God establishes is the "position of authority." Many people fail to notice the position and look at the people in authority; as a result, they dismiss the fact that when they say something about those people, they are instead saying something about the office, not the people.

A person who rebels against authority is rebelling against God's institution. *Institution* refers to an established law, custom, or practice. God does have a Kingdom, and in that Kingdom there are rules known as the law. Thus, if we are rebelling against the authority, we are actually rebelling against God's law. Likewise, if we are rebelling against authority here on earth, we are directly rebelling against God's law.

SISTER SO-AND-SO'S LAW

I graduated from law school in 2008, and since studying law, the Holy Spirit has shown me how God's Word is analogous to the law of America. When we have an injury for which we need the protection of the sovereignty, the government, we have to make our grievance known according to the law. We do not go into a courtroom and tell the judge, "Your honor, I would like to tell you about how I was injured by sister so-and-so. Also, your honor, there was no written law for this so I wrote one up prior to coming to court today, and you can just follow my written law." If this were to happen, trust me, not only would that person's case be dismissed for lack of cause of action, but also that person would most likely be admitted into the psychiatric ward.

Likewise, we have the Word of God to use as the law since we are of the Kingdom of Heaven. For example, we could be coming to Heaven's court with an argument that the enemy is attacking our family. However, the argument against us, if we dishonor authority, would be that we are breaking the Word of God by rebelling against authority. The consequence of rebelling against authority is that we bring judgment against ourselves, and we will be in fear of that authority as well as others on earth. This comes in the form of fearing our boss will fire us, our husband doesn't love us, our pastor is talking about us, and so forth.

TARGETS FOR SATAN

Satan as well is always accusing the brethren day and night before the throne of the Most High God and has the Word to use against us.

The great dragon was hurled down—that ancient serpent called the devil, or Satan, who leads the whole world astray. He was hurled to the earth, and his angels with him. Then I heard a loud voice in heaven say: "Now have come the salvation and the power and the kingdom of our God, and the authority of His Christ. For the accuser of our brothers, who accuses them before our God day and night, has been hurled down. They overcame him by the blood of the Lamb and by the word of their testimony; they did not love their lives so much as to shrink from death (Revelation 12: 9-11 NIV).

If we break the law, disobeying God's Word, we are an open target for the enemy to bring accusation and cause for his attack on our lives.

It is important to become knowledgeable of the Word so that we will not perish. It is vital, therefore, to be armed with the knowledge of walking in obedience to God's authority. Again, do not confuse this with godly authority (godly men and women in office). It is great when we do have godly authority because it says in the Psalms that when we do have a godly king the people rejoice (see Prov. 29:2). However, it is God's authority, which is all authority upon the earth in *everything*. This includes authority in the government, church, business, family, and school.

How Do We Rebel?

How do we rebel against authority? When we disobey God's Word in regard to how we treat authority, we are rebelling. According to *Webster's, rebellion* is to "feel or show strong aversion; be repelled." Analogize this with the disobedience used in Romans 1:28-30, which states that since the people did not find it worthwhile to attain the knowledge of God, they were given over to a depraved *mind*, which would cause them to do what should not be done.

> *Until they were filled (permeated and saturated) with every kind of unrighteousness, iniquity, grasping and covetous greed, and malice. [They were] full of envy and jealousy, murder, strife, deceit and treachery, ill will and cruel ways. [They were] secret backbiters and gossipers, Slanderers, hateful to and hating God, full of insolence, arrogance, [and] boasting; inventors of new forms of evil, disobedient and undutiful to parents. [They were] without understanding, conscienceless and faithless, heartless and loveless [and] merciless. Though they are fully aware of God's righteous decree that those who do such things deserve to die, they not only do them themselves but approve and applaud others who practice them. (Romans 1:29-32 AMP)*

Vine's Dictionary defines disobedience in this verse as *apeithes,* which signifies "unwilling to be persuaded, spurning belief, disobedient."[1]

The word *spurn*, according to *Webster's,* means "to refuse or reject with contempt or disdain." Taking it one step further, *contempt* comes from the Latin word *contemptus,* which according to *Vine's,* is "to scorn," and *scorn* is defined in *Webster's Dictionary* as "to refuse or reject as wrong or disgraceful." Therefore, rebellion is the rejecting of a belief. When people rebel against God's authority, they are rejecting belief in His Word regarding authority. Disobedience is rebellion; it is the disbelief that what God says in His Word is true. Therefore, someone who doesn't respect authority goes against the Word of God.

If we do not obey the Word of God in regard to authority, we are in disobedience (rebellion). Since we understand that disobedience is rebellion against God, shouldn't we find out what His Word says about authority? Yes. It is our duty and benefit to find out what His Word says in *everything,* including authority. Paul states in Titus,

> *Remind the people to be subject to rulers and authorities, to be obedient, to be ready to do whatever is good, to slander no one, to be peaceable and considerate, and to show true humility toward all men* (Titus 3:1-2 NIV).

Here Paul states that we are to be submissive to all rulers and authorities. It is not a conditional Scripture listing only those authorities who are godly or good. To be subject to authority here means to be *under* authority. When we are under authority, we do not usurp the office. *Webster's* defines *under* as "being in an inferior or subordinate position or rank." Thus, we are not trying to usurp the rank of that office. We usurp the rank if we "take or assume and hold in possession by force" the specific office.

I AM RUNNING FOR PRESIDENT

Therefore, if we are talking badly about the President (which is different than using our constitutional privileges of making a change in our government through voting or campaigning appropriately, like the Tea Party, and talking about political issues), we are stepping into the position of president and are trying to usurp his position. This might be laughable, but until we get a picture of what we are actually doing, we will continue to be blind to what is really going on. Likewise, if we are talking badly about our husbands, we are arresting the position of man of the house and taking on the role of husband and are running his office. God is God, and we are not, and it is His place to change the hearts and minds of men and women.

Moreover, if we think that we can do a better job than the preacher or teacher at church on a particular subject, we have removed them from their job and placed ourselves behind the pulpit or podium and made ourselves preacher or teacher. Let me go a step further and state that if we are passing the speed limit or running a red light, we have then placed ourselves in the office of legislation for the municipality in which we are violating the law and have placed ourselves above it. There is a saying: "He is above the law." That means that person is *higher* than the law, and literally they are committing usurpation of the law. This is applicable in *every* arena where there is authority. God is a God of order, and everything that He created has order.

The way we remain subject to authority is to find out what the law is and obey it, not rising "above the law." God's Word requires that we honor all those who are in authority since He established them. We honor them by not talking badly about them, but instead praying on their behalf. Many Christian Americans believe that, because they are Christians, it is their place to denote the wrongs being done in the office of the presidency.

They believe that they should voice their grievances, not to the president, but to all who are within earshot, and they discuss matters as though their opinions carry weight. Moreover, there are television shows on which commentators not only give their opinion, but also bash the president. That is hypocrisy for a Christian. Instead, we must pray for the president and the decisions he has to make according to God's will. Not according to sister so-and-so of the intercessory prayer group, but according to God's will. It is no different from our husbands sitting in the stands at a football game and believing that their screaming at the top of their lungs will cause the quarterback to hear them. Who is the quarterback listening to? The quarterback only listens to his coach. Likewise, the only one the president is accountable to listen to is God. Therefore, we pray the president's ears will be opened to hear God. We pray the president will be surrounded with good counsel and that God's will is fulfilled in the presidential office. It is no different with our employers, husbands, pastors, teachers, and the like.

I would like to add in this section that there are times when we are to seek godly counsel, which would allow the disclosure or discussion of others in authority over us. For instance, some marriages that are in trouble seek marriage counseling in order to get godly counsel for how a wife can be a better wife and a husband can be a better husband. Moreover, new Christians might have questions as to the president's decisions on certain issues regarding law, and they may seek the counsel of a mentor. This is not bashing the person being discussed with the godly counselor, but rather seeking God's Word regarding how to treat the matter. For instance, a woman who is getting abused by her husband might seek godly counsel on whether or not she should stay in the relationship. A woman does not rebel against her husband by inquiring what God's Word is regarding whether or not she should stay and be a punching bag for her husband. Therefore, I want to stress that getting godly counsel is not rebelling against authority.

What if I'm asked to Sin Against God?

It is necessary to lay a foundation in determining when and when not to follow the orders or commands of people in authority. In Constitutional Law, there is a rule known as the Supremacy Clause, which basically states that the Constitution is the Supreme Law of the land and that if anything is in direct conflict with the Constitution, then the conflicting law will be void as a result. Likewise, God's law is the Supreme Law, and if your employer is asking you to lie for him, then you have to follow God's law because it is supreme to your employer's command. that we are not to bare false witness or lie, which is a part of the Ten Commandments (see Deut. 5:20), and his request that you lie is in direct conflict with the Word of God. Anytime there is a direct conflict with the Word of God, you are required to follow the Word, not the command or rule of the authority that is in conflict with the Word.

Now that we understand that we are to be obedient to authority and not disobedient or rebellious, what are we exactly to do in regard to showing obedience? Peter delineates with clarity how we are to live in obedience regarding authority. First, in regard to government officials, Peter delineates what the Lord requires of us. First Peter 2: 13-16 says,

> *Therefore submit yourselves to every ordinance of man for the Lord's sake, whether to the king as supreme, or to governors, as to those who are sent by him for the punishment of evildoers and for the praise of those who do good. For this is the will of God, that by doing good you may put to silence the ignorance of foolish men— as free, yet not using liberty as a cloak for vice, but as bondservants of God.*

Peter states that we are to be submissive to every human ordinance. This includes all the laws made through federal

(Constitution, Internal Revenue Service, Federal Regulations), state (State laws), and local or business regulations (local business offices and ordinances). When we have laws handed to us from authority (federal, state, and local laws), we are to adhere to them. That includes not bad-mouthing the IRS and State Department of Revenue. These tax offices are created out of the power and instructions of governmental authorities, and as such, they are a direct command from those specific offices.

THE INSPIRATIONAL RELIEF SERVICE

For example, when taxes become due each year, you hear many Americans griping and complaining about owing the government money. However, when they are griping, it's as if they are griping about the legislators office. Thus, they are being rebellious because they are saying, "God, I don't like what the legislators are doing by making me pay taxes. I think that I could have done a better job at the nation's taxes, God, than You are doing, because You allowed them to get into office." Since tax is a law enacted by the government and is not in direct conflict with the Word of God, we are required to look it as though the Lord directly is the one we answer to. Instead of griping about taxes, we can approach it God's way, which is by making our requests known to Him (see Phil. 4:6.). If we had people corporately come together to pray over our economy, it would also be a great opportunity to pray that God's will would be done to lower the tax rate and that godly legislators would be elected who would vote on a godly tax plan.

When the Holy Spirit showed me this revelation, He directed me to look at paying taxes as an offering, and I renamed the IRS to mean the Inspirational Relief Service. Every time I respond to anything related to taxes, I say, "Oh, we need to call the Inspirational Relief Service today and give to them." Believe me, if anyone can gripe, my husband and I are in a position according to the world because of his being without work for a while and us borrowing all of his IRA contributions in order to survive. However, we have chosen to look at it positively, and each time we deal with them, we have the favor of God upon us and usually work with very polite people.

Peter states that we are to be submissive to the king, governors, and those appointed to office by these authority figures. This includes policemen, firemen, and other governmental offices that are public in nature. Along with these are schools, which have principals, teachers, janitors, and the like. Everyone who is in an office like these listed is seen as a public servant, and as such, they should be respected and honored by the people they serve (this also includes private schools).

Being submitted to authority is good. *When we are submitted to authority it silences the ignorant people.* One who is ignorant is one who does not have knowledge of something that is established or is law. Laws educate those who are unaware (the foolish) on how to treat people who are in authority. This is advantageous to our nation because, if we have a nation where people are obedient, God promises to bless us. It is God's desire for us to walk in freedom that is given to us by the government.

Radio Commentators Who Bash

One thing that has particularly bothered me in regard to other Christians is their use of their "airtime," either radio or television, to attack the government and personally attack officials who are in public office. That is exactly what the Word addresses in relation to walking in liberty, not for our own evil desires (throwing out our debauched views of our government), but instead as servants to God, praying for officials and using our constitutional privileges in a godly manner (see 1 Tim. 2:1-2.). Do everything as unto the Lord. What we should not do is get on the media airways and complain about our Supreme Court, president, and other officials, stating their "errors" to those who are listening. That is an evil work of satan and is not to be tolerated. In fact, Paul states that people who discuss such things should be avoided.

> *But avoid foolish controversies and genealogies and arguments and quarrels about the law, because these are unprofitable and useless. Warn a divisive person once, and then warn him a second time. After that, have nothing to do with him. You may be sure that such a man is warped and sinful; he is self-condemned* (Titus 3:9-11 NIV).

Therefore, if we are around people who are degrading a public official or the law, we are to admonish them in the Word, as it states "warn them once, and a second time." After the warnings, if they continue in their ways, we are to have nothing to do with such people. It is wise, then, to refrain from talk shows that discuss political controversies because they are sinful in nature.

What we are to do is to look at people like Lou Engle and follow suit. He is gathering young people from all across the nation and teaching them how to be active Christian Americans in regard to the law. His way is walking them through learning the godly approach to changing a law in state and national government. He walks in the plan discussed by Paul in First Timothy.

> *I urge then, first of all, that requests, prayers, intercession and thanksgiving being made for everyone—for kings, and all those in authority, that we may live peaceful and quiet lives in all godliness and holiness. This is good, and pleases God our Savior, who wants all men to be saved and come to the knowledge of the truth* (1 Timothy 2:1-4 NIV).

Lou Engle's ministry is a means by which young people learn about intercession, worship, and standing in the gap between

America and God. Jesus forever makes intercession for us night and day with the Father; we likewise are to do the same for our country, its officials, and the people. It puts me in awe to see such posterity rising up under Lou Engle's effective, godly leadership. It is this type of active role that we Christians should maintain. Moreover, it is being heralded by the young people in our nation, and we who are older would do well to learn from their ways.

I'M AN EPISTLE FOR CHRIST

The whole point of living submissively, interceding and thanking God for our nation's authority, is that it is peaceful and holy, pleasing to God, and it brings others to the knowledge of Christ. Paul states that we are living epistles, which is a New Testament letter written by God's Holy Spirit.

> *You are our epistle written in our hearts, known and read by all men; clearly **you are** an epistle of Christ, ministered by us, written not with ink but by the Spirit of the living God, not on tablets of stone but on tablets of flesh, **that is,** of the heart* (2 Corinthians 3:2-3).

We are a witness to the world of our Lord and Savior Jesus Christ, and that witness comes through living lives of holiness and obedience unto God. As a result of living our lives in this way, others come to the true knowledge of Jesus and are led to salvation.

Pray with me:

God, forgive me for rebelling against the governmental authority you have placed in my life. I ask that You would direct my prayers in order that I may lift up the governmental officials to Your throne of Grace. I pray right now for the President of the United States and ask that you would guide and direct his footsteps. I pray for the legislation and judicial governments of the United States; give them Your wisdom to make laws and legal decisions. I pray for my state, city, and county officials that You would guide them in Your will. I pray that Your Kingdom would come and Your will would be done through all the governmental officials I have lifted up in prayer. In Jesus' name I pray. Amen.

QUESTIONS:

1. Do you have trouble being a submissive citizen? If so, identify areas where you need to allow God to purge you of rebellion.

2. Do you speak poorly about governmental authorities to other people or listen to commentaries that do this? If so, what do you need to stop listening to or speaking about?

3. Can you step out when others are talking poorly about authority and be an epistle read by others, letting them know they are to honor the president?

4. In what areas do you presently show godly respect to authority in your own life?

5. Are there others whom you can impact by teaching them how to pray for and bless those who are in authority?

6. Can you commit to praying for those in governmental authority whom the Lord shows you?

Endnote:

1. http://www2.mf.no/bibelprog/vines?word=%AFt0000763

chapter

5

Employers, Sisters in Christ, Husbands, and Others

HONOR ALL PEOPLE

What about our employers, sisters in Christ, and people in general? The Word tells us to be submissive to employers—those who are kind and those who are harsh. In addition, in regard to our sisters in Christ, it tells us to love each other and honor *all* people.

> *Honor all people. Love the brotherhood. Fear God. Honor the king. Servants, be submissive to your masters with all fear, not only to the good and gentle, but also to the harsh* (1 Peter 2:17-18).

First, in regard to our employers, Scripture states that we are to be submissive to them regardless of their kindness or harshness.

The problem with the western culture is that people find it much easier to talk about how hard and mean their bosses are instead of being submitted to them.

I myself was guilty of this. At one time I was working for a boss who really had it out for me. She only desired to see me fired or dismissed from my position. I found myself so bothered with her treatment that I called the higher-ups to discuss her mistreatment. Her behavior was unwarranted, and I had not done anything to cause her to treat me so harshly. However, the Word does not state that I'm to call those higher in power, but instead it states that I'm to be submitted to her as long as she does not ask me to do anything contrary to the Word of God. *Wait,* you might ask, *What about the unfair treatment? Do you put up with it?* Did Jesus put up with unfair treatment? Did He face things that were unwarranted from those in authority? Yes to both.

Peter states well in Scripture why we are to put up with unfair treatment:

For this is commendable, if because of conscience toward God one endures grief, suffering wrongfully. For what credit is it if, when you are beaten for your faults, you take it patiently? But when you do good and suffer, if you take it patiently, this is commendable before God. For to this you were called, because Christ also suffered for us, leaving us an example, that you should follow His steps: "Who committed no sin, Nor was deceit found in His mouth"; who, when He was reviled, did not revile in return; when He suffered, He did not threaten, but committed Himself to Him who judges righteously; who Himself bore our sins in His own body on the tree, that we, having died to sins, might live for righteousness—by whose stripes you were healed. For you were like sheep going astray, but have now returned to the Shepherd and Overseer of your souls (1 Peter 2:19-25).

Likewise, we are to do the same as Jesus, who is our example. We are to not revile back when we have been reviled, nor are we to pay vengeance for vengeance. Instead we are to suffer as Christ did, not threatening anyone, but committing ourselves to God, who is the righteous Judge.

THE BEAUTY OF SUFFERING

The most beautiful picture of what suffering does to the soul is demonstrated in the life of Jesus, our Lord and Savior. He is our example of how we are to live and walk while on this earth. We are in such a temporary state of being until we meet our eternal destiny after this life. Could it be possible that we need to experience sufferings in this life so that we can be perfected? One might ask why such a good God would want His children to suffer. As God so poignantly puts it, does the clay ask the Potter, "God, what are you doing?"

> *You turn things upside down, as if the potter were thought to be like the clay! Shall what is formed say to Him who formed it, "He did not make me"? Can the pot say of the potter, "He knows nothing"?* (Isaiah 29:16 NIV)

It is not our job to know why we suffer; it is our job only to *trust* God in the midst of our suffering that all things will work to our good (see Rom. 8:28). To further dispel the idea that God does not use suffering to benefit us, let us look at Jesus' portrait prophesied in Isaiah about God's desire for His Son to suffer.

> *Yet it pleased the LORD to bruise Him; He hath put Him to grief: when Thou shalt make His soul an offering for*

sin, He shall see his seed, He shall prolong His days, and the pleasure of the Lord shall prosper in His hand. He shall see of the travail of his soul, and shall be satisfied: by His knowledge shall my righteous servant justify many; for He shall bear their iniquities (Isaiah 53:10-11 KJV).

God desired to bruise Jesus because of what it would produce, which was a beginning of something new. We see this new thing in Jesus' suffering, demonstrated by His travailing. Travailing is seen in a pregnant woman during the labor of childbirth. It means to labor very hard and experience pain. What the Word expresses here is that the suffering Jesus went through produced in Him a travailing of the soul, a hard laboring, which birthed eternal salvation for us.

How many of us mothers know that we do not leave the labor room without a baby? Thus, the birthing that came forth out of the travailing, the suffering, of Jesus was a knowledge that would justify many. This travailing that Jesus had to go through was what was actually putting our sin upon Him. Our sin was put upon Him as He took the lashes for our iniquities. Jesus could have left this earth without going through the suffering. However, if He had not suffered then we would not have an eternity with the Father. It was the very suffering that He went through that birthed eternal life to those who would believe and follow Him.

MADE BEAUTIFUL IN CARRYING OUR CROSS

Jesus has called us to pick up our cross and follow Him. *"And he who does not take His cross and follow after Me is not worthy of Me. He who finds his life will lose it, and he who loses his life for My sake will find it"* (Matt. 10:38-39). He expects nothing less from us than what He Himself did, because He has given us the power to do it by His Holy Spirit. We are able to go through unfair treatment and suffering because the grace and peace to walk through it comes through His Holy Spirit.

The apostle Luke wrote in the Book of Acts about what the apostle Paul said to the church after he had been stoned and left for dead, which was a great suffering he went through. Paul rose up and confirmed the souls of the disciples, exhorting them to continue in the faith and saying, *"We must through many tribulations enter the kingdom of God"* (Acts 14:22). Thus, in order for us to enter into God's Kingdom, we have to go through suffering, and much of that is experienced by being under God's authority. We can see such examples as David and King Saul (see 1 Sam. 13), Hannah and Eli (see 1 Samuel 1), Mordecai and Haman (see Esther 8 and 9), Joseph and his brothers (see Gen. 38), Daniel and King Nebuchadnezzar (see book of Daniel), and so forth. If God demonstrates in his Word that many of His chosen ones suffered under authority, why should we find ourselves exempt?

It is this suffering that produces and births inside of us a deeper knowledge of God, whereby we enter the Kingdom of God. It was the knowledge produced while undergoing suffering that was so vital to the actual purpose behind the suffering. As stated earlier, God does *nothing* without purpose, even if we do not understand the purpose behind His ways. Therefore, the suffering that we go through produces in us the knowledge necessary to carry out His will and plans for our lives.

I have experienced upon many occasions throughout my life persecution from authority (from Christians and non-Christians). I have been falsely accused of doing things that I did not do. My character has been attacked in front of others with almost vile accusation. When these ungodly mistreatments by authority have happened, I must admit that I was only kept by the Holy Spirit restraining my flesh, because I really wanted to dive in and defend myself against the wrong that had been done to me. However, with the Spirit's restraint and the power of the Word, I was able to let God battle for me and not defend myself. As a result, I have received a blessing from unfair treatment. In the midst of the persecution, I am being humbled and learning the revelation that the Lord would have for that moment. Moreover, God has promoted me in front of the very people who have slandered, attacked, and attempted to discredit me.

On the other hand, at times I have judged others wrongly and found myself caught up in deception. For example, I believed that one particular lady was not operating under the direction of God and questioned her actions. However, later the Holy Spirit showed me that I was deceived and gave me a glimpse of how the Father saw this young lady. When I found out what deception I was under and how wrong I was, I grieved over how I had so misjudged this lady and put her off as a "fruit loop." I so felt a touch of the heart of God on how He saw this beautiful daughter of His. After receiving correction by the Holy Spirit, I experienced so much freedom, and God restored my ability to see her as His daughter, versus seeing her as one in error. I was an authority to her, and when I was convicted, I gave her more opportunity to minister than I had previously.

HOORAY PERSECUTION AND SUFFERING!

I am not one to go around jumping up and down when persecution comes my way. It is not my desire to say, "Hooray persecution and suffering!" However, I know that it must come in order for me to be changed from glory to glory and to live a life worthy of the Lord. Paul states to the Colossians:

For this reason, since the day we heard about you, we have not stopped praying for you and asking God to fill you with the knowledge of His will through all spiritual wisdom and understanding. And we pray this in order that you may live a life worthy of the Lord and may please Him in every way: bearing fruit in every good work, growing in the knowledge of God, being strengthened with all power according to His glorious might so that you may have great endurance and patience, and joyfully giving thanks to the Father, who has qualified you to share in the inheritance of the saints in the kingdom of light (Colossians 1:9-13 NIV).

Here we see the word *knowledge,* which is identified in *Vine's Expository Dictionary* as *epignosis,* meaning "exact or full knowledge, discernment, recognition."[1] It is my belief that this is the same knowledge that Jesus obtained, as spoken of in Isaiah 53. Paul writes in Scripture about the importance that the knowledge of Jesus plays in us becoming the Bride of Christ. *"Until we all reach unity in the faith and in the knowledge of the Son of God and become mature, attaining to the whole measure of the fullness of Christ"* (Eph. 4:13 NIV). There is a knowing that we are coming to, through our maturation in Christ, that allows us to attain the *"whole measure of the fullness of Christ." Knowledge* is defined in *Webster's Dictionary* as "all that has been perceived or grasped by the mind; learning; enlightenment." Therefore, there is a knowing that we get through suffering.

It is necessary to undergo suffering as Jesus did. It is through this suffering that we are changed. In the midst of each mistreatment under authority that I have undergone, the Lord has given me fresh revelation of Him. He has shown me who I am in Him. Lately, in the mistreatment that I'm undergoing, the Lord has shown me a much deeper revelation than I've ever experienced that it leaves me in awe of Him. It's as though He has so many secrets, and He reveals them when the opportunity is right, which comes in the midst of suffering.

HONORING HUSBANDS

> *Wives, likewise, be submissive to your own husbands, that even if some do not obey the word, they, without a word, may be won by the conduct of their wives, when they observe your chaste conduct accompanied by fear. Do not let your adornment be merely outward—arranging the hair, wearing gold, or putting on fine apparel— rather let it be the hidden person of the heart, with the incorruptible beauty of a gentle and quiet spirit, which is very precious in the sight of God. For in this manner, in former times, the holy women who trusted in God also adorned themselves, being submissive to their own husbands, as Sarah obeyed Abraham, calling him lord, whose daughters you are if you do good and are not afraid with any terror* (1 Peter 3:1-6).

This is a touchy subject because the western culture has so distorted submission between husband and wife. Let me preface this with discussing the fact that, if there is physical abuse in the relationship, we are not to tolerate that, and in fact, we are not expected by God to suffer from such an atrocity, which was created by satan. The submission here is in reference to a husband that is not physically or verbally abusing his wife.

Submission, in Webster's Dictionary, is identified as a "yielding or surrendering." It is interesting how *yield* is defined, because it gives a different outlook to submission as a wife. *Yield* in *Webster's Dictionary* means "to produce a result." Most people think the definition of *yield* is "to give up," which is true. However, "to give up" is not the fullness of submission. It is God's desire for us to be yielded vessels, and the enemy so many times tries to put a bad taste in our mouths. Satan wants females to rebel against their husband and to be unyielding.

I HAVE YOU COVERED

It is the desire of the Father for us to be covered and protected at all times under Him. In order for us to be covered under God, we must be obedient to His law, the Bible, which delineates expected behaviors and actions. The expected behavior, which is a result, which He desires out of the wife, is that she be submissive to her husband, that she "yields" herself. Although yielding is a surrender, it is also a producing. Therefore, if we look at it a bit differently, it might be easier for us to understand God's desire.

When farmers plant seed, they do it in order to produce a crop. Everything in the Bible is sowing and reaping. There is seed in everything we do, as well as a harvest to reap from the seed that we have sown. The farmer plants seed in the appropriate season so that the seed in the ground will produce a specific crop. They do not plant peanut seeds expecting to get a watermelon. Whatever seeds they plant, that is the crop they will get. Thus, if they plant peanut seeds, they get peanuts. The actual result of the crop is the *yield*. The yield in farming is the result of cultivation, the profit of the seed. Therefore, the *yield* is the end result of the actual process of farming.

Instead of looking at submitting to our husbands as a planting (a seed), which causes us to see a *restrain* on our parts, let us see it as the actual produce (result) of our planting of seeds of obedience prior to the submission showing up. What do I mean? Well, the submission to the husband is not the actual seed, but instead is the produce of some other seed. What seed is submission the produce of? Submission is the produce of the seed of the fear of the Lord. The planting of the fear of the Lord actually produces submission. That is why submission is hard for us, because we see it as the seed. However, it is the produce, the harvest of a former seed. Many of us are trying to plant submission when it is actually the crop, not the seed planted.

GENESIS 3:16

The submission is the produce that tells you if you are under the fear of the Lord; if the fear of the Lord is in you, the natural action would be to be submissive to your husband. Submission is to know your proper place of authority and to maintain your position, as well as not usurping another's position. In Genesis 3, God states what the woman's position is in regard to her husband. To the woman He said,

> *I will greatly increase your pains in childbearing; with pain you will give birth to children. Your desire will be for your husband, and he will rule over you* (Genesis 3:16 NIV).

Here God states that our desire will be for our husbands. *Desire* is to have "a longing for, a craving." Next, He states that our husbands will rule over us, which means that he will lead and guide in decisions. This does not mean that we are not to have input. Quite the contrary; the submissive woman has much input. The husband desires the input of a submissive wife. Remember, submission is the result of a seed of the fear of the Lord. Therefore, the submissive wife demonstrates that she is under God, and as a result, she has knowledge of Him. Remember, Moses knew God's ways because he feared Him, and the Israelites only knew the miracles (acts) of God (see Ps. 103:7).

Therefore, a wife who is submitted to her husband is one who knows the ways of God, and since she does, it is the desire of a husband to discuss matters with his wife.

Husbands, likewise, dwell with them with understanding, giving honor to the wife, as to the weaker vessel, and as being heirs together of the grace of life, that your prayers may not be hindered (1 Peter 3:7).

However, there are times when the husband will not discuss a matter and will make a decision that might be contrary to the wife. The husband might be hearing from God on a specific issue and the wife not. Moreover, the husband might have heard from God and the wife has too, but it is actually a test to see if the wife will be submitted to the husband and thereby maintain a position of the fear of the Lord. Likewise, the husband might miss God on an issue, and the wife hears God. In this instance, she needs to cover it in prayer and ask the Lord for discernment on how to handle the matter.

My Sister

Finally, we are to act in accordance with the Word toward other brothers and sisters in Christ because we can get out of our authority in reference to them.

Finally, all of you be of one mind, having compassion for one another; love as brothers, be tenderhearted, be courteous; not returning evil for evil or reviling for reviling, but on the contrary blessing, knowing that you were called to this, that you may inherit a blessing. For he who would love life and see good days, let him refrain his tongue from evil, and his lips from speaking deceit. Let him turn away from evil and do good; let him seek peace and pursue it. For the eyes of the LORD are on the righteous, and His ears are open to their prayers; but the face of the LORD is against those who do evil (1 Peter 3:8-12).

How do we get out from under God's authority with our sisters in Christ? By not treating them as the Lord would have us, as is demonstrated in His Word. We are to have compassion for our sisters in Christ, not gossiping and talking badly of them. If we are not having compassion for our sisters in Christ and are talking badly of them, then we our out from under God's authority and do not fear the Lord. (This entire subject matter as it relates to Sisters in Christ Jesus is discussed completely in my first book, The Glory to Glory Sisterhood.

PROSPER ME, LORD

In summation of this long and arduous teaching, which is only a snippet of the lengthy, in-depth teaching that we need to pursue, it is my hope that everyone gets an understanding of the fear of the Lord. It is God's desire that we prosper above all. What is the desired outcome of the Lord for us in maintaining a Spirit of the fear of the Lord over our lives? It is to prosper His will, and as His will is prospered in our lives, we prosper. The apostle John states, *"Beloved, I pray that you may prosper in all things and be in health, just as your soul prospers"* (3 John 2).

It is the Lord's desire for us to prosper as our souls prosper. Our souls prosper through our knowledge of God, gained as King Jesus did, by suffering. We gain knowledge of God sometimes through the travailing of our souls (suffering). We get a new revelation of God each time. We are able to pick up our cross and go through this travailing by the Spirit of the fear of the Lord. It is that Spirit of God that urged Moses to step into his destiny (see Ex. 4:14). It is that same Spirit of God that kept David from hurting King Saul and choosing to honor God instead (see 1 Sam. 24:1-13).

I fell into sin as a result of my loss of the Spirit of the fear of the Lord. I exchanged it for the fear of people. We cannot have both, because they are contrary to each other. Therefore, I had to let the fear of people go in order to experience the fullness of the fear of the Lord. Oh that we would all be like Moses, knowing our shortcomings and being so overwhelmed at the call upon our lives that we would remain in a position of humility, knowing that without God we are unable. Without His hand, we are nothing. God desires to work with a contrite heart, which grows out of a fear of the Lord.

When I started studying the fear of the Lord, I was addicted to alcohol and would binge drink on occasion. Binge drinking, although not a desire to drink every day, is just as deadly as drinking daily. When I would drink, I would drink in large consumption. I was reading John Bevere's teaching on the fear of the Lord and knew that I wanted what he was writing about. I would read his teachings, and when I found myself wrenched in my sin and so mad at myself, I would pray in the midst of it, "Lord deliver me, deliver me. I know that You have the power." God, one day, all of a sudden, delivered me from it. My deliverance did not come instantaneously; it was something I had to contend for. The love of God kept me contending for my deliverance.

When I was delivered and set free, God's Spirit of the fear of the Lord set me on a "fast track" in the spiritual realm, and I was able to accelerate my spiritual growth in a short time. I am by no means anywhere near where I want to be. However, I do know that I am so much farther than I had ever dreamt of being.

It was the fear of the Lord that pressed me into a holy lifestyle. One day while reading the Bible, I saw in Isaiah about a road that was made for those who are holy. When I read the Scripture, I knew the Holy Spirit was directing me to understand why I had come so far in such a short time. I had done so because, by the Spirit of the fear of the Lord, I was able to pursue holiness. This pathway is available for you, too if you pursue holiness. It is impossible to pursue holiness without the Spirit of the fear of the Lord. Therefore, I want to close this chapter out with this verse and in prayer.

And an highway shall be there, and a way, and it shall be called The way of holiness; the unclean shall not pass over it; but it shall be for those: the wayfaring men, though fools, shall not err therein. No lion shall be there, nor any ravenous beast shall go up thereon, it shall not be found there; but the redeemed shall walk there (Isaiah 35:8-9 KJV).

Dear Lord, forgive me for being rebellious toward authority that You have placed in my life. I ask You to place in me a delight for the fear of the Lord. Father, give me a knowledge of You that will give me a desire to be obedient and submissive to those who are in authority over me. Give me Your mercy for carrying my cross and following King Jesus. Help me to see any suffering I might have as the beauty of knowing You in Your holiness. I yield myself to the fear of the Lord and the work that You want to do in me. In Jesus' name I pray. Amen.

QUESTIONS:

1. Do you have trouble being submissive to any authority within your family (husband, parents, grandparents, aunts, uncles, and so forth)? If so, what do you need to do to allow God to purge this out of you?

2. Do you speak badly about your sisters in Christ Jesus? If so, what can you do to overcome this deadly

habit? Can you confess only what the Word of God says about your sisters in Christ Jesus?

3. What are some other areas in you in which you want God to do a deeper work in the fear of the Lord?

Endnote

1. http://studybible.info/vines/Know,%20Known,%20Knowledge,%20Unknown

SECTION 2

Spiritual Warfare

Spiritual Warfare:
Push, Pursue, and Recover

Let me preface this chapter with the fact that when I first sat down to write this series of books in 2004 (four books in all) the Holy Spirit laid out the table of contents for each section. I found myself finishing a section, and then I would move by the Holy Spirit to the next thing that I desired to write and found out by looking at the table of contents that this was the very next section on the table of contents. God has been giving me the next section for book three as He laid it out from the very beginning. Moreover, I have been walking through the sections in my personal life as I write them. Therefore, the spiritual warfare that I have been experiencing, to say the least, has been at an all time high over the past couple of weeks. While undergoing these attacks, I've been looking at the table of contents, contemplating my next few weeks of walking through this book series and I laugh. I see that the next sections are forgiveness and rejection, and I'm already praying for an anointing to walk through both (laugh out loud).

chapter

6

Becoming a Princess Warrior

Well, let's get to work warriors, because this is a serious subject, and the approach we need to take, as with all of God's Word, is one of being teachable and pliable in the hands of the Great Potter. God is the potter, and we are the clay. The desired end is to be an honorable vessel crafted out of the hands of God and filled with the Holy Spirit, while walking in the fullness of who we are in Christ Jesus. We will not walk in our fullness in Christ unless we address spiritual warfare, because the blood He shed was for *everything,* not some things. He didn't die just for our salvation so we could anticipate going to Heaven when we die. He died for *everything!* He died to bring us fullness in Him.

For in Christ all the fullness of the Deity lives in bodily form, and you have been given fullness in Christ, who is the head over every power and authority. In Him you were also circumcised, in the putting off of the sinful nature, not with

a circumcision done by the hands of men but with the cir-
cumcision done by Christ, having been buried with Him
in baptism and raised with Him through your faith in the
power of God, who raised Him from the dead. When you
were dead in your sins and in the uncircumcision of your
sinful nature, God made you alive with Christ. He forgave
us all our sins, having canceled the written code, with its
regulations, that was against us and that stood opposed to
us; He took it away, nailing it to the cross. And having
disarmed the powers and authorities, He made a public
spectacle of them, triumphing over them by the cross (Colossians 2:9-15 NIV).

In order to experience the fullness of Christ, we have to appropriate our God-given authority to take dominion over the
earth. Jesus Christ disarmed satan and his demons, making them
a public spectacle due to His triumph through the cross. As a result, we have been given all authority through Christ Jesus.

DON'T BE SPOOKED

Many people are spooked to some degree when it comes to
spiritual warfare, and in the beginning, I must admit I was too.
I had been a Southern Baptist all of my life, and the thought of
doing spiritual warfare spooked me. It was something I had never
been exposed to when I was in the Baptist church. However, I had
been a social worker and worked with the seriously mentally ill
for a short time. During the time that I worked with that population, I saw things that were abnormal based on what I would term
as natural. The behaviors demonstrated were not of this world,
of natural people, but were what I perceived to be of some "dark"
entity outside of this natural realm we call earth. As a result, I began to seek God's Word on what I was experiencing through my
discussions and visits with the mentally ill population. In order

to address spiritual warfare and the mentally ill, I suggest you get an appropriate book. One I would suggest is, *Pigs in the Parlor: A Practical Guide to Deliverance*, by Frank and Ida Hammond.[1]

After reading many books, attending many programs, and experiencing abnormal confrontations, I woke up one day and found myself in the middle of spiritual warfare. Through my pursuit of finding the truth regarding spiritual warfare and meeting others who did as well, I didn't realize that all the while I was walking in the midst of what I was seeking. For instance, it had become common for certain words to be used around my house and on the telephone with others. Discussions about deliverance (which we will discuss later), demons, and strongholds were normal. Before I knew it, people were calling me to assist in "deliverances" for those seeking deliverance and asking me questions on spiritual warfare, as well as borrowing my library media in reference to it.

I did not plan this; it just happened. This is only something to whet your appetite, as in the section on the fear of the Lord. What I would encourage you to do is to get further teaching on this area from those Christian teachers who are very experienced and knowledgeable in spiritual warfare. Some of my favorite teachers are Neil T. Anderson, John Paul Jackson, Anna Mendez Ferrell, Rebecca Brown and George Bloomer.

In order to address this area, I would like to begin this chapter with a prayer and ask you to go through this chapter at your own pace. We will embark on a quest to find out what we are to do in the spiritual realm in terms of warfare.

Dear Lord, I plead the blood of Jesus over me, my mind, my family, and my home. I declare that I will come forth with the full knowledge by Your Holy Spirit in regard to warfare in the spiritual realm. You said that Your Word would not return void, and I declare that the truth that You give me will be implanted in and covered by the blood of Jesus and that it will produce fruit for the Kingdom. I bind any hindrances or distractions that would cause me to not fully attain the knowledge that You have set for me in this section. I declare that all lying spirits that would make me believe that this is not of You and that I do not have the power that You placed in me when You died on the cross would be bound. I loose Your Holy Spirit to have His way. I declare that I will walk in the boldness and knowledge of God and not deny the power of the Word that operates inside of me. I bind the spirit of intimidation and the spirit of fear, and I loose the spirit of the fear of the Lord. You said, Father, that whatever is bound in Heaven will be bound on earth and whatever is loosed in Heaven will be loosed on earth. I ask this in the awesome, powerful name of Jesus Christ and know that it is so. Amen.

WE ARE TO RULE THE EARTH

We have established the fact that in Christ's death all fullness of measure was obtained for us. What is included in the fullness of measure is what Almighty God bestowed on us in the beginning.

Then God said, "Let us make man in our image, in our likeness, and let them rule over the fish of the sea and the birds of the air, over the livestock, over all the earth, and over all the creatures that move along the ground." So God created man in his own image, in the image of God he created him; male and female he created them. God blessed them and said to them, "Be fruitful and increase in number; fill the earth and subdue it. Rule over the fish of the sea and the birds of the air and over every living creature that moves on the ground" (Genesis 1: 26-28 NIV).

Man (I don't like the word "people" here because that is not what it says in the Word and I will not try and be politically correct and compromise God's word. God made Adam who is a man in His image) were made in the image of God, Jesus, and Holy Spirit, as we discussed in the section on the fear of the Lord. In that time, God gave all power over the earth to man, commissioning them to fill it and subdue it. He gave us ruling power over the earth. The power given was to *fill* the earth and *subdue* it. *Webster's* defines *subdue* as "to conquer and bring into subjection; to bring under control especially by an exertion of the will." Therefore, God gave people the authority to control the earth (creatures of the sea, air, and ground).

It was not until the fall of humanity that all power was then subjugated to another entity, satan. It was through satan's craftiness that he took the power given only to humanity, when Adam and Eve disobediently ate of the tree of the knowledge of good and evil. In doing so, their eyes were opened to both good and evil, and satan took their power from them. It was necessary for Jesus to leave His throne, come to earth, and pay the price to take away the curse that fell upon man and the earth when satan took over, which is the curse of death.

LIFE OR DEATH

There are only two positions in existence, life and death. Christ came to give life and give it abundantly. Satan came to bring death. The fight that Jesus fought on earth was the victory over death. When Adam and Eve sinned and their knowledge was opened to evil, death began on earth. Nature was never intended to die; it was to live without decay.

The creation waits in eager expectation for the sons of God to be revealed. For the creation was subjected to frustration, not by its own choice, but by the will of the one who subjected it, in hope that the creation itself will be liberated from its bondage to decay and brought into the glorious freedom of the children of God. We know that the whole creation has been groaning as in the pains of childbirth right up to the present time (Romans 8:19-22 NIV).

Creation was subjected to decay by Adam and Eve's sin, and it eagerly waits for the sons and daughters of Christ to be revealed. I picture it as though creation, if it were possible, is sitting at the edge of its chair ready to jump up at the moment when the sons and daughters of Christ are revealed and leap for joy that it would no longer be subject to decay.

We know that the position of life is that which is offered by God, and the position of death is offered by satan. Since satan is not a creative being, he cannot create, he can only mimic or copy what has been created by God. Therefore, the opposite of life is death, and as Christ brought life abundantly, satan has brought death abundantly. Since satan took humanity's authority and position in subduing the earth and brought creation on earth under the power of death, life exists only when we use the power given to us to overcome death. Power is given to us by the blood of Jesus Christ when He was offered as a guilt offering for our sins, making us joint heirs with Him, seating us in heavenly places, and giving us the keys to the Kingdom of Heaven (see Eph. 2:6; Matt. 16:19). It is resurrection power!

Princess Warrior

Everything that is taken by death is done so violently. As the Scripture states, the Kingdom of Heaven suffers violence and the *violent* take it by force:

And from the days of John the Baptist until the present time, the kingdom of heaven has endured violent assault, and violent men seize it by force [as a precious prize—a share in the heavenly kingdom is sought with most ardent zeal and intense exertion] (Matthew 11:12 AMP).

This Scripture is not referring to the enemy taking the Kingdom of Heaven, God's Kingdom. Instead, it is saying that violent Christians are going to be the ones who literally take back what was given to man and stolen by satan. Believers do this by appropriating the power given to them as joint heirs of Christ, who have the keys to the Kingdom of Heaven and power to take dominion over the earth. In order to have a deeper revelation of this violence coming from God's people we have to look at the scripture in context. The word in Matthew 11:12 was identifying an opposition that we could stand in confidence and oppose. The Word identified that Heaven was suffering violence, heaven was being assaulted and the opposition to that was darkness, satan's kingdom. However, this is where the revelation comes in. We did not have access to the Kingdom of Heaven until something shifted on earth. Let us look at this scripture further by going to the next verse. *"For all the Prophets and the law prophesied up until John"* (Matt. 11:13 AMP). Therefore, when John the Baptist entered the scene something shifted for the Kingdom of Heaven. John was cloaked with the mantle of Elijah that would prepare the way of the Lord to turn many to the Lord Jesus (see Luke 1:17). John's message was *"Repent for the kingdom of Heaven is at hand"* (Matt. 3:2). John's message came as a result of Jesus being on the earth as Messiah, King of kings and Lord of Lords, Son of God and Son of Man! Jesus states that He is the door to the Father (see John 10:9). *"I am the Door; anyone who enters in through Me will be saved (will live). He will come in and he will go out [freely], and will find pasture"* (John 10:9 AMP). Moreover, Jesus' message also was: repent for the Kingdom of

Heaven is near (see Matthew 4:17). Heaven became accessible to man (woman and man) again when Jesus entered the earth. Up until John the Baptist, accessing heaven was only prophesy, not yet a reality. However, when John, entered the scene something shifted something happened! John was one who prepared the way of the Lord Jesus, therefore His message was *repent for the Kingdom of heaven is near!* John knew the door, Jesus, to the Kingdom of Heaven was now on the earth, thus making heaven accessible again to us! Therefore, when the Kingdom of Heaven became accessible to us, satan saw the open door to heaven, the heavenly access and began to put many adversaries around that door so that it would be a hindrance to man obtaining his rightful inheritance. Satan saw that the Kingdom of Heaven would be obtainable and began a violent assault in attacking it once it became accessible on earth again through Jesus Christ. We as women have access to the Kingdom of heaven; we have the keys of the kingdom! Therefore, since we have the keys of the kingdom we have access to our inheritance through Christ Jesus as we come to the Father, God, in order to appropriate what is already ours. Once we obtain our inheritance and bring it into the earthly realm by God's Holy Spirit we become a weapon in the hands of our God (see Zech 9:13). We women are to become Princess Warriors being a weapon in God's hand to take dominion over the earth along with God's men and bring the Kingdom of Heaven near to all those in the earth and make the kingdoms of this world the kingdom of our God.

Who is a princess warrior? She is a daughter of the most High God who has appropriated salvation through confessing that Jesus is her savior, that He died for her sins, and that He was resurrected (see Rom. 10:9-10). This woman is then entitled to appropriate her position as a daughter of God, walking in her authority in Jesus Christ; she is a Princess Warrior.

Who do we violently take back the Kingdom of Heaven on earth from? This is answered in Ephesians, where it states:

For our struggle is not against flesh and blood, but against the rulers, against the authorities, against the powers of this dark world and against the spiritual forces of evil in the heavenly realms (Ephesians 6:12-13 NIV).

Thus, this mandate is for us to fight in the spiritual realm. We are given power over the earth, and it is our duty to subdue the earth.

When I first got into spiritual warfare, I started praying whatever my flesh felt like, and I opened a door to spiritual attacks from the enemy. I started praying against dark rulers over cities and regions. I basically challenged them immediately because I was so zealous. This is not wise; it is like an infant deciding to drive a car. If an infant begins to drive a car then that infant and many others will get hurt. Therefore, to avoid spiritual warfare backlash, do not go up against any territorial demons until you do further reading on that matter because it is necessary to have what Holy Spirit has given me knowledge of knowing when I have the "green light" to come against territorial demons as I go from glory to glory in God's authority in spiritual warfare. Read the suggested authors in order to operate in a knowledgeable understanding about doing warfare, especially John Paul Jackson's book, *Needless Casualties of War*.[1] Here we will be discussing spiritual warfare strategies and plans that you can carry out now related to individuals, families, schools, and so forth.

Our position then is to bring life (light) to earth where there is death (darkness) and to bring God's Kingdom to its rightful position on earth, overcoming satan's kingdom by rightfully taking back what God gave humanity—the earth. In order to do this, it is important to read the Word and believe in it. Belief during the Bible days was not as we see it today, which is to "hope for." Instead, it was to "trust and obey!" When Abraham, King David, and Esther believed God in the Old Testament, they trusted His Word to be truth, and they obeyed it.

BELIEVE THE WORD!

The Bible has not changed in regard to believing the Word. We are to trust that the Word brings life and that anything contrary to it brings death. Moreover, we are to *obey* the Word of God, which is an action. If obeying is an action, then our obedience to God is demonstrated in our day-to-day lives (our action). Therefore, if we believe God's Word on spiritual warfare and subduing the earth, we are to be demonstrating that in our day-to-day lives.

Let me ask you, are you violently taking back the Kingdom of God in your life from the enemy? You can answer a few questions that will let you know if you are. Is your house saved? Are your finances free from attacks by the enemy? Are you and your loved ones in good health? Are your marriage and family relationships on solid ground? Is your spiritual relationship with God on solid ground? Is your school free from drugs, gang violence, and crude media? If you answered no to ANY of these questions, you need to get more violent in your spiritual warfare. However, before you can get violent, you have to know something about spiritual warfare and what authority you have.

Understand that the minute you were birthed into the Kingdom of God you were put into a war. The war is between the Kingdom of God (light) and satan (darkness). Everything that is going on in the earth is between God and satan. We are simply to choose whom we will serve.

In order to understand the fullness of what Jesus was speaking about in praying for the Kingdom of Heaven to come to earth (see Matt. 16:19) and binding and loosing things on earth so that they will be done in Heaven (see Matt. 16:18-20), we have to understand a couple of concepts. We have to understand the Kingdom and binding and loosing. The Kingdom that Jesus is referring to is the Father's Kingdom, God's Holy Dominion. What makes up a kingdom is not necessarily the land that it possesses; a country can possess a land, but not necessarily be in dominion over it. Rather, a kingdom is a ruling authority. Therefore, we have to understand God's Kingdom so that we can bring His ruling authority to earth. This is seen when Jesus made a statement to Peter.

> *He said to them, "But who do you say that I am?" Simon Peter answered and said, "You are the Christ, the Son of the living God." Jesus answered and said to him, "Blessed are you, Simon Bar-Jonah, for flesh and blood has not revealed this to you, but My Father who is in heaven. And I also say to you that you are Peter, and on this rock I will build My church, and the gates of Hades shall not prevail against it. And I will give you the keys of the kingdom of heaven, and whatever you bind on earth will be bound in heaven, and whatever you loose on earth will be loosed in heaven"* (Matthew 16:15-19).

Peter had a revelation that Jesus is the Christ, and on that revelation Jesus stated that He would build His church. The Greek translation for *church* in this Scripture is *ekklesia*. The word *ekklesia* in the time of Jesus Christ did not refer to church, but instead it meant "a governing body, a legislative assembly." Therefore, Christ was saying to Peter, "On the revelation that you have of Me as Jesus Christ will I build My government." Governments duplicate themselves in the culture by having the people talk the language and abide by their rules and by maintaining control and authority over everything within that area. Jesus, therefore, was telling Peter and His disciples that His government is to be established

This government of Jesus is prophesied by the prophet Isaiah. This same government, the Kingdom of Heaven, Jesus tells us is inside of us.

> *Once, having been asked by the Pharisees when the kingdom of God would come, Jesus replied, "The kingdom of God does not come with your careful observation, nor will people say, 'Here it is,' or 'There it is,' because the kingdom of God is within you"* (Luke 17:20-21 NIV).

The prophet Isaiah further explained the nature of the Kingdom when he prophesied about Jesus:

> *For to us a child is born, to us a son is given, and the government will be on His shoulders. And He will be called Wonderful Counselor, Mighty God, Everlasting Father, Prince of Peace. **Of the increase of His government and peace there will be no end.** He will reign on David's throne and over his kingdom, establishing and upholding it with justice and righteousness from that time on and forever. The zeal of the LORD Almighty will accomplish this* (Isaiah 9:6-7 NIV).

The prophet Isaiah here prophecies that Christ would be given to the earth and with Him would be the coming government of Heaven. In this prophecy, it foretells that the government of Christ will continually increase.

QUESTIONS:

1. Do you have trouble being a Princess Warrior, one who does spiritual warfare? If yes, then describe why.

Is it because of your upbringing, because it is unearthly, or for some other reason?

2. Describe what character traits add to you being a Princess Warrior. Are you bold, a warrior, fearless, and so forth?

Endnotes

1. Frank Hammond and Ida Mae Hammond, *Pigs in the Parlor: A Practical Guide to Deliverance* (Impact Christian Books, 1973).

2. John Paul Jackson, *Needless Casualties of War* (Flower Mound, TX: Streams Publications, 1999).

Spiritual Warfare: Where Do I Begin?

In order to do spiritual warfare, we have to know about God's Kingdom and His Kingdom principles. This is the crux of spiritual warfare. If we do not know this, it's as if we are throwing darts aimlessly into the air with no likelihood of hitting a target. It would be as though we signed up for the Army, walked in and grabbed a gun, were transported to the war in the Middle East, and began shooting at anything we discerned to be an "enemy." That is not a good idea, and in fact, it is reckless. I have discovered in law school that *recklessness* is used as an element under certain rules of law in proving that someone has broken the law. Therefore, if we are reckless with God's law, it is disobedience, and we have to repent and turn our minds to understanding it. What do we need in order to understand God's law and be obedient to it in regard to spiritual warfare? We need an understanding of what His Kingdom is and what principals govern spiritual warfare.

While on this earth, Jesus brought the news of the Kingdom of God. Everywhere He went He taught the Kingdom, whether it was in parables, symbolism, discipleship, or miracles. All around Jesus the word *Kingdom* was spoken. Jesus stated,

> *My kingdom is not of this world: if My kingdom were of this world, then would My servants fight, that I should not be delivered to the Jews: but now is My kingdom not from hence* (John 18:36 KJV).

In the Book of Daniel, we see a closer look at God's Kingdom, which Jesus spoke of in His day.

> *But throughout the history of these kingdoms, the God of heaven will be building a kingdom that will never be destroyed, nor will this kingdom ever fall under the domination of another. In the end it will crush the other kingdoms and finish them off and come through it all standing strong and eternal* (Daniel 2:44 MSG).

This Scripture was an interpretation the prophet Daniel gave to King Nebuchadnezzar's dream. Daniel informed King Nebuchadnezzar that his kingdom (Babylon) had been established through him by God and that after it passed away there would be other kingdoms to succeed it.

GOD'S KINGDOM

However, while the earthly kingdoms were rising and being overtaken by others, God's Word identified that there would be one Kingdom created by God, which would not be under human rule. In the end, the Kingdom of God would stand alone, crushing the other kingdoms. It is a Kingdom set up by God, ruled by

God, and it would be the only one standing to last throughout eternity. Jesus discussed this Kingdom with His disciples when He stated that He is going to help in the preparations of this Kingdom. He stated,

Do not let your hearts be troubled. Trust in God; trust also in Me. In my Father's house are many rooms; if it were not so, I would have told you. I am going there to prepare a place for you. And if I go and prepare a place for you, I will come back and take you to be with Me that you also may be where I am (John 14:1-3 NIV).

Therefore, the Kingdom is not an earthly Kingdom, rather it is in Heaven being built up and prepared for our arrival.

Daniel saw in the interpretation of King Nebuchadnezzar's dream that several earthly kingdoms would be established and that during their rise and fall that God's heavenly Kingdom would be built. There is a set time identified in the dream that God's Kingdom would come down on earth and crush all of the earthly kingdoms. However, in between now and that appointed time, there is the opportunity for us, being daughters of God in Christ, to actually bring down the heavenly Kingdom into the earthly realm. Thus, the Kingdom that we fight for is the heavenly Kingdom of God most high, established in the heavens.

Since we know where the Kingdom is and what it is, how is it then that we are to fight for the Kingdom? This is displayed in the Lord's Prayer. While on earth, Jesus taught us how to pray.

And He said to them, When you pray, say: Our Father Who is in heaven, hallowed be Your name, Your kingdom come. Your will be done [held holy and revered] on earth as it is in heaven. Give us daily our bread [food for the morrow]. And forgive us our sins, for we ourselves also forgive

everyone who is indebted to us [who has offended us or done us wrong]. And bring us not into temptation but rescue us from evil. (Luke 11:2-4 AMP).

Jesus taught us to pray that the Father's Kingdom would come to earth *as it is* in Heaven. This Kingdom is one that Jesus has given us access to; He wants us to pray that the Kingdom come. *Come* is an action word, a verb. Therefore, it denotes some form of action taking place. *Miriam-Webster's Dictionary* defines *come* as "to move toward something." We are praying that God's heavenly Kingdom move toward the earth to be established in our world as it is in Heaven through the will of the Father.

Therefore, this shows that the Kingdom is not here on earth, but has the propensity to come to earth. How does the Kingdom of Heaven come to earth? It requires us bringing it here through the will of God. God gave people dominion over the earth; therefore, we have to be the conduits whereby Heaven is established on earth by the power God gave us at the beginning of time. Our Lord and Savior Jesus Christ restored this power, after we lost it in Adam. Jesus restored our power to bring God's Kingdom to the earth. This can be seen further in God's Word when Jesus speaks a parable to the disciples in the book of Luke.

And he said to them, Which of you who has a friend will go to him at midnight and will say to him, Friend lend me three loaves [of bread]. For a friend of mine who is on a journey has just come, and I have nothing to put before him. And he from within will answer, Do not disturb me; the door is now closed, and my children are with me in bed; I cannot get up and supply you [with anything]? I tell you, although he will not get up and supply him anything because he is a friend, yet because of his shameless persistence and insistence he will get up and give him as much as he needs. So I say to you, Ask and keep on asking and it shall be given you; seek and keep on seeking and you shall find; knock and keep on knocking and the door shall be opened to you. For everyone who asks and keeps on asking receives, and he who seeks and keeps on seeking finds; and to him who knocks and keeps on knocking, the door shall be opened. (Luke 11:5-10 AMP).

God wants us to press in with all our heart, mind and soul to Him and as we seek God and His righteousness (see Matt. 6:33), He will add everything to us! God leads and guides us by His Holy Spirit!

THE HOLY SPIRIT

This power is recognized at Pentecost in the Book of Acts. The apostles were given directions by Jesus to wait upon the Holy Spirit, whom they would receive from God.

On one occasion, while he was eating with them, he gave them this command: "Do not leave Jerusalem, but wait for the gift My Father promised, which you have heard Me speak about. For John baptized with water, but in a few days you will be baptized with the Holy Spirit (Acts 1:4-5 NIV).

While Jesus was on earth, the authority that He gave to the disciples to do spiritual warfare was the power He possessed during His time on earth. However, in this passage, Jesus was about to ascend to the heavens and return to the Father. Therefore, He had to have a way for God's people to receive the same power in His absence.

This power was given to us after Jesus ascended by the receiving of God's Holy Spirit. Power came from the baptism of the Holy Spirit. Remember, we are baptized into salvation's plan, and at that time we are saved and have the right to the gift of God's

Holy Spirit. We go from death to life in the Kingdom of God when we accept Jesus Christ as our Savior. The baptism of the Holy Spirit happens when we are empowered to walk out our Christian lives in fullness.

> *But you will receive power when the Holy Spirit comes on you; and you will be my witnesses in Jerusalem, and in all Judea and Samaria, and to the ends of the earth* (Acts 1:8 NIV).

This power that we receive when the Holy Spirit comes upon us is to do all the incredible signs and wonders that Jesus spoke of regarding true believers.

> *He that believeth and is baptized shall be saved; but he that believeth not shall be damned. And these signs shall follow them that believe; in My name shall they cast out devils; they shall speak with new tongues; they shall take up serpents; and if they drink any deadly thing, it shall not hurt them; they shall lay hands on the sick, and they shall recover* (Mark 16:16-18 KJV).

This power is only received from above, not of this world, and it is only the work of God's Holy Spirit and none other. This power gives the believer the authority to cast out demons, cleanse the leapers, heal the sick, and raise the dead.

DON'T GO PICKING UP SNAKES!

A side note: *"They shall take up serpents"* is used as a symbol in the English translation and does not literally mean picking up serpents (snakes). Some translations state that the believers will pick up snakes (serpents), which is not helpful in getting the revelation of what the Scripture is referring to here. The translation here in the KJV addresses the serpent (snake) issue more in detail. The Word states, *"they shall take up serpents,"* not pick up or hold. The word *take* in the Strong's Concordance is *airō,* which means "to take up or away, to lift or raise."[1] *Serpent* here is translated from *ŏphis,* which means "sharpness of vision as a type of sly cunning," such as satan.[2] Satan and his demons intend to use their malicious and deceitful lies against people and place put it on them as a yoke of bondage. Therefore, the Word of God is speaking to believers being able to bring the Kingdom of God into other people's lives or a geographic area by lifting up or taking away the malicious lies of satan and his demons by the Word of God's truth and anointing destroying the yoke of satan (take up or lift off the yoke of satan, the serpent).

Many of you may have questions regarding the Holy Spirit. There are many books on the Holy Spirit; my favorites are *Experiencing the Holy Spirit* by Andrew Murray and *Holy Spirit My Senior Partner* by David Yonggi Cho and Paul Yonggi.[3] I am writing about Spiritual Warfare; if you need further guidance on the baptism of the Holy Spirit and the work of the Holy Spirit, seek further reading and pray to the Lord regarding the baptism of His Holy Spirit. I will emphasize this, you can ask for God's Holy Spirit being a believer of Christ Jesus, a Christian, and God will baptize you in His Holy Spirit if you want it now. Simply pray "Father God in Heaven, I ask for the infilling of Your Holy Spirit to be upon me now in Jesus Name." It is that simple, it is not a difficult thing because in God's Word in Luke 11 it states:

> *What Father among you, if his son asks for a loaf of bread, will give him a stone; or if he asks for a fish, will instead of a fish give him a serpent? Or if he asks for an egg, will give him a scorpion? If you then, evil as you are, know how to give good [gifts that are to their advantage] to your children, how much more will your heavenly Father give*

the Holy Spirit to those who ask and continue to ask Him!
(Luke 11:11-13 AMP).

Now that we understand what Kingdom we fight for and what our part is in fighting for the Kingdom of God, let's discuss the power for spiritual warfare. We are to bring the Kingdom of God to earth through the power that we have. This use of the power of the Holy Spirit requires that we first have a relationship with God, not a religion. It requires intimacy with God and listening to what He wants us to do. This could be compared to a commander in the military who desires to give orders to his troops. If the commander is at the command post and the troops are in the field, how are they going to know what orders the commander wants them to carry out. They have a form of communication, usually a radio, which allows transmission from the commanding officer to the troop. It is the same with us.

THE COMMANDER AND CHIEF

God has orders for us while we are at war here on earth. However, the only way we can hear from Him is to have a transmission of His commands for us. This transmission is through God's Holy Spirit. It's as though we have a receptor, and God has a communicator that sends out signals. If we do not have a receptor in a location that allows the incoming signals to be received, we will not get the message. Therefore, the receptor is activated by God's Holy Spirit. The Holy Spirit gets the communications from God the Commander and Chief to run through our receptor and be translated. This is what I call Hearing God, which is discussed in full detail in book four of this series, *Destiny*.

How are we to bring the Kingdom of God from Heaven to earth? We do this as demonstrated through the life of Jesus. He went about preaching and proclaiming the Kingdom.

But He said, "I must preach the good news of the kingdom of God to the other towns also, because that is why I was sent." And He kept on preaching in the synagogues of Judea (Luke 4:43-44 NIV).

Jesus was *sent* to preach the *news* of the Kingdom of God. *"After this, Jesus traveled about from one town and village to another, proclaiming the good news of the kingdom of God..."* (Luke 8:1 NIV). Jesus proclaimed the Kingdom of God. While preaching and proclaiming the Kingdom, Jesus was taking dominion in the earth realm for the Kingdom of God, and this is where spiritual warfare is involved. The warfare is over the good news that Jesus came to give about the Kingdom of God. It was the spoken Word of the Kingdom (the news) that brought it into earth, thereby taking dominion of the earth away from the kingdom of darkness wherever Jesus went. The Kingdom is spread throughout the world by the *news,* and as a result of spreading the news, we are going to come into contact with the enemy, which involves spiritual warfare. Also, spiritual warfare comes because when we bring the news of the Kingdom of God, we then free people who are in bondage to the kingdom of darkness.

For example, Operation Enduring Freedom involved America spreading the news of freedom that we desire to maintain in our own country and to offer to those who are not free in the Middle East. In order to carry out that operation, military warfare is involved. The President of the United States is not going to send over the best-looking people of America (most handsome and beautiful people) to go to the Middle East and tell a hostile government that they can be free and "hey man, freedom is where it is at." I have seen many high profile celebrities think that this was the way to go.

On the contrary, the President is spreading a message (news) about freedom through a trained, submissive, and skilled military. It is this news of freedom that threatens our enemy. In order to reach those who are in need of freedom, we have to fight the hostile militants who do not want the civilians in the Middle East to receive freedom. Moreover, the militants want to take freedom away from others outside of their country, as in the attack on the trade towers in September 2001, which was spreading the news of fear. We in America are not truly free unless there is no threat of attack against us by the enemy. If the enemy can come into our country and wreak havoc, then we are not free, but are living in fear instead.

Those who are not truly empowered by God's Kingdom are already in bondage to the enemy and need the Kingdom of God to free them. While we are spreading the news about the Kingdom and are trying to reach others for Christ, those in bondage, we will come into contact with a hostile kingdom (satan's kingdom) that wants to terrorize us and does not want the news of God's Kingdom to be spread to those who are in bondage. As a result of a hostile enemy, we will experience attacks by him to prevent that news from being spread and received. He wants to keep us paralyzed in the same way that our nation was paralyzed when the attack came upon America with the trade towers. The enemy wants us to fear and avoid stepping out to even fight the war. If he can keep us in fear, it will paralyze us, and in the end he will come and take what freedoms we do have. The Word of God puts it so well in Isaiah 61.

ISAIAH 61

The Spirit of the Sovereign LORD is on Me, because the LORD has anointed Me to preach good news to the poor. He has sent Me to bind up the brokenhearted, to proclaim freedom for the captives and release from darkness for the prisoners, to proclaim the year of the LORD's favor and the day of vengeance of our God, to comfort all who mourn, and provide for those who grieve in Zion—to bestow on them a crown of beauty instead of ashes, the oil of gladness instead of mourning, and a garment of praise instead of a spirit of despair. They will be called oaks of righteousness, a planting of the LORD for the display of His splendor (Isaiah 61:1-3 NIV).

When God's Holy Spirit is on us, "the Spirit of the Sovereign Lord," it will be in order to "preach the good news to the poor." In the King James Version, it uses the word *meek* instead of poor. *Strong's Concordance* identifies the *poor* as "those who are depressed in mind or circumstances."[4] This is where we can use the guiding of the Holy Spirit to help us take away the lies of the enemy on people experiencing this attack.

When people are depressed in their minds or circumstances, it is because satan and his devils are feeding them lies that they are different than the Word says they are. For example, when people are not able to manage their finances well and have bounced checks, the enemy might tell them, "See, you can never manage finances." That is contrary to the Word of God, because if I am in Christ and my Kingdom is of God then God owns the cattle on thousand hills (see Ps. 50:10). Moreover, I have the mind of Christ (see 1 Cor. 2:16), which means I am more than able to manage my finances. This is an example of us taking serpents up (lies), as identified earlier. We are not handling snakes with our hands, but are taking away or lifting off the malicious lies of the enemy.

Attacks can take many forms. There are attacks on us, our families, our churches, and those whom we are fighting for. For example, we might be attacked from the very moment we receive Christ. It might be that after receiving salvation through Christ, you leave the church and end up having something go terribly wrong. It could be that you've been a Christian for a while, and you find that you and your husband are living almost separate lives, without marital bliss. You might discover that your teenager, who has been raised in church since he was 2 months old, is doing drugs. The list can go on. Remember, we war not against flesh and blood (see Eph. 6:12.). If there are negative occurrences in our lives, and they are not a result of disobedience on our part, it is most likely an attack by the enemy. Keep in mind that some occurrences happen because of living in this fallen earth, such as your grandparents dying, having your air conditioner unit blow, and so forth.

The very attack that is coming against us by the enemy will turn out to our benefit because *all things God works for the good of those who love Him, who have been called according to His purpose."* (Rom. 8:28 NIV). God has given me a slogan: "The enemy has a plan, but God has an appointment that will disrupt the enemy's plans." We will go through trials and tribulations while we are on earth. (see 1 Pet. 1:6-7) The whole purpose of going through spiritual warfare, going through the trials and tribulations is to see Christ Jesus clearer than ever before, to have a revelation of Christ in you the hope of glory! (see 1 Pet. 4:12-13). However, when we go through things, we simply must trust God and know that His Word is true, trusting that no matter what bad things are going on in our lives—God will work them out to our benefit. Moreover, it is through hearing God that the enemy's plans are exposed and we receive instruction on overcoming the enemy. I will give you an example of this later, along with the spiritual warfare that I did to fight for my eldest son's life. Job is the best example of attacks being allowed by the enemy against

God's people. Satan came before God to get permission to come against Job (see Job 1:12; Job 2:7).

The whole purpose of the attack by the enemy is to stop the spreading of the news regarding the Kingdom of God. Jesus gave us a protocol in spreading the news of the Kingdom and doing spiritual warfare.

> *When Jesus had called the Twelve together, He gave them power and authority to drive out all demons and to cure diseases,* **and** *He sent them out to preach the kingdom of God* **and** *to heal the sick* (Luke 9:1-2 NIV).

It appears in the Book of Luke that Jesus had a protocol in order that we might spread the news about the Kingdom. He gave power and authority (as given to us by the Holy Spirit) to drive out *all* demons and cure diseases. Jesus first gave power, which we get now from the baptism of the Holy Spirit. Therefore, we are not to even consider doing spiritual warfare without the power of the Holy Spirit. After they were given power, Jesus then sent out the disciples to preach the Kingdom of God and heal the sick. After we are empowered with God's Holy Spirit, we can then go preach and proclaim the Kingdom in the earth. It is in carrying the news of the Kingdom of God that we will need to use the power given to us by the Holy Spirit to do spiritual warfare for ourselves and the troops (our Christian sisters and brothers), as well as for those who are in bondage by satan in casting out demons and curing diseases. In order to operate against the attacks of the enemy, we will do so by using spiritual warfare.

We are to drive out demons, lift away the lies of demons (satan and his devils) off of people and circumstances, and cure diseases—all the while proclaiming and preaching the news of the Kingdom. The truth is established by proclaiming the Kingdom of God to set people free from oppression by satan. Those in bondage hear the truth of the Kingdom, which breaks the oppression they are experiencing. Jesus stated, *"And ye shall know the truth, and the truth shall make you free"* (John 8:32 KJV).

Remember, the Kingdom brings forth life, and the enemy brings forth death. Therefore, we will come into contact with and overcome death with our Holy Spirit-given power. We will learn principles from Jesus in using our authority to come against oppressive demonic spirits. Below we will learn principles of spiritual warfare and also some terms that we must become familiar with.

QUESTIONS:

1. Who is our battle against?

2. What are the signs of a believer of Christ Jesus?

3. Are we to handle snakes? If not, what does the Word of God mean when it talks about taking up serpents?

4. What Scripture in the Old Testament signifies the call that demonstrates believers operating in spiritual warfare?

5. Assignment: Profess the Scriptures in this section, and if you are not filled by God's Holy Spirit then seek the baptism of the Holy Spirit. Study Isaiah 61 and decree and declare Isaiah 61 over you each day. I sometimes read the entire chapter out loud, or at other times I simply say, "I decree Isaiah 61 over me in the Name of Jesus."

Endnotes

1. James Strong, *Strong's Exhaustive Concordance of the Bible* (.142 GREEK..), #.

2. Ibid., #GREEK 3789.

3. Andrew Murray *Experiencing the Holy Spirit* (Pittsburgh, PA: Whitaker House, 2000); David Yonggi Cho, *Holy Spirit, My Senior Partner: Understanding the Holy Spirit and His Gifts* (Lake Mary, FL: Charisma House, 1996).

4. James Strong, Strong's Exhaustive Concordance of the Bible Strong, #. HEBREW 6035

8

Tearing Down Strongholds and Binding and Loosening

TEARING DOWN STRONGHOLDS:

We demolish arguments and every pretension that sets itself up against the knowledge of God, and we take captive every thought to make it obedient to Christ (2 Corinthians 10:5 NIV).

To tear down a stronghold, we need to understand what a stronghold is. "A stronghold is a strongly fortified defensive structure."[1] If the enemy captures the stronghold, basically the entire city is captured because the stronghold is the defense structure. Therefore, if we are demolishing a stronghold that has been set up by the enemy, we are demolishing satan's defense fortress.

Does a fortress pop up overnight? No, it has to be built. Likewise, a stronghold by satan is built in our lives when we receive his lie that contradicts the Word of God. The next thing that happens is that another lie comes in the same area where the stronghold is and builds upon what is already there. Before long, we have a building, a fortress, which has been established by the enemy in our lives and needs to be demolished. Strongholds of satan are built in our minds, which are part of our souls. Our souls are made up of the mind, will, and emotions. Therefore, the stronghold of the enemy in our minds will affect both our wills and our emotions.

I went through much rejection in my life, in high school, in my college sorority, and in former relationships in my life. The enemy had built up a defense fortress inside of me that was a stronghold of rejection. Some demonic spirits can link together to set up a stronghold. I had received the enemy's lies all throughout the years that I was rejected because I truly didn't know who I was in Christ and, therefore, didn't value myself, believing that satan's lie was the truth. You might think this absurd, but this is exactly how a stronghold is built in your mind by the enemy.

Moreover, when one stronghold is built, others can be built with it, as well. For example, what happens when people experience rejection time after time? They try to numb the pain by using alcohol, by overworking, by pleasing people, and so forth. Therefore, in order to overcome the alcoholism, workaholic behaviors, people-pleasing, and the like, they have to bring down the strongman that is behind all of that in order to demolish the stronghold. *"Or again, how can anyone enter a strong man's house and carry off his possessions unless he first ties up the strong man? Then he can rob his house"* (Matt. 12:29 NIV). The strong man is at the core of any stronghold that is operating in our lives and has the other strongholds of oppression under him.

If we only treat the alcoholism and workaholic behaviors, we have not gotten to the root of the problem causing the behavior.

When a strong man, fully armed, guards his own house, his possessions are safe. But when someone stronger attacks and overpowers him, he takes away the armor in which the man trusted and divides up the spoils (Luke 11:21-22 NIV).

We have to overpower the strong man in order to take away his armor. The enemy's armor could take on a few forms. A besetting sin, a generational stronghold (in the family line), or belief in the enemy's lies could all allow him to stay. If we believe in satan's lies, he has a right to be there because we are in agreement with the lie and in disagreement with the Word of God. Therefore, we must get out of agreement with the lie, repent, and put our minds on the things of God, the truth.

A MOLDY HOUSE

A demonstration in the natural regarding strongholds can be seen in the home that I lived from 1994-2005. It was beautiful to behold, but underneath the beauty was mold, which had gotten in and attached to the interior of the home, causing the wood to rot. What led to the rotting was water coming from outside through the window frames and anything else that provided an opening when it rained. After a long period of time, with continued water damage, mold began to grow in the interior of the wall, and the wood began to rot. Could we have cured the problem if my husband and I had gotten a new exterior and simply put it on top of the old exterior? From an aesthetic perspective, it would have appeared so, and those who drove by would have thought it to be the case. However, after time, the rot would have gotten to the outside of the new exterior.

It is the same way with getting the strong man when it comes to spiritual warfare. You can stop the drinking and other undesired behaviors, but unless you get to the root (the mold), you will not have solved the problem. Now imagine that my husband and I would have gotten the entire exterior stripped and the wood treated and replaced by a builder and then a new exterior put up in its place. Would the problem have been solved? Yes, because the lumber would be uncontaminated and have no reason to affect any part of the house inside and out.

The strongman is like the mold behind all of our symptomatic behaviors, which are strongholds. Unless it is taken out of our "houses," we can keep putting on a "new exterior" and appear to have it together, but eventually our rejection will take us back into other strongholds. We have to take down the exterior—the behaviors apparent in our lives. For example, alcoholism, workaholic behaviors, addictions, and other unhealthy behaviors can be the apparent behaviors others see in our lives (the symptoms). The interior of the home where the strongman is set up is not as apparent because we only see the symptoms, the exterior. However, the strongman that is causing those apparent behaviors is "the mold" (in my life, rejection was the strongman).

I had been engulfed in alcoholism and promiscuous relationships when I was a single mom. When others looked at me, they thought, *Oh, look at that alcoholic woman who cannot get it together.* I had several people who came up to me and said, "Why can't you just get yourself together?" These people had only been observing the exterior part of me (my house) and could not see into the interior of my soul. All they saw were my addictions and unhealthy behaviors.

However, if someone were to look really deep, they would have realized that what was producing those apparent behaviors was a root of rejection that had been established in my life at a young age. The "mold" in my home (my mind) had so entrenched my soul (will and emotions) that I could not separate me from rejection. I was rejection in my mind. I was rejected. I did not see myself as accepted because I had bought the enemy's lie so much that a huge stronghold was established in my life.

I had gone through time after time when I stopped drinking and started "living right." Most people who looked at me would have agreed that I had it all together. However, after some difficult circumstances, rejection would work its way even stronger into my life, whereby I returned to my unhealthy behaviors. I returned to drinking, eating disorders, and the like. The strongman was rejection, and underneath him were the addictions to alcohol and eating disorders, which were the apparent behaviors that others saw. In order to ensure that I would not return to unhealthy behaviors, I had to address the strongman, rejection, and evict him out of my mind, my soul. (Moreover, I do have a teaching series, The Healing of the Soul, on the healing of the soul, bringing people inner healing after deliverance from strongholds).

When the strongman rejection had been evicted, the new exterior could be put up. I did not need to worry that I would fall back into unhealthy behaviors. That is what happens when we go through deliverance and bring down strongholds. Anything that is not of God is of satan and is considered an evil stronghold and, therefore, needs to be demolished. (Generational strongholds, besetting sins, and deliverance are addressed in detail in book three of the series, *At His Feet.*)

We demolish arguments and every pretension that sets itself up against the knowledge of God, and we take captive every thought to make it obedient to Christ (2 Corinthians 10:5 NIV).

What is it that we are demolishing when we attack a stronghold? We are demolishing every argument and pretension that is contrary to the Word of God. According to *Webster's*, an argument is "a reason given in proof or rebuttal or discourse intended to persuade." *Pretension* is defined as "a claim or an effort to establish a claim." Both an argument and a pretension are thoughts that are being argued to be the truth against the Word of God. We have no true idea of who we are in Christ, so when an argument comes that says, "You are worthless," or, "You can never do anything right," we believe that it is true. However, God's Word says, "You are fearfully and wonderfully made" (see Ps. 139:14).

The enemy's lie; that we are worthless and unable to do anything right, is contrary to the truth about us in Christ. When we accept the lie that we are worthless and cannot do anything right, we are disagreeing with the truth that says we are wonderfully and fearfully made. We gradually allow the enemy to build up a stronghold in our lives when he comes in time after time, telling us lies contrary to God's Word.

We demolish a stronghold that has been built up by the lies of Satan with the truth of the Word of God, and we repent for our belief of the lie. We confess that we are who God says we are, and every time the enemy's lie comes up, we "take that thought captive." We take a thought captive by arresting it and not allowing it a place in our minds. We arrest it so that it can no longer wreak havoc in our minds, and we make it bow down to the Word of God. It might look like this:

MARY, MARY

Mary is driving to work one morning, and on the way she gets a phone call from the daycare saying that her child is screaming and is unable to be controlled because Mary forgot the teething medicine for her baby, who is cutting a new tooth. All of a sudden

Mary thinks, *I'm a horrible mom and can never do anything right. I cannot be a good mother; I don't know why I had children because I'm so horrible at it.* Mary turns around to go get the teething medicine for her baby.

She walks into her house only to find her husband on the telephone talking to another woman in a way that he should only talk to her. She asks him what he is doing, and he says to her, "You are not the woman for me because you cannot possibly satisfy me." Mary, who is totally shocked, is standing there with her mouth open because she didn't know there was a marital problem. She knew that they had arguments, but nothing so devastating as to cause her husband to leave her. She asks him why he is leaving, and he says, "I cannot please you. You are too hard to please." Mary, begins to think, *I am a hard woman to love and really am unlovable. I'm unattractive and undesirable. No wonder he wanted to leave me.*

It would appear that Mary has had a horrible morning with arguments and pretensions that have come up in her mind. This might seem a bit dramatic. However, I want us to see the small thing, like leaving the teething medicine, and the big thing with her husband leaving her. Both offer opportunity for satan to bring lies to her about who she is in Christ. In addition, he brings arguments and pretensions about other people and who they are in Christ. Mary now feels like the most horrible mother and unloved wife who deserves nothing but to become a recluse.

The manner in which Mary has to demolish these arguments is to take them captive (arrest them) and demolish them with the truth in the Word of God. She would arrest the thought, *I'm a terrible mother and can never do anything right,* with, *He has made me more than a conqueror in Christ Jesus* (see Rom. 8:37). Then she would arrest her husband's argument that she is unable to satisfy him and is never pleased with him by reminding herself, He *has made me accepted in the beloved,* and *God is able to do exceedingly, abundantly above all that I could ever hope or imagine according to the power that is inside of me* (see Eph. 1:6; 3:20).

When a lie comes into our thoughts we have to take it captive by using the Word of God, His truth, in the scriptures. Demolish the lie with the truth. We must do this whenever a lie comes into our minds. If we do not take the thought captive at the point of entry, a stronghold will start to build.

In summation, you have to demolish strongholds that have been set up by the enemy in your life. Look through your life and see what lies of the enemy you have believed that are contrary to the Word of God. Invite the Holy Spirit to open your eyes to the truth about the beliefs you have that are contrary to God's Word. Spend a few days pondering them and writing them down so as to address finding the truth in the Word of God that the argument is contrary to. (Make sure that you get book three to get into some specific spirits that set up strongholds, like rejection, unforgiveness, jealousy, control, and so forth.) Moreover, you have to eat and digest (read) the Word of God so that you get more and more truth in you to take captive every thought.

BINDING AND LOOSING

And I tell you that you are Peter, and on this rock I will build My church, and the gates of Hades will not overcome it. I will give you the keys of the kingdom of heaven; whatever you bind on earth will be bound in heaven, and whatever you loose on earth will be loosed in heaven (Matthew 16:18-19 NIV).

The next principle is binding and loosing. As the above passage shows, Jesus gave us the authority to bind and loose as it is done in Heaven. What is binding and loosing? Binding is seen well in the healing of the demon possessed man at the Garasenes.

> *They went across the lake to the region of the Gerasenes. When Jesus got out of the boat, a man with an evil spirit came from the tombs to meet him. This man lived in the tombs, and no one could **bind him** any more, not even with a chain. For he had often been chained hand and foot, but he tore the chains apart and broke the irons on his feet. No one was strong enough to subdue him. Night and day among the tombs and in the hills he would cry out and cut himself with stones* (Mark 5:1-5 NIV).

We see here a man who was uncontrollable. He was such a distraction and wreaked such havoc that the community tried time after time to handcuff him in chains (bind him). He would cry out and cut himself without being chained. Therefore, *binding* happens when something that needs to be tied up is tied up so that there will be no disorder. *Miriam-Webster's Dictionary* defines *bind* as "to make secure by tying; to confine, restrain, or restrict as if with bonds; to put under an obligation; to constrain with legal authority."

BE QUIET!

For example, if you knew a murderer was loose in your neighborhood and the police were looking for him, you would want the felon arrested. He cannot be fired upon by the police because there is a protocol to follow before they can even think about pulling their guns out. They have to make sure that it is the right circumstances in order to trigger their use of guns.

The binding is our God-given power by the Holy Spirit that exists 24-7. We can use it anytime and anywhere. However, we have to receive discernment through the Holy Spirit in order to know what spirit to bind. Therefore, in our example, after the police find the felon and arrest him, he cannot kill anyone or wreak havoc in the neighborhood. This situation is considered "binding." If we know that there is a certain demonic spirit attacking us, our families, our businesses, our finances, our marriages, and so forth, we can bind that spirit from wreaking havoc or causing a scene.

When the man in the tomb, was unbound, he cried and cut himself. This caused a disturbance to the community. Likewise when we bind a spirit, it will not be able to cause a scene or disturbance in the place or time where we have bound it. It will be bound to where it cannot operate the way it wants to through a person's life. However, this can be distinguished from the flesh in that the spirit is bound but if the person who has the stronghold gives over to their flesh, they might be operating in the flesh still, in the carnal nature and although the spirit is bound the carnal nature might be pronounced in the person's behavior and character.

For example, if you are experiencing trouble with a son who might be using drugs and acting rebellious, he is probably under an oppression of a rebellious and lawless spirit. In addition, many other spirits might be oppressing him. In dealing with this troubled child, remember that it is not the child who you are in battle with; we do not fight against flesh and blood (see Eph. 6:12). You need to discern through the Holy Spirit what oppressive spirit it is that is coming against your child. First and foremost, you want your child delivered from the oppressive spirit. However, before you go through deliverance, you might have to do binding and loosing until you get the green light from the Holy Spirit regarding deliverance.

Deliverance happens when the spirit no longer has a place around your child and has left him, whereas binding means that the oppressive spirit is still around your child, but cannot act out. In order to keep this spirit from wreaking havoc on your child's life and in your home, you have to bind it. You have to speak it out in order for it to be done; as Jesus gave you power to do.

With the discernment of the Holy Spirit, you will bind the spirit that is oppressing your child. It might sound something like this, "I bind you spirit of rebellion and spirit of lawlessness in the name of Jesus Christ." When you bind these spirits, they cannot wreak havoc the way they desire. If the man that was at the Gerasenes would have been chained with chains that he could not break, he would have been subdued and under the control of the community. Likewise, we have the authority to subdue and control our environment from the power of darkness.

TRANSFER THE SERVICE, PLEASE

I was paying one of our monthly bills at the actual sight of the business one day. While I was in there, I felt in my spirit that there was tension in the room as soon as I walked in. It tightened on my chest the closer I got to the window to speak with the young lady at the desk. Immediately, I could discern in my spirit that the spirit of intimidation was operating through her and that the spirit wanted to come through her in order to intimidate me. This spirit is a familiar spirit in my life because I have had so many circumstances occur in which people have allowed this spirit to operate through them in order to cause me to become timid.

The lady I was seeking help from was rude and would not listen to my explanation of my prior telephone conversation with her company. I had called to confirm a transfer of our service from our prior home to our new home. The lady insisted that it was not a transfer and that she would have to set up new service (this all had to be corrected later when the technician came to "transfer" our service, not set up "new" service). I knew that she was mistaken because of my thorough conversation with the other workers over the telephone.

However, she started raising her voice and making a scene in this small office that was the size of many public bathrooms. It was a small location, and this spirit was trying to act out against me and cause me to have a most miserable day. I then started speaking in tongues under my breath because I was feeling anxious and knew that this spirit was trying to come against me. Suddenly, the Holy Spirit told me to bind the spirit of intimidation. I bound it, and all of a sudden the Holy Spirit flooded me with such a peace that you would have thought I had recently been at an all day spa. Where the enemy wanted to take dominion, I used my authority in binding the spirit and loosed peace. It flooded that entire room and quieted the other lady. I know others could initially feel the tension and then the peace of God afterward because it was such a small room.

Therefore, when there is any hint of a scene, it could mean that there is a spirit trying to operate, and you need to bind it (there are times when it is actually a person's flesh and not a demonic spirit). My husband and I continually bind up spirits that try to come into our house through visitors, our children, or us. I do a lot of ministry in our home, and as a result, there are many women who come in with strongholds operating in their lives. In order to maintain order, many times I bind the spirit of control so that it will not operate through another person trying to control my work for God.

To *loose* is "to release." It is the opposite of *bind* since *bind* means "to tie and restrain." Jesus tells us that He has given us the keys, and with the keys we have access to the Kingdom of Heaven to bind and to loose. Whatever we bind will be bound, and whatever we loose will be loosed on earth and in Heaven. The loosening that is referred to can be either loosing things of God into people or areas or loosing the enemy off of someone (which is discussed in the next chapter and further understanding is provided under the Key of David chapter).

Also, Holy Spirit at times instructs me on what to bind in the second heavens by God when I am lead to bind the demonic power in the second heavens giving power to the demonic spirit in the earth. God's word says we can bind up whatever is bound in heaven! Therefore devils are not permitted to operate in God's heavenly kingdom but in the second heavens they might be wreaking havoc on God's people. As Holy Spirit instructs me, He will show me demonic princes operating against a person, ministry or region to bind up. The kings/princes are all listed in God's word and Holy Spirit is having me do an entire teaching series on those kings. Presently get into God's word and understand demonic kings and powers that He shows you by Holy Spirit that are operating and He will instruct you on when to bind them. (loosing demons off of people will be discussed in next chapter on deliverance).

LOOSING THE WORD OF GOD!

What is bound in Heaven that is not allowed to operate there? Death, destruction, disease, poverty, plague, devastation, depression, divorce, anger, gossip, control, malice, and so forth. What is loosed in Heaven that is of God? In Heaven we see life, healing, prosperity, joy, peace, kindness, and so forth. Therefore, we also loose the good things of God on the earth and into people's lives. The only way to know the good things of God is to read the Word and, by the eating and tasting of His Word and the knowledge of the truth, we can call forth His goodness to be loosed on earth.

For example, the Word of God states that He is love (see 1 John 4:8); therefore, you should loose love. He states that some of the fruits of the Spirit are kindness, joy, longsuffering, patience, self-control, and forbearance (see Gal. 5:20). Loose one of the fruits of the Spirit if the Holy Spirit prompts you. Loose peace when you've bound up intimidation or strife. Loose patience when you've bound up impatience or anxiety. Search the Word and find out all the good things of God and loose them; every good and perfect gift comes from the Father of lights (see James 1:17).

QUESTIONS:

1. Do you have oppressive strongholds operating in your mind? Can you identify them through the Holy Spirit? If not, continue to speak the Word of God until you know that you know it; then ask the Holy Spirit again. Usually a word or picture might pop up in your mind, indicating the stronghold or strongman.

2. Do you have spirits operating against you in your home, workplace, environment, or other places that you need to bind? Can you identify how they are operating and through whom they are operating?

Endnote

1. http://en.wikipedia.org/wiki/Stronghold

c h a p t e r

9

Deliverance

Whoever believes and is baptized will be saved, but whoever does not believe will be condemned. And these signs will accompany those who believe: In My name they will drive out demons; they will speak in new tongues; they will pick up snakes with their hands; and when they drink deadly poison, it will not hurt them at all; they will place their hands on sick people, and they will get well (Mark 16:16-18 NIV).

DELIVERANCE FROM A DEMONIC SPIRIT

Let me preface this with the truth I believe regarding demonic possession. I believe by the understanding I have of God's word that Christians cannot be demonically possessed, but can be oppressed. Once we are born again, our spirit is born of God, it is born from above we are a new creation (see John 3:2-7). Once a person is born from above their spirit cries out Abba

Father, as one who is a son or daughter of God (see Rom. 8:15). Therefore, our spirit is given to God; we are His. However, we still have strongholds of the enemy in our life where we need healing and deliverance which is part of the great commission (see Mark 16:17). Therefore, many Christians can still be oppressed by demons but not possessed by them, where satan possesses your soul because your soul is born from above of God. Much oppression comes in the form of strongholds that we have allowed to take root in our lives. The strongholds are so great that we have allowed a home for an oppressive spirit to take residence in our souls (mind, will, and emotions), which then becomes the strongman.

Jesus did not leave deliverance from demons only to the disciples and apostles. He did not leave the casting out of demons to the Catholics. He stated that *those who believe* will have certain signs that will accompany their lives. The first sign stated is that they will drive out demons. You may find this a bit spooky or scary. However, it is like gravity, which exists whether you acknowledge it or not.

We have been so blinded by our natural eyes that we have not opened our spiritual eyes. If we were to open our spiritual eyes, we might be as the prophet Elisha, who saw what his servant could not when they were outnumbered in the natural.

"Don't be afraid," the prophet answered. "Those who are with us are more than those who are with them." And Elisha prayed, "O LORD, open his eyes so he may see." Then the LORD opened the servant's eyes, and he looked and saw the hills full of horses and chariots of fire all around Elisha. As the enemy came down toward him, Elisha prayed to the LORD, "Strike these people with blindness." So he struck them with blindness, as Elisha had asked (2 Kings 6:16-18 NIV).

Not only would we see the angels of God, who are fighting along with us and who have been given charge by God, we would also see the hordes from hell that are sent on assignment to come against us. Satan tries to get us to stay in our flesh, seeing with our natural eyes so that we will be ignorant of his demons that are at work against us.

This can be likened to a night war that is fought between the good battalion and bad battalion. If they are engaged in battle and it is dark outside, how is it that the good battalion will know where the enemy's position is? They have what is called a night goggle which can detect the enemy with clarity. Now, if the good troop did not possess the appropriate equipment to detect the enemy at night time, would it mean that the enemy was not there? No. It would simply mean that they did not employ the correct method in detecting the enemy and his location. If the good troop went out, they would risk being shot upon without possible success of delivering an effective blow to the enemy.

What if the good troops had the appropriate equipment and left it on their sleeping bags? Would they still be able to detect the enemy with accuracy and deliver a tactical blow? No. The good troops not only have to possess the right equipment, but put it on as well. Therefore, it takes possessing something (a noun) and doing something (a verb). Thus the noun would be the right weapon given to us by the Holy Spirit. The Holy Spirit enables us to discern the spiritual weapon needed to employ against the enemy. The verb would be the action we take in carrying out the method that is most effective.

FLEAS AND A RODENT

A good example of knowing what spiritual weapon to use can be seen in an incident that happened with my first mentor, Sheila. I had given her a rug to put in her house and, although

I had vacuumed it, there were still some fleas left in it from my dog. Therefore, a week after I had given her the carpet, she called me to let me know that her house was now flea-infested. In addition to the flea infestation, she had also been experiencing a rodent (a cute mouse—she hated it, and I loved it). I had to buy flea bombers to kill the fleas, and she bought mouse traps to catch the mouse. With the fleas, the noun (weapon) that we possessed was the flea bombers. With the mouse, the noun we possessed was the mouse trap.

What if we tried to use the mouse trap against the fleas; would it work? Of course not; the fleas need a specific chemical to kill them. If we used the flea spray to kill the mouse; would that work? Most likely not; a mouse is much bigger than a flea and actually needs to be caught in order to be terminated. Moreover, after the mouse is caught, another method has to be employed to kill it since it is suffering in the trap. There were two different pestilences that we had to tackle. Each one was a different type of pestilence and had to be dealt with in a different manner in order to get rid of it. In addition, if we had the flea bombers and never activated (action) them, they would not have been effective. Or, if we had the mouse traps and never took them out of the bag, how effective would we be at catching the mouse? Not effective at all because an action is required on our part after we have the right method to fight them.

If we are Christians and have been baptized with the Holy Spirit, we now possess what is necessary to help us get the right weapons to get rid of our enemy. The Holy Spirit will give us discernment as to which weapon to use in order to destroy the enemy. As demonstrated with the two different instrumentations that were used to rid my mentor of the pestilence, different tactics are needed for different enemies. Therefore, in order to discern the instrumentation (noun/weapon) needed to employ against the enemy, we have to first discern the weapon from the Holy Spirit and then employ that method (action). As discussed, we can have the right instrumentation or method and not ever employ it, which will not yield results.

I had much demonic oppression to be delivered from when I was on a quest to be set free from the enemy. I had a binge drinking problem. I was suicidal and depressed. I had irrational thinking, and the list goes on. I was such a basket case and had so much oppression that I had to seek deliverance or life was not worth living. This was when I began seeking information on deliverance from demonic oppression. Along with this, I was reading the Bible and attending as many anointed Bible studies as I could.

With all of this, I was able to be delivered from the demonic oppression that I was experiencing and walk in true freedom from the deadly grip of satan. I discovered that I was truly victorious and that life was worth living; it was joyful, peaceful, and full even though all around me might appear bleak. There was a song in my heart because Jesus had delivered me from the nighttime terror. We were meant to walk in the light and not the darkness.

In my first deliverance, there was no manifestation of a demon or the like. My eyes would simply fog up during the deliverance session, which is a common occurrence for some people who go through deliverance. However, when I have gone through some supernatural deliverance, where God simply came on me in His power, I have actually had a more pronounced manifestation that I was set free from the spirit that was attacking me. I have known people to have manifestations from demonic oppression through yawning, burping, coughing, crying, or laughing. Afterward, there is a "lifting," so to speak, and the person then feels lighter. What I experienced after going through deliverance is really hard to explain because there are no words to describe it other than it is supernatural.

When this happens, a demon has been "loosed" off of a person. In regard to loosing demons off of others, we have to know by Holy Spirit that it is time to loose that demon off of a person. Again, the demoniac at the Gerasenes was tormented by the devils. People would tie him up (bind him) to keep him from causing havoc. However, when Jesus entered the area, Jesus loosed the devils off of him and they went into the pigs.

Cutting Cords and Loosing Demons!

There are two ways to loose. You can loose a devil from a person when you are doing deliverance or you can loose, "release" God's Word, promises, and plans into a person.

For example we see the loosing of a spirit from a person with Jesus in the scripture.

Now Jesus was teaching in one of the synagogues on the Sabbath. And there was a woman there who for eighteen years had had an infirmity caused by a spirit (a demon of sickness). She was bent completely forward and utterly unable to straighten herself up or to look upward. And when Jesus saw her, He called [her to Him] and said to her, Woman, you are released from your infirmity! Then He laid [His] hands on her, and instantly she was made straight, and she recognized and thanked and praised God. But the leader of the synagogue, indignant because Jesus had healed on the Sabbath, said to the crowd, There are six days on which work ought to be done; so come on those days and be cured, and not on the Sabbath day. But the Lord replied to him, saying, You play actors (hypocrites)! Does not each one of you on the Sabbath loose his ox or his donkey from the stall and lead it out to water it? And ought not this woman, a daughter of Abraham, whom

Satan has kept bound for eighteen years, be loosed from this bond on the Sabbath day? Luke 13:10-16 AMP.

Here the loosing that Jesus is describing is being set free from the spirit of infirmity. Jesus saw a woman that was bound by a spirit of infirmity that had kept her bent over. Jesus saw the spirit of infirmity and commanded it to loose her, laying His hands upon her. The woman immediately was released from the demon that had kept her bound. When I minister to others in prophetic ministry Holy Spirit will show me different demonic spirits that have people bound. As I see them and engage Holy Spirit on the instruction of the Lord for releasing the person from bondage He will many times have me cut "cords" that I see in the spirit realm first before I command a spirit to loose someone. Holy Spirit has shown me that many times there are cords of the enemy coming from the second heaven, where satan and his kingdom has much operation over the earthly realm as we see in Daniel when the angel tells Daniel that he had to withstand the prince of Persia in the second heavens.

> *And [the angel] said to me, O Daniel, you greatly beloved man, understand the words that I speak to you and stand upright, for to you I am now sent. And while he was saying this word to me, I stood up trembling. Then he said to me, Fear not, Daniel, for from the first day that you set your mind and heart to understand and to humble yourself before your God, your words were heard, and I have come as a consequence of [and in response to] your words. But the prince of the kingdom of Persia withstood me for twenty-one days. Then Michael, one of the chief [of the celestial] princes, came to help me, for I remained there with the kings of Persia* (Daniel 10:11-13 AMP).

Here in Daniel we see warfare with Michael the Arch Angel against the Prince of Persia in the celestial realm, the second heavens. Therefore, in knowing this Holy Spirit taught me how to cut cords that I would see attached from the powers of satan in the second heavens coming to earth to give power to the demonic spirit on the earth before I commanded a spirit to loose someone. I saw the "cords" of the enemy Holy Spirit was teaching about later in God's word.

> *The kings of the earth take their places; the rulers take counsel together against the Lord and His Anointed One (the Messiah, the Christ). They say, Let us break Their bands [of restraint] asunder and cast Their cords [of control] from us. He Who sits in the heavens laughs; the Lord has them in derision [and in supreme contempt He mocks them]* (Psalm 2:2-4 AMP).

> *I will call upon the Lord, Who is to be praised; so shall I be saved from my enemies. The cords or bands of death surrounded me, and the streams of ungodliness and the torrents of ruin terrified me. The cords of Sheol (the place of the dead) surrounded me; the snares of death confronted and came upon me* (Psalm 18:3-5 AMP).

> *The cords and sorrows of death were around me, and the terrors of Sheol (the place of the dead) had laid hold of me; I suffered anguish and grief (trouble and sorrow).*

> *Then called I upon the name of the Lord: O Lord, I beseech You, save my life and deliver me!* (Psalm 116:2-4 AMP).

> *And if they are bound in fetters [of adversity] and held by cords of affliction* (Job 36:8 AMP).

The Holy Spirit, after showing me cords with my spiritual eyes, instructs me to cut the cords to demonic spirits coming from the second heaven before I loose someone. It might look like this. As I am ministering over someone I see cords coming from the second heaven to a lying spirit that is telling someone they are a failure, a looser, and will never make anything of themselves. I will pray "I take the Sword of the Spirit and cut the cords to the lying spirit off of Mary. I command the lying spirit that has Mary bound to loose her in Jesus' Name." This example is a demonstration of many ways in which I command spirits to loose people. In spiritual warfare there are different beliefs by people on where to send the spirit and there is much debate and argument. I listen to Holy Spirit about where to command the spirit to go once the person is loosed from them. I would again recommend the other spiritual warfare books to add to your library to get a thorough understanding in spiritual warfare. I only ask for you to seek God, His wisdom, knowledge and understanding and He will give you further instruction on casting out demons.

When I do deliverance with others, I bind up devils that Holy Spirit tells me to bind, and I loose devils that Holy Spirit tells me to loose. The person with whom I am working has to be a willing vessel when it comes to loosing the devil. This is very important because if a demon is loosed off of someone who is not spiritually mature to have that deliverance, then the person could actually get worse than before. If a person is not filled up with the Word of God, it's as though that person is a house with nothing there. Loosing a devil off of such people can actually harm them more than help them. When you loose a devil off of someone, it roams in arid places searching for rest. When that spirit does not find rest, it comes back to the place it once occupied, and if that place is empty, it calls seven more spirits that are *more wicked* than the first. Therefore, a person's condition in the latter state is worse. We can only do deliverance when Holy Spirit tells us; we are being reckless otherwise.

> *But when the unclean spirit has gone out of a man, it roams through dry [arid] places in search of rest, but it does not find any. Then it says, I will go back to my house from which I*

came out. And when it arrives, it finds the place unoccupied, swept, put in order, and decorated. Then it goes and brings with it seven other spirits more wicked than itself, and they go in and make their home there. And the last condition of that man becomes worse than the first. So also shall it be with this wicked generation (Matthew 12:43-45 AMP).

Other times I have actually seen manifestations of demonic spirits during deliverance where they have talked through the person or caused disturbance. However, I have come to know that it is nothing to be afraid of, but rather to stay in the Holy Spirit in order to do the necessary deliverance. However, this book is not intended to go into detail about deliverance; it is best to acquire a video, audio, and book library on the subject from different teachers. Again, my favorites are John Paul Jackson, Neil T. Anderson, Benny Hinn, Anna Mendez Ferrell, Don Dickerman, Rebecca Brown and George Bloomer.

ASSIGNMENTS:

1. Read the Book of John chapters 14 through 17. It is necessary when doing spiritual warfare to make sure that you realize that God in you is bigger than any devil. God is bigger, and Jesus Christ in you has made you a conqueror. Continue to read these chapters for a month.

2. Read the book of Ephesians in order to understand the power of Jesus in you and that you're fighting a spiritual battle. This is an awesome book and should strengthen your confidence in Christ Jesus in you.

Pick Your Weapons

Finally, be strong in the Lord and in his mighty power. Put on the full armor of God so that you can take your stand against the devil's schemes. For our struggle is not against flesh and blood, but against the rulers, against the authorities, against the powers of this dark world and against the spiritual forces of evil in the heavenly realms. Therefore put on the full armor of God, so that when the day of evil comes, you may be able to stand your ground, and after you have done everything, to stand. Stand firm then, with the belt of truth buckled around your waist, with the breastplate of righteousness in place, and with your feet fitted with the readiness that comes from the gospel of peace. In addition to all this, take up the shield of faith, with which you can extinguish all the flaming arrows of the evil one. Take the helmet of salvation and the sword of the Spirit, which is the word of God. And pray in the Spirit on all occasions with all kinds of prayers and requests. With this in mind, be alert and always keep on praying for all the saints (Ephesians 6:10-18 NIV).

Prayer is the first line of defense for the Kingdom of God. Without prayer, we are helpless to fight against the schemes of the enemy because, as Jesus stated, we are to pray that the Kingdom come (see Matt. 6:10). Therefore, bringing the Kingdom to earth happens through the vehicle of prayer. The prayer is answered in the heavens and sent to us by God the Father who gives us good gifts. Every perfect gift comes from the Father of lights:

Every good and perfect gift is from above, coming down from the Father of the heavenly lights, who does not change like shifting shadows (James 1:17 NIV).

Therefore, if we get blessed with a child, a good job, a nice home, and so forth, it is from God. He tells us that we do not have because we do not ask (see James 4:2). We have to make our petitions to God through prayer. Prayer can sometimes be petitions or declarations. We put on the armor of God by knowing each part of it and appropriating the gift that God has given us in that piece of armor.

SUIT UP!

God has presently given me much revelation about the armor of God, and I will be finishing a book on it identifying the revelations about each piece of the armor that reveals a trait of Jesus Christ *(A Revelation of Jesus Christ: God's Key to His Armor)*. The Word of God tells us in Ephesians that we are to put on (which means understanding and applying the revelation) the full armor of God so that when the day of evil comes we can stand our ground (see Eph. 6:10-11). This revelation shows us that without the armor of God we cannot stand during the evil day.

The first piece of armor is the Belt of Truth. The Belt of Truth is the Word of God that will last for all eternity. Truth is poured into us through God's Word. We have to have faith in the Word, and faith comes by hearing and hearing by the Word of God (see Rom. 10:17). Therefore, while reading and listening to the Word, we have to have faith that it is the truth.

The next piece of armor is the Breastplate of Righteousness. After we have the Belt of Truth and know the Word of God, we have to fight against evil in the righteousness (right standing with God) of Christ Jesus. Our righteousness is but filthy rags to God, and satan knows it. That is why we appropriate the righteousness of Christ when we put on the Breastplate of Righteousness. If we do not appropriate the righteousness of Christ in our spiritual warfare, then we are open for attack. We have no authority on our own, and instead we have to come in the authority given us by Christ Jesus.

The Shoes of the Gospel of Peace are to be on our feet in order to stand against evil. The enemy is after our peace, and if he can get our peace, then doubt and unbelief will harass us. There have been many times when I have been in a season in which the enemy is telling me that I'm going to fall and that "this will happen" or "that will happen." It is at that time that I confess to God that I will become a fool for Him and that if He needs to take me through something that is going to give me endurance in the Fight of Faith, then I'm willing. At that moment, God's peace comes over me because I am no longer considering my reputation, but instead am looking to God's reputation. I'm putting on the shoes of peace, choosing to walk in His power and not my own. It is the peace of God that surpasses our understanding that will *"guard your hearts and minds in Christ Jesus"* (Phil. 4:7 NIV).

The Shield of Faith is the next piece of armor and is used to strike down the arrows of the enemy. Remember, the enemy's number one job is to get us to doubt God, to kill our faith. The fight that we fight is the Fight of Faith. There are two positions in this world, life and death. In choosing to fight for the position of life, God's side, we are fighting for the Faith that His Word is what it says it is. We do not believe the lie of the enemy because it is contrary to the Word of God. When satan throws a flaming arrow at us, we put it out by holding up our shield of faith. This flaming arrow can come through the enemy, who uses circumstances and others in our lives to come against who we are in Christ Jesus. For example, when my oldest son went through a rough period when the enemy was trying to take his life, it was a flaming arrow. My faith was being challenged as to if I would listen to the doctor's report or God's report on my son's healing. I had to put up my shield of faith to come against that flaming arrow.

Next, we put on the Helmet of Salvation, which covers our minds. It is usually at the times when I get deeper in the Lord that satan tries to come against my mind, trying to overwhelm me with who I am in Christ. The Helmet of Salvation guarantees me that I am who God says I am. Many times the enemy tries to cause me to doubt my salvation or harasses me with the lie that I have committed the unpardonable sin. This is all a ploy to get me distracted and paralyzed, to prevent me from pushing forward and doing the work that God has called me to do.

The Lord has brought to my remembrance the time when I worked with the elderly population in social work and the Alzheimer's program. Many people would come to me and say

"I'm worried that I might have Alzheimer's. How do you know if you have it or not?" I would respond with the statement I had heard from the medical arena, "If you are worried you have it, you probably don't have it." Likewise, if the enemy harasses us with thoughts that we are not saved or have committed the unpardonable sin, then most likely we have not. The Holy Spirit has no problem with finding us and putting us on the right track. However, we have to put on that Helmet of Salvation because it is in our salvation that we discover who we are in Christ.

Finally, we need the Sword of the Spirit, which is the Word of God. The Sword of the Spirit is to be wielded at a time when we have been compelled by God's Holy Spirit to open our mouths and release the Word of God. I imagine my own mouth with a sword coming out of it when I use this weapon. It is not my words, by any means, which defeat the enemy. It is the Holy Spirit's Words, which come out of my mouth as a sword to do God's work.

I usually know when I'm using this weapon because I get such an unction and restlessness to get a word out of my mouth, which is the very Word of God. It is a rushing in my heart, a pounding so deep that I feel as though I am literally going to explode if I don't open my mouth and speak it out. Sometimes I even feel as though fire is in my chest. Jeremiah describes it so well,

> *But if I say, "I will not mention Him or speak any more in His name," His word is in my heart like a fire, a fire shut up in my bones. I am weary of holding it in; indeed, I cannot* (Jeremiah 20:9 NIV).

That is not to say that everyone should feel the Sword of the Spirit this way. (This weapon is discussed more in the symbols for Princess Warriors.)

Fasting

Fasting is a strong weapon of God. It is what helped save my son from the attack that satan used to try to kill him. It is a denying oneself of something, usually food, and coupling it with prayer. You need to get a book on fasting before you even consider a fast, one I recommend is Jentezen Franklin's book, *Fasting*.[1] Do not go into fasting without the right knowledge and without consulting your physician because it could lead to death if done incorrectly.

I will briefly describe how fasting saved my son's life; however, I encourage you to do further study on this weapon of warfare. It can be used for many warfare techniques, in identifying the direction to take, discovering the identity of the demon that is attacking, and so forth. People who are going to work in deliverance ministries (casting out demons) have to live fasted lives.

As stated earlier, satan tried to kill my oldest son with a demonic attack against his health in 2003. My oldest son, Christopher, nearly died from a severe staph infection. It started out to be what looked like a local strain on his joint from participating in middle school football summer training camp. I took him to the doctor for an examination, and the doctor told me that it was a sprained ankle.

The Holy Spirit told me to begin a partial fast that week. My husband and I fasted from all food until five o'clock, and during that time we would intercede (pray). I wasn't sure why we were to fast because, on the surface, everything appeared alright. On the first day of our fast, I felt urgency, and all that kept coming up in my spirit was "danger, danger, danger." I didn't know what I was feeling urgent about. On the second day of our fast, the Holy Spirit told me to pray over Christopher while he was sleeping. Then the next day Christopher started running a severe temperature that was over 103 degrees, going nearly to 104 degrees. I took him to the doctor again and told the clinicians that I believed there was a correlation between his ankle pain and the fever he was experiencing. They assured me that there was no correlation and that I was only to watch Christopher for his fever and treat it as a virus.

The week continued, and my son was getting sicker. He was unable to walk, his whole leg in pain, and I was continually hearing, "danger, danger, danger." My son went to his father's house that weekend, and I was glad because he is a physician. However, I received a phone call from his father about Chris' temperature, which alarmed me. I then got Chris the next day, and the Holy Spirit told me to take him to the emergency room. I took him to the hospital. My son was deteriorating, faster and faster; he had severe pain and a fever of 105 degrees. We stayed in the emergency room all night, and in the morning they admitted him into the hospital. We had to go two days while my son was tested for all sorts of things in order to find out what was wrong with him.

I knew as a mother that something was seriously wrong with my son and that the medical staff did not understand the serious nature of what was wrong with him. I stepped up as a mother and a former social worker to inform them that they would no longer treat him the way they thought best. Instead, if they were to perform further testing, they would increase his pain medication from something that was almost over-the-counter to something that would be substantial. Moreover, I told them that they would no longer transfer him from his bed to a wheelchair for transporting him in the hospital, but instead would transfer him to another stretcher because of his enormous pain.

With some resistance, they finally met my requirements for treating my son.

We found out after a couple of days that my son had a deadly staph infection, which had already created pockets of infection inside of the bone in his leg, had settled in his lungs and throat, and was on its way to his heart. I knew that his illness was critical because of listening to the Holy Spirit. Moreover, the pain he had been experiencing in his leg from the bone infection required him to be on morphine in order to tolerate the pain. He was seriously ill, and although the medical staff could not determine that until further tests were done, two days worth, I knew this information from the onset of the fast that my husband and I had been on.

A demonic spirit, the spirit of death, was attacking my child, and my husband and I fasted and prayed in order to expose the schemes of the enemy and to know what we were fighting against. The fasting revealed the strategy and kept my husband and me spiritually sharp to hear what the Spirit of God was saying. That is why it is life and death to know what is going on in the spirit realm. It could mean the premature death of your child. *"And He said unto them, this kind can come forth by nothing, but by prayer and fasting"* (Mark 9:29 KJV).

I heard from several people during this time that many other children had this same infection and did not make it. My son was the only person I heard about that year who survived that infection. The Holy Spirit showed me that it was satan coming against the children, just as he did during Moses and Jesus' infancy, killing all the infants. My son stayed in the hospital for two weeks, had two surgeries, and an intravenous (IV) line put in his vein leading to his heart in order to pump in the antibiotics he needed to overcome this infection. He had to have the IV in his arm and was on home health for three months.

It was horrific, dangerous, and severely urgent. I shudder to think of what would have happened had Rich and I not fasted. I don't want to know, because all I care about is the fact that my son, who was battling a deadly infection, survived when many other children that year did not. The weapon was fasting, and in order to use it appropriately, we had to actually fast the way the Holy Spirit wanted us to.

THERE IS POWER IN THE BLOOD OF CHRIST

This is the most important weapon of warfare that we have. It is through Jesus giving Himself as a sacrifice for our sins that we have crossed from death to life.

How much more, then, will the blood of Christ, who through the eternal Spirit offered Himself unblemished to God, cleanse our consciences from acts that lead to death, so that we may serve the living God! (Hebrews 9:14 NIV)

The blood of Jesus Christ protects us as it symbolically did when the Israelites put the blood of the lamb over their doorposts so the death angel would pass over them—which is where we get Passover. I apply the blood of Jesus each morning over my sons, husband, relatives, and friends. In addition, I apply the blood of Jesus over me and others whom I minister too. The enemy cannot cross the blood line, and that is why it is so important to apply the blood of Jesus spiritually when Holy Spirit tells us to. When I have the Princess Warriors or 22 IS 22 (Isaiah 22:22 Company) meetings, I go to the doors and anoint them, declaring that I apply the blood of Jesus and that no demons can cross the blood line.

In addition, many times when I minister to people, Holy Spirit will have me apply the blood of Jesus in different areas. For example, when I pray for healing, Holy Spirit many times will have me call in the blood of Jesus over that person's body part that I am praying for at the time. This past Friday night when I ministered, Holy Spirit told me that God wanted to heal the woman I was praying for and said she had problems with her hip, which had been a challenge for her her whole life. The woman was in her late 50s and she carried a struggle with her hip since she was in her youth. As I prayed, God told me that He was bringing His fire into her hip and told me to declare that as well as the blood of Jesus in her hip. Today, I received a phone call that the woman's hip was healed by the next morning, and she no longer has pain. The blood of Jesus is powerful! Glory to God!

When you pray for others and yourself, as well as the church, community, city, state, and much more, be sensitive to how Holy Spirit wants you to apply the blood of Jesus over someone or something. The enemy hates the blood of Jesus and knows that it is the blood of Jesus that defeated him, because the blood of Jesus paid for our sins.

I also pray the blood of Jesus Christ over myself before I minister to others, and I pray the blood of Jesus over *everyone* I minister to. The blood of Jesus Christ is so powerful, and I encourage you to get more knowledge, wisdom, and understanding regarding the blood of Jesus. (There is not enough room to discuss this fully here, so please get a book on the Blood of Jesus by Perry Stone, Benny Hinn, Mahesh Chevda, or Anna Mendez Ferrell.)

PSALM 91 PROTECTION

Along with the blood of Jesus Christ, I declare Psalm 91 Protection over the same people each day and over others I minister to. It is an awesome protection Psalm. In the midst of warfare, we have to make sure that we are protected. This happens when we apply the blood of Jesus over ourselves and declare Psalm 91 protection. Psalm 91 Protection is a powerful weapon for Christians.

Many times I say, "I declare Psalm 91 Protection over _____" and I fill in the blank. Then other times I declare parts of the Scripture out loud, if not the entire Scripture.

PSALM 91

He who dwells in the secret place of the Most High shall remain stable and fixed under the shadow of the Almighty [Whose power no foe can withstand].

I will say of the Lord, He is my Refuge and my Fortress, my God; on Him I lean and rely, and in Him I [confidently] trust!

For [then] He will deliver you from the snare of the fowler and from the deadly pestilence.

[Then] He will cover you with His pinions, and under His wings shall you trust and find refuge; His truth and His faithfulness are a shield and a buckler.

You shall not be afraid of the terror of the night, nor of the arrow (the evil plots and slanders of the wicked) that flies by day,

Nor of the pestilence that stalks in darkness, nor of the destruction and sudden death that surprise and lay waste at noonday.

A thousand may fall at your side, and ten thousand at your right hand, but it shall not come near you.

Only a spectator shall you be [yourself inaccessible in the secret place of the Most High] as you witness the reward of the wicked.

Because you have made the Lord your refuge, and the Most High your dwelling place,

There shall no evil befall you, nor any plague or calamity come near your tent.

For He will give His angels [especial] charge over you to accompany and defend and preserve you in all your ways [of obedience and service].

They shall bear you up on their hands, lest you dash your foot against a stone.

You shall tread upon the lion and adder; the young lion and the serpent shall you trample underfoot.

Because he has set his love upon Me, therefore will I deliver him; I will set him on high, because he knows and understands My name [has a personal knowledge of My mercy, love, and kindness—trusts and relies on Me, knowing I will never forsake him, no, never].

He shall call upon Me, and I will answer him; I will be with him in trouble, I will deliver him and honor him.

With long life will I satisfy him and show him My salvation (AMP).

Praise God!

PRAISE

In addition to these weapons of warfare, there is the weapon of Praise. God inhabits the praises of His people (see Ps. 22:3). Therefore, a great weapon against the enemy is that of praise! The Word so poignantly paints a picture of what praise does to the enemy. When Israel (formerly Jacob) was dying and passing out the blessings upon his sons, He spoke over Judah, whose name means praise, a blessing: *"Judah, you are the one whom your brothers shall praise; **your hand shall be on the neck of your enemies...**"* (Gen. 49:8 AMP). This message depicts literally that our praise will place our hands on the enemy's neck. If we are being attacked in the spiritual realm and want to put a chokehold on the enemy, we can do it with praise.

What happens when you put your hand on the front of someone's neck? If your hand is on the front of your enemy's neck, where did you come from, the front or the back? Think about it; if I'm in a confrontation, which means I'm facing the enemy face-on with what he is doing to me, and I grab his neck, where is my position to the enemy? My position is face-to-face; I would put my hand on the front of his neck. However, I will have to wrestle him (fight him) in order to put it on the front of his neck because we will be facing each other. Instead, I will gain a greater advantage if I come from behind the enemy and put my hand on the back of his neck because I will not have to struggle and instead will catch him by surprise.

A good example of this would be if an attacker jumped out of a van and came directly in front of you to get you. You would see him and he would see you. There would be a face-to-face confrontation and a struggle. If you could not fight your attacker off and were weak, he might grab you and put you in the van. He would watch you until he was comfortable with the thought that you were not going to fight. That is what satan does.

When the attacker is comfortable with the fact that you are not fighting him back, he might walk off and do things, like making phone calls, getting a drink, making plans and the like, without having to keep his eye on your every move. It is at that time that his back is turned to you, which is exactly the time he least expects you to do anything. Likewise, when we appear at our weakest and satan thinks that he has wearied us down, that is when we belt out *"Thank You, Lord! I was lost, but now I'm found! You brought me up from a pit! You are the God who provides, the God who saves, the God who restores, and the God who sees all! You are my foundation and solid rock!"*

It is at that moment, when the enemy least expects it, that we have grabbed him from behind, put our hands on his neck, and have taken back the fight that he thought we lost. He cannot see it coming; it is like a left hook in a boxing match, and the enemy has no clue that we have it in us. I don't know how many sisters saw *Rocky* with Sylvester Stallone. In the first movie, he fought Apollo Creed in the boxing ring. Apollo, who had been victorious over other boxers, was expecting the same victory against Rocky, and he expected it to be an early defeat, as well. However, Rocky surprised him because he had more "fight" in him than Apollo had expected. Moreover, when Rocky's own manager wanted him to throw in the towel and the crowd expected him too, Rocky surprised them. He found a well (a reservoir) of fight left in him that he pulled from and fought Apollo to a point when Apollo told him, "There will be no rematch."

We have that same reservoir in us that the enemy cannot see and, even when our sisters in Christ might expect us to lie down and give up, that reservoir of praise must start turning over and stirring in us. All of a sudden, we shoot out and take on the enemy, throwing that left hook. I want to hear the enemy say, "There will be no rematch," because my role in fighting the enemy by the Spirit of God is such that he will have no desire for a rematch. In a boxing match, there is no punch, wait, punch. There is a punch, punch, punch, punch, punch, ding (the bell goes off). It is a flood-like attack from the enemy, not a dribble of rain. The Word of God says, *"...When the enemy shall come in like a flood, the Spirit of the Lord will lift up a standard against him"* (Isa. 59:19). Our God has not called us to throw in the towel, as Rocky's manager impulsively wanted him to do. Rather, our God raises a standard against the enemy, and when He raises the standard, the enemy is set to flight.

THE DEVIL IS UNDER MY FEET.

Joshua's pursuance of the enemy is an incredible illustration of how God places us in a position to be in the "rear" of our enemy, coming up behind him and thereby grabbing him without his knowledge. Moreover, in Joshua's battle strategy, he taught his men where the neck of the enemy was to stay—under their feet. Therefore, if we are not grabbing the enemies' necks with praises, then in other warfare, we are putting the enemy's neck under our feet.

> *So it was, when they brought out those kings to Joshua, that Joshua called for all the men of Israel, and said to the captains of the men of war who went with him, "Come near, put your feet on the necks of these kings." And they drew near and put their feet on their necks. Then Joshua said to them, "Do not be afraid, nor be dismayed; be strong and of good courage, for thus the LORD will do to all your enemies against whom you fight"* (Joshua 10:24-25).

The Word of God tells us to praise the Lord at all times.

*I **will** bless the Lord at all times; His praise shall continually be in my mouth. My life makes its boast in the Lord; let the humble and afflicted hear and be glad. O magnify the Lord with me, and let us exalt His name together* (Psalm 34:1-3 AMP).

King David belted out this praise. Also, in the New Testament, Paul in his letter to the Hebrews states,

*Through Him, therefore, let us constantly and at **all times** offer up to God a sacrifice of praise, which is the fruit of lips that thankfully acknowledge and confess and glorify His name* (Hebrews 13:15 AMP).

It is the Lord God who trains our hands to war; therefore, we do not lean on our own understanding regarding spiritual warfare. David puts it so well when he declares that God trains him for battle. *"He teaches my hands to war, so that my arms can bend a bow of bronze"* (Ps. 18:34 AMP). *"Blessed be the Lord, my Rock and my keen and firm Strength, who teaches my hands to war and my fingers to fight"* (Ps. 144:1 AMP). Therefore, through our praise, God trains us in how we are to battle; this is spiritual warfare.

The Holy Spirit has shown me through this teaching a method that allows me to go into every spiritual battle with a reverent approach, ensuring my success. In the next chapter we will discover the approach to spiritual warfare application. Remember that all things we do are to be carried out by our spirit and not by our flesh. As God had different battle victories with Israel, requiring them to follow a different method in winning the battle, He also has different methods of instruction for us each time. This is why we consult Him about every battle we are to fight. The battle is the

Lord's; He is our commander and chief, and as such, He is to give us instructions on carrying out our assignments, just as the general of a troop gives orders to them to carry out the battle plan.

QUESTIONS:

1. Is there a method identified in this chapter in which you need to mature?

2. Is there a method identified in this chapter that you have been implementing?

3. Continue to read the assignments in the prior chapter in John and Ephesians.

Endnote

1. Jentezen Franklin, *Fasting: Opening the Door to a Deeper, More Intimate, More Powerful Relationship with God* (Lake Mary, FL: Charisma House, 2007).

11

Push, Pursue, and Recover

King David was faced with a situation that was beyond all natural hope in fighting his enemy. His only possibility of overcoming the enemy was dependent upon God. In his gaining victory over the enemy, the Word of God demonstrates how we ourselves are to approach our own battles against our enemies. Here the enemies I'm referring to are not people who cannot stand us or those we do not like. We war not against flesh and blood, but against principalities and rulers in high places (see Eph. 6:12). Therefore, we have to become spiritually-minded and not fleshly-minded. If we cannot get in our spirits during battle, the enemy will win because he can only overcome us if we are in our flesh.

Therefore, let's look at the example that David gives us so that we too can overcome our enemy, ensuring us victory in our battle.

David and his men reached Ziklag on the third day. Now the Amalekites had raided the Negev and Ziklag. They had attacked Ziklag and burned it, and had taken captive the women and all who were in it, both young and old. They killed none of them, but carried them off as they went on their way. When David and his men came to Ziklag, they found it destroyed by fire and their wives and sons and daughters taken captive. So David and his men wept aloud until they had no strength left to weep. David's two wives had been captured—Ahinoam of Jezreel and Abigail, the widow of Nabal of Carmel. David was greatly distressed because the men were talking of stoning him; each one was bitter in spirit because of his sons and daughters. But David found strength in the Lord his God. Then David said to Abiathar the priest, the son of Ahimelech, "Bring me the ephod." Abiathar brought it to him, and David inquired of the Lord, "Shall I pursue this raiding party? Will I overtake them?" "Pursue them," he answered. "You will certainly overtake them and succeed in the rescue." David and the six hundred men with him came to the Besor Ravine, where some stayed behind, for two hundred men were too exhausted to cross the ravine. But David and four hundred men continued the pursuit. They found an Egyptian in a field and brought him to David. They gave him water to drink and food to eat- part of a cake of pressed figs and two cakes of raisins. He ate and was revived, for he had not eaten any food or drunk any water for three days and three nights. David asked him, "To whom do you belong, and where do you come from?" He said, "I am an Egyptian, the slave of an Amalekite. My master abandoned me when I became ill three days ago. We raided the Negev of the Kerethites and the territory belonging to Judah and the Negev of Caleb.

And we burned Ziklag." David asked him, "Can you lead me down to this raiding party?"

He answered, "Swear to me before God that you will not kill me or hand me over to my master, and I will take you down to them." He led David down, and there they were, scattered over the countryside, eating, drinking and reveling because of the great amount of plunder they had taken from the land of the Philistines and from Judah. David fought them from dusk until the evening of the next day, and none of them got away, except four hundred young men who rode off on camels and fled. **David recovered everything** *the Amalekites had taken, including his two wives. Nothing was missing: young or old, boy or girl, plunder or anything else they had taken. David brought everything back. He took all the flocks and herds, and his men drove them ahead of the other livestock, saying, "This is David's plunder." Then David came to the two hundred men who had been too exhausted to follow him and who were left behind at the Besor Ravine. They came out to meet David and the people with him. As David and his men approached, he greeted them. But all the evil men and troublemakers among David's followers said, "Because they did not go out with us, we will not share with them the plunder we recovered. However, each man may take his wife and children and go." David replied, "No, my brothers, you must not do that with what the Lord has given us. He has protected us and handed over to us the forces that came against us. Who will listen to what you say? The share of the man who stayed with the supplies is to be the same as that of him who went down to the battle. All will share alike." David made this a statute and ordinance for Israel from that day to this. When David arrived in Ziklag, he sent some of the plunder to the elders of Judah, who were his friends, saying, "Here is a present for you from the plunder of the Lord's* *enemies." He sent it to those who were in Bethel, Ramoth Negev and Jattir; to those in Aroer, Siphmoth, Eshtemoa and Racal; to those in the towns of the Jerahmeelites and the Kenites; to those in Hormah, Bor Ashan, Athach and Hebron; and to those in all the other places where David and his men had roamed* (1 Samuel 30:1-31 NIV).

PUSH

First, we are to push. When David and all of his men were weak, what set him apart from his men was that he tapped into the spiritual realm. His men were weak and unable to find strength. However, unlike his men, David found strength in His God. He asked the priest to bring the ephod, and he inquired of the Lord, "Shall I pursue, and will I overtake them?" David pushed through to talk to God and ask the questions that were relevant to his situation, to his present battle. The enemy tries to weary us in well–doing, and at times it feels as though there is no strength in us. However, if we push into hearing from God, we will find Him!

For example, an attack I underwent during 2007 and 2008 was so heavy that I felt as close as I could imagine to King David in this instance. My husband and were being attacked on every side from false accusations coming against us through others in regard to my oldest son. Moreover, I was undergoing persecution for the way I believed in the prophetic mandate God had given me regarding our ministry 22 IS 22 (Isaiah 22:22 Company). In addition, our finances were hit yet again, and we were down to one car.

There were times after ministry when I would leave the meeting and it would be 12 A.M. I had to pick Rich up at 3 A.M. each morning during that time since we had one car. So I would leave the meeting where I ministered and go sleep in the car at his job for a couple of hours until Rich got off of work. Therefore, needless to say, I was stretched beyond measure when the blow came regarding my oldest son, and I felt as though King David must have. I didn't realize I was in a pit, the dark night of the soul, and was in a time when I only saw the darkness because the attack was so great against us. For me to get up and start praising God was not what God had for me in that hour. Rather I had to seek God in the darkness and find the riches He had for me in this attack.

> *And I will give you the **treasures of darkness and hidden riches of secret places**, that you may know that it is I, the Lord, the God of Israel, who calls you by your name* (Isaiah 45:3 AMP).

I was in a dark time because of the attack, and by Holy Spirit, I was determined to seek God even in the midst of my darkness. Literally during this time, I often had no strength and felt as though I was a rag doll plopping myself on the chair and many times staying on the floor. In the midst of that time, all Holy Spirit would let me do is declare over and over John 1:5, "The darkness does not overcome the *light*!!" I would many times muster up enough strength to whisper it, because that was all I could do. However, day by day I got through this difficult time, and finally one day the enemy was crazy enough to do one more thing against me, and at that moment, I felt a switch go off in me. All of a sudden my strength was renewed. I received a new anointing, and I came out of that pit like superman! I became like a wild ox! *"But my horn (emblem of excessive strength and stately grace) You have exalted like that of a wild ox; I am anointed with fresh oil"* (Ps. 92:10 AMP). I came out of that pit victorious and with a fresh anointing! However, if I had not sought God and pushed through to find Him during that hard time, the new anointing would not have come upon me.

When we push through our warfare, we ask the Lord how to fight the present spiritual battle. It is arrogant to presume that if we won a former spiritual battle in a certain way then we can put into action that same method and win the present battle we are in. Instead, we must wait on God regarding what we are to do. The response David got from God was that he was to pursue, and on top of that, God said he would recover all that the enemy had taken from he and his men.

All throughout the Bible we see God telling His people to wait on Him; *"But you must return to your God; maintain love and justice, and wait for your God always"* (Hos. 12:6 NIV). Many times, because of our microwave age society, we desire to put a request into a microwave and have it immediately answered by God. Moreover, there are times when we play God's role, and we ourselves decide on what is to be done and never push into asking and receiving from God regarding our battle assignment.

My husband and I went through a major attack regarding the property where we at one time lived. Initially, I had in my own strength, and from my prior professional background as a social worker, I started playing God's part in fighting the battle against our home. This occurred through my decision to do research and make several telephone calls on what strategy would best help us. However, what I came to find out was that God was not in any of it; I had not pushed through to hear from Him regarding the situation. All I could see, as in King David's scenario, was that without a major miracle from God, my husband and I would shortly be in a detrimental situation.

My flesh screamed like a toddler, and all I could do was "something." The something that I was doing was not of God, but of Robin. Therefore, the Lord brought me to a brokenness to see that without Him I could do nothing In the midst of that brokenness, I sought Him and waited to hear from Him. He told me clearly to *"Be still and know that I am God"* My husband and I remained in a position of being still and waiting upon His hand to move. While this was going on, I didn't know what God was doing behind the scenes. I came to find out that He was rearranging some files for us that would work in our favor. This is similar to what happened when David was in his battle. He was weak and had need of a great miracle from God in order to ensure victory.

In the midst of this, the enemy sent a person to our home that was by no means evil. In fact, he was a Christian, but he was acting out of his flesh. This man came to our home unannounced, and it appeared as though God had sent this man. However, the enemy revealed himself through this man's visit when this man almost tried to pressure us into working with him. This exposed that this in fact was not from God, but was instead from the enemy to cause us to move outside of God's plan for our lives. As a result, I told the man that I would not move on his response at all until I heard clearly from God, and until then I would not budge. Immediately, the man saw the faith of God inside of me and actually asked me to pray for him. God's Holy Spirit showed me, through the gift of discernment, how this man was really acting out of his own desperation and distrust in God.

Was this a divine appointment? At first it would not appear so. It was a divine appointment, but not for us to get help from him. Three months later after this meeting, on the day my husband and I were moving out of that house into a new home, the man drove up in our driveway. When I went out to meet him, he got out and said that he didn't know why he came to our home; he wasn't there on business, but out of need. I knew that I was to direct him to my husband to be ministered to by God. They talked for nearly two hours. It was a divine appointment; not for us, but for this man to receive from God.

As a result of not moving or wavering until we heard from God, we heard and knew what to do and had favor, blessing, and money come in. Moreover, God brought us out of a situation where we would be financially devastated, had we not waited upon Him and listened for His instruction.

David, likewise was being pressured by his men to act out of his flesh. His men were angry and wanted to kill him. In circumstances like this, most of us would immediately go to the "let me satisfy my flesh" solution and make everyone happy. However, most of the time it is in the pleasing of the flesh that we are ensured total defeat. As stated earlier, satan can only defeat us if we are in our flesh because when we walk in our God-given authority (the Spirit), he cannot stand against us. Therefore, circumstances will occur in order to pull us out of our Spirit walk and into our flesh walk. We have to stay on guard and be watchful so the enemy does not pull us from walking in the Spirit. *"Watch, stand fast in the faith, be brave, be strong"* (1 Cor. 16:13).

David's men wanted him to react, but reaction is only done in the flesh. Instead, God wants us to respond, which is carried out by walking in the Spirit. David called for the priest, which demonstrated his stepping into his spirit man. Likewise, we cannot be moved by people or circumstances, but rather be still and wait upon the Lord in order to get a response from Him.

When we walk in the Spirit, we are actually pushing through to hear from God. We do not move due to how our circumstances appear, but instead we push through and get an answer from God. If we are having trouble hearing from God, the biggest struggle that we might have to overcome is being still. Again, due to our fast-paced culture, we have to go against the grain of our culture and learn to be still and trust that God will work things out and send our answer.

In the situation that my husband and I experienced with our home, we pushed through to hear from God. After pushing through in order that we might hear from God, we asked the right questions and were obedient to His Word. That brings up an issue. Can you ask the wrong question? Absolutely. *"[Or] you do ask [God for them] and yet fail to receive, because you ask with wrong purpose and evil, selfish motives..."* (James 4:3 AMP). We see throughout the Bible times when people have asked the wrong question, and it was because they were in the flesh, not in the Spirit.

When we come to God, we have to come humbly with a broken and contrite heart. If we come to God haughtily and ask something that is contrary to His Word, we should not expect the answer we might hope for or be ready to say "woe is me!" This is seen in the story of Balaam in the Book of Numbers and King Ahab in the Book of First Kings. Therefore, when we come to God, before we jump in and ask any question, we need to ask the one in which the Holy Spirit is guiding us. It is fine to let God know of our insecurity, concerns, worries, and so forth. However, when we ask Him something, we need to ask Him out of brokenness and humility, not out of pride or wrong motives.

For example, if you are angry with a woman who might be trying to usurp your authority in a specific job and get you fired, would you come to God and ask Him how you can get rid of her? No. That is in your flesh. Instead, come to God and let Him know that you are angry because He already knows. Confess that you need help with overcoming your anger toward her. If you were to do anything presently, it would most likely be ungodly. Ask Him to show you how you can win the battle you are in and to give you the wisdom to come to Him and ask of Him what it is that you need. The Bible states that you have not because you ask not (see James 4:2). Therefore, if you have a need, you have to ask.

In addition, when we come to God and ask, we should *expect* Him to answer! There are so many people who come to God, and when they ask Him for something, they come with an attitude of, "If You want to God...." Thus, they pray prayers like, "Lord, I need help in overcoming this horrible attack against me at my job, and I'm being falsely accused by another lady. If you want to, God, please deliver me from this trap that the enemy has set."

We do not have to ask God if He wants to do something because His Word says that He *will!* Therefore, when we come to Him, asking for a need, we have to expect that He will meet it.

> *But without faith it is impossible to please Him: for He that cometh to God must believe that He is, and that He is a rewarder of them that diligently seek Him* (Hebrews 11:6 KJV).

We have to have *faith* that God will answer us, and He will reward us for diligently seeking Him for the answer.

PURSUE

Next, we are to pursue. In pursuing, we go after the enemy according to the strategy God gives us. God answered King David's request by telling him that he would pursue the enemy and overtake them in order to recover all that the enemy took from him and his men. The enemy burned their homes, took their families, animals, and valuables. David pursued the enemy with confidence, knowing that the battle had already been won. Likewise we are to go in confidence with the Word we have received from the Lord, knowing that He is faithful and will keep that Word that He has given us (see Heb. 10:23). He is not a man that He would lie to us, but a God who changes not (see Num. 23:19). Therefore, when He gives us answers regarding the attack against us, we need to believe His Word and confess it as true.

When my husband and I received the Word from the Lord to be still and wait upon Him, we pursued that Word with tenacity. We were tenacious about pushing through that battle with the Word. The enemy would send people to us, telling us things that were contrary to the Word we received in order that we would let go of it and not be still and wait. However, we hung on to that Word as a lion hangs on to a piece of meat that is being pulled out of his mouth. There was no letting go of His Word, and our pursuit of the enemy involved us putting on the armor of God, declaring the Word that He had given us, and not turning from His promise. It involved binding up lying, fearful, anxious, and intimidating spirits from the enemy and loosing a sound mind, an overcomer anointing, and peace.

RECOVER

Finally, after we pursue the enemy with the Word that God has given us, we are to expect to recover what the Lord has spoken. In David's case God demonstrates that not only will we recover what the enemy stole from us, but we will in addition, plunder his camp and have such an overabundance of it that we will also be giving to others in need and to those who have given to us. God has promised that we will receive sevenfold from the enemy what he has taken from us (see Prov. 6:31).

If we receive sevenfold, do we get to keep all of it for ourselves? Usually, the sevenfold is not for our own keeping, because it is abundantly above what we could use. David gave some of the plunder to those who stayed at the camp because of their weakness and inability to go with him in pursuing the enemy and going into battle, as well as to others. Sometimes we might be weak when another sister in Christ is strong in pursing the enemy in spiritual warfare. She is not only going to get "hers," but she will also get "yours." We need to have a "we mentality" because no one can be an island unto themselves. We are one Body in Christ Jesus. There may be a weaker vessel that God has asked us to give some of our plunder from the enemy to.

Moreover, David went to the elders who were his friends to give them the enemy's plunder. When the Lord brings us into a position of plundering the enemy's camp, He wants us to bless those elders who have planted into our lives. Elders are not old people. Rather, they are people or ministries who are mature in the Lord and who have prayed for us, taught us, encouraged us, and been in the fight with us. Elders who have sown into us can be television ministries, leadership or mentors at church, our local church, and so forth. There have been times when my husband and I have been blessed, and we have certain elders (individuals and ministries) whom the Lord requires us to give to. We do and, in so doing, experience joy that we are giving to the Lord. An elder is not necessarily defined by age, but by position in Christ.

I want to close this chapter out with a Scripture that one of my dear friends, Holly, brought to my attention, which demonstrates so well the position of spiritual warfare that we in Christ are to take.

But as for me, I watch in hope for the LORD, I wait for God my Savior; my God will hear me. Do not gloat over me, my enemy! Though I have fallen, I will rise. Though I sit in darkness, the LORD will be my light (Micah 7:7-8 NIV).

Though you may be sitting in darkness right now while in the middle of a spiritual battle—such as, a divorce, bankruptcy, foreclosure, addiction, a rebellious child, AIDS, homosexuality, malicious gossip, or illness—know that in the midst of the darkness the Lord is your light. It is He who will lift you up out of it. He will direct your footsteps and, in the midst of what looks like an impossible situation, He will train your hands to war so that you will recover all and then some.

Here's an important reminder: One of the most important things about doing spiritual warfare and working to get free from strongholds is that once you are free from the enemy, you have to get full of the Word of God. If you do not, you can find yourself in a worse state than what you were in before.

> *When an evil spirit comes out of a man, it goes through arid places seeking rest and does not find it. Then it says, "I will return to the house I left." When it arrives, it finds the house unoccupied, swept clean and put in order. Then it goes and takes with it seven other spirits more wicked than itself, and they go in and live there. **And the final condition of that man is worse than the first**. That is how it will be with this wicked generation* (Matthew 12:43-45 NIV).

In order to keep your house (your soul) from being unoccupied, you have to fill it with the Word of God.

QUESTIONS:

1. Where do you have needs for which you need to push through and hear God to meet your need?

2. Do you pursue once you hear from God, or do you give up? (Many people give up before they recover.)

3. When you recover, do you have people whom you intend to bless when you get the sevenfold blessing?

4. Confess the Scriptures in Ephesians that encourage you in the Lord and His power in you. Continue to read John chapters 14–17. When you do spiritual warfare, it is necessary to increase your love tank with the Lord because perfect love casts out fear and you can battle unafraid.

c h a p t e r

12

The Key of David: Isaiah 22:22

The Key of David is an important weapon in bringing Heaven to earth. This small teaching helps us to understand how we are to steward our authority for the Kingdom of Heaven. It is binding and loosing as explained earlier, but in more detail. *"I will place on his shoulder the key to the house of David; what he opens no one can shut, and what he shuts no one can open"* (Isa. 22:22 NIV).

The Key to the House of David is an important revelation for all Christian soldiers in walking in their God-given authority. In order to be effective in bringing the Kingdom of Heaven, God Almighty's Kingdom, to earth, we have to understand our authority as associated with the Key of David.

The Key of David is given only to those wise stewards on earth who will open up the door for the Kingdom of Heaven to be released on the earth and will also shut the door to the kingdom of darkness. In order to understand this fully, we have to look at the Scripture in context. Context means that we have to look at the Scripture regarding the circumstances it was used in during that time, the time of the prophet Isaiah. Moreover, we then have to transmute the Scripture into our time and apply it to us.

King David (who had already passed away) is in the lineage of the Messiah, Jesus Christ (who had not yet been born on the earth), and David's throne had been given to another in the lineage. Isaiah the prophet states that the throne of King David will have no end when he prophecies the coming rule of King Jesus. *"...He* [JESUS] *will reign on David's throne and over his kingdom, establishing and upholding it with justice and righteousness from that time on and forever..."* (Isaiah 9:7 NIV).

Therefore, the key to David's House is important because it is the key to the king's treasury. During Isaiah's time, King Hezekiah was ruling the House of David.

Below the Scripture is used in context. Before you read the Scripture, here is some background. The man Shebna in this passage is the holder of the key to the king's house, to the treasury of the king's house. This position was basically a governor for the home of the king. Shebna had a lot of power. However, because of his wickedness, he ended up getting demoted. Shebna used to be a scribe, and everywhere else in the Bible you see Shebna in the position of scribe (see 2 Kings 18:18). A scribe was a writer and recorder of everything that occurred during that time.

Eliakim ended up taking Shebna's position because Eliakim was an honorable man. He became the governor of the king's palace and held the key to his entire home, which included all of the king's wealth.

This is what the Lord, the LORD Almighty, says: "Go, say to this steward, to Shebna, who is in charge of the palace: What are you doing here and who gave you permission to cut out a grave for yourself here, hewing your grave on the height and chiseling your resting place in the rock? Beware, the LORD is about to take firm hold of you and hurl you away, O you mighty man. He will roll you up tightly like a ball and throw you into a large country. There you will die and there your splendid chariots will remain—you disgrace to your master's house! I will depose you from your office, and you will be ousted from your position. In that day I will summon my servant, Eliakim son of Hilkiah. I will clothe him with your robe and fasten your sash around him and hand your authority over to him. He will be a father to those who live in Jerusalem and to the house of Judah. I will place on his shoulder the key to the house of David; what he opens no one can shut, and what he shuts no one can open. I will drive him like a peg into a firm place; he will be a seat of honor for the house of his father. All the glory of his family will hang on him: its offspring and offshoots—all its lesser vessels, from the bowls to all the jars. In that day," declares the LORD Almighty, "the peg driven into the firm place will give way; it will be sheared off and will fall, and the load hanging on it will be cut down." The LORD has spoken (Isaiah 22:15-25 NIV).

Here Shebna was the governor to the king. However, in verse 15, God tells Isaiah to talk with Shebna and refers to him as a steward. A steward is someone who has been entrusted something and manages the provision of what he has. Shebna was entrusted with the entire estate and wealth of King Hezekiah.

In verse 16 the Lord says, *"Who gave you permission to cut out a grave for yourself here."* Back in the day of Isaiah, famous and important people had tombs up in the hills, and the bigger you were while you lived, the bigger your tomb would be. Have you ever gone to a cemetery where they had tombs above the ground; New Orleans has many because of the high water levels. At any rate, the bigger and more expensive looking the tomb a person had built, the more important it showed that they were. The Lord was angry with Shebna because he was entrusted with the wealth of the king, and instead of being a good manager of what was in the king's home, he was spending the money on himself.

Shebna was not managing king Hezekiah's kingdom correctly and instead was building somewhat of his own Shebna kingdom. The Lord was angry at Shebna, and He continued to describe Shebna's arrogance by being rhetorical, asking Shebna, *"What are you doing here and who gave you permission to cut out a grave for yourself here hewing your grave on the height and chiseling your resting place in the rock."* Shebna was building his own dynasty by first of all showing everyone in the kingdom how important he was by the location and expense of the tomb he was building himself.

Shebna was misappropriating the key to the house of David that he was given. God instructed Shebna through the prophet Isaiah that He was going to take Shebna out of office.

Beware, the LORD is about to take firm hold of you and hurl you away, O you mighty man. He will roll you up tightly like a ball and throw you into a large country. There you will die and there your splendid chariots will remain— you disgrace to your master's house! I will depose you from your office, and you will be ousted from your position (Isaiah 22:17-19 NIV).

Shebna's name means "to grow." Shebna was to grow in the position of governor of the house of David, but he did not grow in God's way, but in his own selfish way. He grew to take what was of the king's kingdom in the house of David and appropriate it for himself, in his tomb. He was in essence burying the Kingdom of God.

Jesus describes this in a parable that He gave about three servants and the talents given to them by their master.

THE PARABLE OF THE TALENTS

Again, it [the Kingdom of Heaven] *will be like a man going on a journey, who called his servants and entrusted his property to them. To one he gave five talents of money, to another two talents, and to another one talent, each according to his ability. Then he went on his journey. The man who had received the five talents went at once and put his money to work and gained five more. So also, the one with the two talents gained two more. But the man who had received the one talent went off, dug a hole in the ground and hid his master's money. After a long time the master of those servants returned and settled accounts with them. The man who had received the five talents brought the other five. "Master," he said, "you entrusted me with five talents. See, I have gained five more." His master replied, "Well done, good and faithful servant! You have been faithful with a few things; I will put you in charge of many things. Come and share your master's happiness!" The man with the two talents also came. "Master," he said, "you entrusted me with two talents; see, I have gained two more." His master replied, "Well done, good and faithful servant! You have been faithful with a few things; I will put you in charge of many things. Come and share your master's happiness!"' Then the man who had received the one talent came. "Master," he said, "I knew that you are a hard man, harvesting where you have not sown and gathering where you have not scattered seed. So I was afraid and went out and hid your talent in the ground. See, here is what belongs to you." His master replied, "You wicked, lazy servant! So you knew that I harvest where I have not sown and gather where I have not scattered seed? Well then, you should have put my money on deposit with the bankers, so that when I returned I would have received it back with interest. Take the talent from him and give it to the one who has the ten talents. For everyone who has will be given more, and he will have an abundance. Whoever does not have, even what he has will be taken from him. And throw that worthless servant outside, into the darkness, where there will be weeping and gnashing of teeth"* (Matthew 25:14-30 NIV).

What Shebna had been given was the Kingdom of Heaven, and instead of using it wisely, he was burying it. He was to grow in the knowledge of how to use the key to the house of David in order to go into the treasury room and appropriate wisely the king's treasure for his kingdom.

God knew of one who was righteous who would appropriate the key to the House of David in a manner that would bring honor to the kingdom. This wise servant was Eliakim. *Eliakim* means "the Lord raises up." God in essence was saying that He would raise up a servant who would know how to use the key wisely to the house of David.

"In that day I will summon my servant, Eliakim son of Hilkiah. I will clothe him with your robe and fasten your sash around him and hand your authority over to him. He will be a father to those who live in Jerusalem and to the

house of Judah. I will place on his shoulder the key to the house of David; what he opens no one can shut, and what he shuts no one can open. I will drive him like a peg into a firm place; he will be a seat of honor for the house of his father. All the glory of his family will hang on him: its offspring and offshoots—all its lesser vessels, from the bowls to all the jars. In that day," declares the LORD Almighty, "the peg driven into the firm place will give way; it will be sheared off and will fall, and the load hanging on it will be cut down." The LORD has spoken (Isaiah 22:20-25 NIV).

"That day" was the day that Shebna would be removed and Eliakim would be placed in office. Eliakim was to be clothed in royal garments that signified his position over the king's wealth and treasury. Moreover, he would become a father to those under the king's rule.

Eliakim, which means "God raises up," is a personification of the Messiah Jesus Christ. We see Jesus with the Key of David in Revelation when He was talking to the Church of Philadelphia.

To the angel of the church in Philadelphia write: These are the words of Him who is holy and true, who holds the key of David. What He opens no one can shut, and what He shuts no one can open (Revelation 3:7 NIV).

Moreover, Hilkiah, who was Eliakim's father, had significant meaning to his name, too. *Hilkiah* means "a portion of God." Therefore, God Himself would "give a portion of God" into His Son Jesus Christ, who would be raised up by God to bring in a new government that would allow the Kingdom of Heaven to be opened up in the earthly realm. Isaiah prophecied this in Isaiah 9:

For to us a child is born, to us a son is given, and the government will be on His shoulders. And He will be called Wonderful Counselor, Mighty God, Everlasting Father, Prince of Peace. Of the increase of His government and peace there will be no end. He will reign on David's throne and over his kingdom, establishing and upholding it with justice and righteousness from that time on and forever. The zeal of the LORD Almighty will accomplish this (Isaiah 9:6-7 NIV).

When Adam disobeyed God in the Garden of Eden, the rule of this world left humanity and went to satan. The Kingdom of Heaven was not being opened up after that time to get into the earthly realm except through designs given by God to man (the power had not yet come into people to be a door for Heaven). Rather satan himself was busy taking what had been given to people by God and building his own kingdom through "death, death, death."

When Jesus entered into earth, He could not come by a priest line (although He is the High Priest) because He had to legitimately be the heir to a throne already established in earth in order to build His Kingdom through that line. That is why Jesus is called the Son of David in the Scriptures. Jesus was heir to the throne of David, and thereby, He had rights to build up that lineage of royal DNA from God through claiming the throne of David. This is how Jesus establishes His Kingdom.

We are joint heirs with Christ.

The Spirit itself beareth witness with our spirit, that we are the children of God: And if children, then heirs; heirs of God, and joint-heirs with Christ; if so be that we suffer with him, that we may be also glorified together (Romans 8:16-17 KJV).

Therefore, we have to come into the revelation of the power that we have in possessing the Key of David. We have authority as joint heirs to take the Key of David and open the doors of the Kingdom of Heaven to be released into this earthly realm and shut the door to the kingdom of darkness.

How do we get the key? Jesus gives us the key when we have a revelation of Him as *the Christ*. This is seen in Matthew 16, when Peter is asked who Jesus is.

When Jesus came to the region of Caesarea Philippi, He asked His disciples, "Who do people say the Son of Man is?" They replied, "Some say John the Baptist; others say Elijah; and still others, Jeremiah or one of the prophets." "But what about you?" He asked. "Who do you say I am?" Simon Peter answered, "You are the Christ, the Son of the living God." Jesus replied, "Blessed are you, Simon son of Jonah, for this was not revealed to you by man, but by My Father in heaven. And I tell you that you are Peter, and on this rock I will build My church, and the gates of Hades will not overcome it. I will give you the keys of the kingdom of heaven; whatever you bind on earth will be bound in heaven, and whatever you loose on earth will be loosed in heaven." Then He warned His disciples not to tell anyone that He was the Christ (Matthew 16:13-20 NIV).

On the revelation of Jesus being the Christ, Peter was given the keys of the Kingdom of Heaven, and he was given authority to bind and loose. When we come to a revelation of who Jesus really is, then we likewise have that same power, and we become wise stewards. We are then stewards of the Key of David and can open up the Kingdom of Heaven into our cities, schools, communities, homes, friends, and everything. Moreover, we can shut the door to the kingdom of darkness with this same key.

Jesus describes well how the Pharisees shut the Kingdom of Heaven to the people instead of releasing it; they were like Shebna, building their own kingdoms.

> *Woe to you, teachers of the law and Pharisees, you hypocrites! You shut the kingdom of heaven in men's faces. You yourselves do not enter, nor will you let those enter who are trying to* (Matthew 23:13 NIV).

We are to take dominion of the earth through the Key of David, which is opening up the door to the Kingdom of Heaven into earth and shutting the door to the kingdom of darkness. How do we do this? We start praying prayers like this:

> *I take the Key of David in Isaiah 22:22 and open up the door to the Kingdom of Heaven to my school in Jesus' name, that no man can shut. I shut doors to the kingdom of darkness in Jesus' name that no man can open.*

> *I take the Key of David in Isaiah 22:22 and open up the door to the God-ordained relationships for _____ [name] and declare that those doors will not be shut in Jesus' name. I take the Key of David in Isaiah 22:22 and shut the door to every relationship that no man can open in Jesus' name to relationships that are not of God.*

> *I take the Key of David in Isaiah 22:22 and shut the door to drugs, fornication, gangs, and rebellion in my school that no man can open. I open the door to holiness and purity from the Kingdom of God that no man can shut into my school in Jesus' name. Amen.*

> *I take the Key of David in Isaiah 22:22 and open up the door to my destiny that no man can shut, and I take the*

Key of David and shut every door that is not of God to my destiny that no man can open. In Jesus' name. Amen.

I take the Key of David in Isaiah 22:22 and open up the door to my promotion in my work place that no man can shut and take the Key of David and shut every door that would stop my promotion that no man can open in Jesus' name.

Do this for everything that the Spirit of God prompts you. I pray it over homes, jobs, destiny, relationships, property, and so forth—over *everything*.

This is what God wants you to do. Will you stand with King Jesus and open up the Kingdom of Heaven and take dominion of the area you walk and also shut up the kingdom of darkness?

If so, pray this prayer:

Dear Lord, I ask that You wouldgive me wisdom, under-standing, revelation, and knowledge on how I am to use the Key of David in Isaiah 22:22 and be one whom You raise up to bring the Kingdom of Heaven to earth. I pray for boldness to walk in the authority that You have given me through Christ Jesus. I ask for a revelation of the royal heav-enly DNA in my body so that I can stand like King David, a giant killer, against anything that profanes You. In Jesus' name I pray Amen.

The ability to be a Princess Warrior for the Most High God comes through being a Christian. God empowers you with His Holy Spirit so that you will be able to be taught, counseled, and led into all the truths of God in your spiritual warfare. No spiritual warfare can be done effectively without a true fear of the Lord, because it is the fear of God that keeps you from sin and brings you to a place of reverence. In this place of reverence, you desire God's will to be done on earth as it is in Heaven. Your will fades away, and you walk as a reproducer of the seed of Jesus Christ, desiring for all darkness to be pushed back and for the light of Jesus to be released into the lives of others.

Moreover, the most powerful weapon that a Princess Warrior uses, above all, is the love of God that pours out of her heart toward a lost and dying world. She does not judge by her own eyes, but with righteousness she judges (see Isa. 11:3). She sees what God sees and calls those things that are not as though they are (see Rom. 4:17). Therefore, we are to look through the eyes of love at everyone and every circumstance and call forth the Kingdom of Heaven into those people and circumstances.

From my own experience, this growth in spiritual warfare has come by increasing my prayer life and worship time with the Lord. Moreover, I continually ate and fed myself on the Word of God. All of these personal devotions to the Lord allowed me to grow strong in my spirit (see Luke 1:80; 2:40) so that I would pray with more accuracy.

I am going to do the Princess Warriors meetings on a bigger level as the doors open for me to do so. Therefore, please consider joining with your other sisters and look for the Princess Warriors Website and Facebook page as they come forward.

This is my prayer for you, Princess Warrior:

I pray that God fills you into overflow with His love and His Holy Spirit so that you might walk in His will, plans, and purposes only for the spiritual warfare He has assigned to you. I plead the blood of Jesus over you as you walk obediently into your call. I declare Psalms 91 protection over you. I declare that you will walk in the full armor of God.

I ask for God to rest the Spirit of the fear of the Lord upon you. I declare that you will walk in knowledge, wisdom, and understanding regarding deliverance, binding and loosing, and the Key of David. I declare that you will be a reproducer of the seed of Jesus Christ, and you are anointed as King Jesus was prophesied in Isaiah 61. I declare that you will set the captives free. I declare that you will spread the knowledge of the Gospel by spreading the knowledge of the Kingdom in Jesus' name.

Symbols to Princess Warriors

When God gave me the vision for Princess Warriors, He later instructed me on what the symbols would be and the meaning behind the symbols. The symbols are the sword of the Spirit and crown forming the "P" for princess and the fire forming the "W" for warriors. I believe God instructs with purpose even today as He did several thousand years ago when God instructed Moses on everything that was to be in the tabernacle (see Ex. 25). These symbols were used in at the beginning of the book. As the angel, Hieremias, gives Robin the sword, crown, and ball of fire in the short story, Holy Spirit likewise offers God's Princess Warriors these three weapons of warfare, too. I pray that the revelation of each symbol is infused into your inner woman, providing greater God confidence in your spirit woman to walk in the authority of Jesus Christ.

13

The Sword of the Spirit

WIELDING THE SWORD OF THE SPIRIT

Princess Warriors put your seat belts on and buckle in because Holy Spirit is going to give you a full revelation of the Sword of the Spirit! Holy Spirit does not want to waste one drop of this revelation to God's Princess Daughters. In order to bring about the full revelation, there has to be a foundation laid to bring you forward into the fullness of this revelation. God bless you and welcome to the revelation of God's "Sword of the Spirit" which is the first symbol in Princess Warriors.

Paul wrote, *"And take the helmet of salvation and the sword that the Spirit wields, which is the Word of God"* (Eph. 6:17 AMP). Here the Sword of the Spirit represents, as Paul states, *"the Word of God."* The Sword of the Spirit is Jesus, because Jesus is the Word:

In the beginning was the Word, and the Word was with God, and the Word was God. He was in the beginning with God. All things were made through Him, and without Him nothing was made that was made. In Him was life, and the life was the light of men. And the light shines in the darkness, and the darkness did not comprehend it...And the Word became flesh and dwelt among us, and we beheld His glory, the glory as of the only begotten of the Father, full of grace and truth (John 1:1-5; 14).

Jesus is the Word and was in the beginning with God. Through Jesus all things were made.

He is the image of the invisible God, the firstborn over all creation. For by Him all things were created that are in heaven and that are on earth, visible and invisible, whether thrones or dominions or principalities or powers. All things were created through Him and for Him. And He is before all things, and in Him all things consist (Colossians 1:15-17).

Jesus came full of life and light, being the Word of God, and created all things in Heaven and earth. The Word of God is powerful beyond measure. We have no clue the depth of the power of the Word of God in and over our lives, families, communities, nations, and the earth. It was the spoken Word that formed the earth and all that it is in it. That is *power!*

When we look at the beginning and how God formed the earth and the existence of all that is in it, we have a clearer revelation of how God the Father, Jesus the Son, and Holy Spirit work together as one. It is the relationship of the Trinity, the Godhead (Father God, Jesus, and Holy Spirit) that we see a great demonstration of the authority and creative power of God.

In the beginning God (prepared, formed, fashioned, and) created the heavens and the earth. The earth was without form and an empty waste, and darkness was upon the face of the very great deep. The Spirit of God was moving (hovering, brooding) over the face of the waters. And God said, Let there be light; and there was light (Genesis 1:1-3 AMP).

Here in Genesis 1 we see God creating the heavens and earth by having His Holy Spirit hover (move) over the place into which He was about to release His powerful words. Then God spoke, "Let there be light," and light was manifested. What God spoke was already in His mind prior to Him speaking it. God had already completed the entire earth in His mind before it was ever released through the Word.

Also to enlighten all men and make plain to them what is the plan [regarding the Gentiles and providing for the salvation of all men] of the mystery kept hidden through the ages and concealed until now in [the mind of] God Who created all things by Christ Jesus (Ephesians 3:9 AMP).

God's mind contains the structure whereby He formed earth and all that was in it. As we see in the Bible, God's ways are higher than our ways, and His thoughts are higher than our thoughts (see Isa. 55:9). God's thoughts contain the structure, the DNA so to speak, of the form of everything.

As God thought the entire universe in His mind, He then wanted to see the form come forth outside of Himself. In order to do that, He used the Word, Jesus, to bring that form forth. God spoke, "Let there be light"—that was Jesus, the Word. God's Holy Spirit was waiting upon Jesus before He could finish the plan of God and actually bring the existence of what was spoken. The Godhead is intricately connected, more than we can ever imagine. They work cooperatively with each other in unity to bring forth God's plan and purposes. In watching the working of the Godhead, we see, as Jesus the Word formed everything that is made, that there is power in the Word!

In understanding how God's Holy Spirit and Jesus work together to bring about God's plans and purposes, we will see how God wants us to be baptized in the Holy Spirit and work cooperatively with the Word, Jesus, in bringing about God's plans and purposes on the earth, too. The Sword of the Spirit is exactly that, the Word of God, Jesus, moving forth with the spoken mind of God in our lives to speak His plans and purposes forth and work in conjunction with God's Holy Spirit to manifest them, bring them into existence.

BAPTIZED WITH WATER AND THE HOLY SPIRIT

Therefore, in using the Sword of the Spirit, the Word, as Princess Warriors, we have to be in relationship with Christ just as God and Holy Spirit are in relationship with Jesus. When we are born again into relationship with Christ, we enter the Kingdom of God, a different dimension of living. We leave one kingdom, the kingdom of this world, and then become born from above, born into the Kingdom of God.

Jesus answered, I assure you, most solemnly I tell you, unless a man is born of water and [even] the Spirit, he cannot [ever] enter the kingdom of God (John 3:5 AMP).

The Kingdom of God is all of who God is; it is His essence, His glory. As discussed in *The Glory to Glory Sisterhood*, it is God's glory. That is why the devil is so angry at us—because of the threat we are to his kingdom, the kingdom of darkness. When we become born again of water and the Spirit, what we are doing is: 1. being baptized with water unto repentance, which is turning away from the sins of this world and changing our minds to be born of God, and 2. being baptized unto the Spirit, which is the essence of God.

There is much debate on baptism in water and in the Holy Spirit, and it is necessary to make a demarcation about the matter here because of the importance of baptism. Why do you think that so many people in the Church are divided on the matter of baptism? It is because of the importance of baptism and what it means that the enemy has created such division on the matter. Let's look at God's Word on the matter.

The messengers had been sent from the Pharisees. And they asked him, why then are you baptizing if you are not the Christ, nor Elijah, nor the Prophet? John answered them, I [only] baptize in (with) water. Among you there stands One Whom you do not recognize and with Whom you are not acquainted and of Whom you know nothing. It is He Who, coming after me, is preferred before me, the string of Whose sandal I am not worthy to unloose. These things occurred in Bethany (Bethabara) across the Jordan [at the Jordan crossing], where John was then baptizing. The next day John saw Jesus coming to him and said, Look! There is the Lamb of God, Who takes away the sin of the world! This is He of Whom I said, After me comes a Man Who has priority over me [Who takes rank above me] because He was before me and existed before I did. And I did not know Him and did not recognize Him [myself]; but it is in order that He should be made manifest and be revealed to Israel [be brought out where we can see Him] that I came baptizing in (with) water. John gave further evidence, saying, I have seen the Spirit descending as a dove out of heaven, and it dwelt on Him [never to depart]. And I did not know Him nor recognize Him, but He Who sent me to baptize in (with) water said to me, Upon Him Whom you shall see the Spirit descend and remain, that One is He Who baptizes with the Holy Spirit (John 1:24-33 AMP).

John the Baptist baptized with water, which was a baptism unto repentance, which is delineated in Matthew 3.

*And already the ax is lying at the root of the trees; every tree therefore that does not bear good fruit is cut down and thrown into the fire. **I indeed baptize you in (with) water because of repentance [that is, because of your changing your minds for the better, heartily amending your ways, with abhorrence of your past sins]**...* (Matthew 3:10-11 AMP).

That is why there is a demonstration of our coming out of the world and coming into the Kingdom of God through a baptism of water. It is an outward sign that we are repenting of our past sins and changing our minds to live as God says we should live in His Word. This baptism is powerful and can only be determined or chosen by the person who is getting baptized. There are many denominations that believe that sprinkling an infant in their baby dedication is a baptism, but that is not the baptism discussed in God's Word. Rather that sprinkling the infant with the water is a demonstration of the parent's dedication to train the child in God's way. *"Train up a child in the way he should go [and in keeping with his individual gift or bent], and when he is old he will not depart from it"* (Prov. 22:6 AMP).

Instead, the baptism with water unto repentance happens when people decide in their lives to repent of sin and accept Jesus as their Savior, identifying that He is the Son of God who came to this earth, died for our sins, and arose from the dead.

Because if you acknowledge and confess with your lips that Jesus is Lord and in your heart believe (adhere to, trust in, and rely on the truth) that God raised Him from the dead, you will be saved. For with the heart a person believes (adheres to, trusts in, and relies on Christ) and so is justified (declared righteous, acceptable to God), and with the mouth he confesses (declares openly and speaks out freely his faith) and confirms [his] salvation (Romans 10:9-10 AMP).

NOT BY POWER OR BY MIGHT, BUT BY THE SPIRIT

When the individual makes a decision and confirms her salvation, she then makes an outward demonstration of that decision through a water baptism, which is a baptism as John the Baptist states unto repentance. Afterward, there is still another baptism of which John the Baptist testified—the baptism of the Holy Spirit.

And I did not know Him nor recognize Him, but He Who sent me to baptize in (with) water said to me, Upon Him Whom you shall see the Spirit descend and remain, that One is He Who baptizes with the Holy Spirit (John 1:33 AMP).

In the Gospel of Matthew, it describes that Jesus will baptize us in the Holy Spirit and with fire. We will discuss the fire part in chapter 15, "God's Fire." Therefore, here there is still another baptism that remains, one of the Holy Spirit, which Jesus baptizes us into. Once we accept salvation and come into the knowledge of Jesus being the Son of God, we then are positioned to receive the baptism of the Holy Spirit. The baptism, where we are immersed in water, turning away from our old lives of sinning and coming into the Kingdom of God is demonstrative of the same baptism of the Holy Spirit.

As discussed in *Glory to Glory Sisterhood,* receiving the Holy Spirit baptism is a free gift from God and shows that we choose to walk out our Christian walk in the power of God's Holy Spirit and not our own might or strength. This is demonstrated so clearly in the book of Zechariah.

As Zerubbabel, the governor of the Persian province of Judah, was leading around 42,360 of his countrymen out of Babylonian captivity during 538 B.C., he was instructed by the Lord to rebuild the temple that had been destroyed. Zerubbabel's grandfather, Jeconiah, was King of Judah, before the Babylonian capture; therefore, Zerubbabel was from the royal lineage of the tribe of Judah, from which the Messiah was prophesied to come. The prophet Zechariah was instructed by God to go encourage Zerubbabel in his efforts of rebuilding the second temple.

> *And the angel who talked with me came again and awakened me, like a man who is wakened out of his sleep. And said to me, What do you see? I said, I see, and behold, a lampstand all of gold, with its bowl [for oil] on the top of it and its seven lamps on it, and [there are] seven pipes to each of the seven lamps which are upon the top of it. And there are two olive trees by it, one upon the right side of the bowl and the other upon the left side of it [feeding it continuously with oil]. So I asked the angel who talked with me, What are these, my lord? Then the angel who talked with me answered me, Do you not know what these are? And I said, No, my lord* (Zechariah 4:1-5 AMP).

Zechariah was instructed by the angel to see the Holy Spirit of God before there was such a baptism available on the earth. The lampstand—all of God with bowls for oil and the seven pipes—

demonstrated the dimensions of God's Holy Spirit. During the ancient days, oil was used in a lampstand to keep the lamps lit.

The lampstand represents the sevenfold Spirit of God, as prophesied in Isaiah 11:2.

The Spirit of the LORD will rest on Him—the Spirit of wisdom and of understanding, the Spirit of counsel and of power, the Spirit of knowledge and of the fear of the LORD (Isaiah 11:2 NIV).

God's Holy Spirit is in front of His throne and ever ready to do the work of God.

Out from the throne came flashes of lightning and rumblings and peals of thunder, and in front of the throne seven blazing torches burned, which are the seven Spirits of God [the sevenfold Holy Spirit] (Revelation 4:5 AMP).

The sevenfold dimension of Holy Spirit is demonstrated by the lampstand here in Zechariah.

The Scripture in Zechariah is a demonstration of how The Word, Jesus, comes forth with power, bringing the mind of God forth to the earth. Remember, God, Jesus, and Holy Spirit work cooperatively and intricately with each other to bring about God's plans and purposes on the earth. Therefore, as God's vision was manifested to Zechariah, Zechariah was seeing the mind of God, what was in God's thoughts and mind.

The lampstand is a picture of what was in God's mind when Zechariah was awakened to the vision of God by the angel.

Next Zechariah saw God's Holy Spirit by the representation of the lampstand. And in conjunction with the vision of the Holy Spirit, Zechariah saw a representation of the relationship between the Holy Spirit and Jesus.

> *Then he said to me, This [addition of the bowl to the candlestick, causing it to yield a ceaseless supply of oil from the olive trees] is the word of the Lord to Zerubbabel, saying, Not by might, nor by power, but by My Spirit [of Whom the oil is a symbol], says the Lord of hosts* (Zecheriah 4:6 AMP).

The vision given to Zechariah about the power of God's Holy Spirit was translated from the mind of God, the vision, and became "the Word of the Lord!" It became Jesus manifested from God's mind, becoming the spoken word. And the Holy Spirit waited upon the spoken word to manifest, bring into existence, God's plans and purposes on the earth! It is Genesis 1:1-2! God was bringing forth what was already in His mind through Jesus, the Word, with God's Holy Spirit waiting upon the Word to do God's will! That is the power of Jesus, the spoken Word, from whom everything that was made is made (see Col. 1:15-17).

Zechariah had to encourage and exhort Zerubbabel, governor of Judah, who was bringing forth a most impossible task in his time; he had been in Babylonian captivity for many years. Now Zerubbabel was being commissioned by God to do something beyond his own strength for God's people—rebuilding the temple. This in itself was a representation of Jesus. The first temple, which King Solomon built in 960 B.C., was destroyed prior to the nation of Judah going into Babylonian captivity in 587 B.C. It demonstrated the crucifixion of Christ. However, we know that Christ arose from the grave! Therefore, a demonstration of that

(God's prophesy in the earth) had to be completed by having a rebuilding of the temple, which prophesied Jesus being buried and resurrected.

> *Then the Jews retorted, What sign can You show us, see-ing You do these things? [What sign, miracle, token, indi-cation can You give us as evidence that You have authority and are commissioned to act in this way?] Jesus answered them, Destroy (undo) this temple, and in three days I will raise it up again. Then the Jews replied, It took forty-six years to build this temple (sanctuary), and will You raise it up in three days? But* **He had spoken of the temple which was His body. When therefore He had risen from the dead, His disciples remembered that He said this. And so they believed and trusted and relied on the Scripture and the word (message) Jesus had spoken** (John 2:18-22 AMP).

God was encouraging Zerubbabel that it was not going to be by Zerubbabel, but rather by God's Holy Spirit that the temple would be completed! The encouragement came from the spoken Word, Jesus, bringing forth *life* to Zerubbabel in order to carry forth the plans and purposes of God in the earth. Jesus came to bring life and life abundantly (see John 10:10). We see that the devil comes to steal us from operating in God's plans and pur-poses. *"The thief does not come except to steal, and to kill, and to destroy. I have come that they may have life, and that they may have it more abundantly"* (John 10:10). If we look deeper, this verse is saying that Jesus is bringing life to the plans and purposes of God that the enemy tries to steal, kill, and destroy. We are the temple of the Holy Spirit now (see 1 Cor. 6:19).

Therefore, when Jesus came, as John the Baptist said, He came to baptize us with the Holy Spirit, which is the mighty working power of God in our lives! We receive the Holy Spirit through being saved in Jesus and being filled with the Holy Spirit in power to walk out God's plans on this earth. The baptism of the Holy Spirit is covered in detail in *The Glory to Glory Sisterhood,* where I write about how it brings us power in walking out godly lives before God. I know for me personally, the Holy Spirit came upon me one day as I went into worship, and all I knew was that my life was changed, and where I once was in bondage to alcohol, by the baptism of God's Holy Spirit, I now had power to overcome it!

Other people have had a similar experience, in which they were baptized in the Holy Spirit through seeking God with all their hearts! As His Word says in Jeremiah 29:13:

> *For I know the thoughts and plans that I have for you, says the Lord, thoughts and plans for welfare and peace and not for evil, to give you hope in your final outcome. Then you will call upon Me, and you will come and pray to Me, and I will hear and heed you. Then you will seek Me, inquire for, and require Me [as a vital necessity] and find Me when you search for Me with all your heart* (Jeremiah 29:11-13 AMP).

NEVER THE SAME

As I was seeking God with all my heart one day in worship at my church, Kingwood Church, during the offertory time, I encountered God and was never the same! It was Resurrection Sunday at Kingwood Church 2002, and I was sitting in the very back of the church. We had already done worship that morning; however, I could still feel my heart beating a million miles an hour, such that I felt as though I was going to burst if I could not worship God more and more! The pastor was coming by greeting everyone at their seats, as he so wonderfully did in each service to share with people the love of God.

As the offering was being made from the platform and Pastor Cox was walking by, I felt as though I was going to explode across the entire sanctuary into a million pieces. I did not want to get up before he passed by because I was worried that he might think I was trying to show off and let him see how spiritual I was. If only I had known what was about to happen to me, I would have never been concerned. To preface what is coming next, I want you to know that I had told God several times I would be a fool for Him no matter what.

It was during this time that I was still in bondage to alcohol, and I would binge drink on occasion, drinking half a case of beer in a day with no problem. I constantly asked God to deliver me from the bondage and would constantly prophesy over myself that I was not an alcoholic. Rather, throughout the weeks prior to this experience, I would declare God's Word over my life, that I had the mind of Christ, was the righteousness of Christ Jesus, and was seated in heavenly places with Christ (see Eph. 2:6). Moreover, I constantly declared Jeremiah 29:11-13 over myself time and time again daily. I was *not a drunk!* I refused to believe it or give in to the devil's plan to steal, kill, and destroy me, which was contrary to God's Word. I continued to speak the Word over my life, the Scripture. The entire time, God's Holy Spirit was hovering over me waiting to manifest the plans and purposes of God. The Word, Jesus, was coming out of my mouth the entire time, confessing the Scripture even when I was still in bondage.

After the pastor walked past me, I then had to stand up or I knew I was going to explode. Only when I stood up, I immediately began to shake violently under the power of God's Holy Spirit, not knowing or understanding what was going on with my body. I knew that since I was the only one standing up that everyone in the choir could see me shaking like crazy, and I had never seen anything like this or witnessed this in my life. I was in total ecstasy in the love of God, feeling such a power beyond my human ability to contain it, and although I knew I looked like a fool to everyone, I didn't care because I felt *God!* I felt His Holy Spirit inside of me, going into the very crevices of my heart! I received *power* to walk out the will of God in my life, which at that immediate time was to get free from alcohol.

My drinking decreased, and daily I confessed the Scriptures, the Word, in my life over and over from that point forward with even a greater measure, and within seven months, the power of God's spoken Word, Jesus, manifested in my life. I kept speaking that I was not a drunk, but rather had the mind of Christ, was the righteousness of Christ Jesus, and was seated with Jesus in heavenly places. In one day, everything changed because the mighty working of God's Holy Spirit *manifested the Word* in my life! It came into existence! I was free from the bondage of alcohol forever at the end of 2002! I had *power* by God's Holy Spirit to walk out God's will in my life!

Without the spoken Word, Jesus, the Holy Spirit does not operate because they are uniquely different, but they are one and connected. As the mind of God comes forth, it does so by the power of the spoken Word, Jesus, being released into the atmosphere. Then, as the Holy Spirit is the receptor of that Word, the manifestation, coming into existence, of God's plans and purposes is seen.

Anointed to Prophesy

Therefore, as we are baptized with the Holy Spirit, we are anointed to use the Sword of the Spirit, the Word of God to bring forth God's plans and purposes in this earth. God is waiting for us to speak His mind in the earth with the spoken Word so that His Holy Spirit will come forth and manifest what we have spoken. That is power!

As in Ephesians, we are to use the Sword of the Spirit as a weapon of warfare in the earth. It is the spoken Word, Jesus, being released into earth. What does this look like? It is prophecy!

> *...Worship God! For the substance (essence) of the truth revealed by Jesus is the spirit of all prophecy [the vital breath, the inspiration of all inspired preaching and interpretation of the divine will and purpose, including both mine and yours]* (Revelation 19:10 AMP).

Here, God's Word states that the *"substance, essence of truth"* that is revealed by Jesus (the spoken Word) is the Spirit (Holy Spirit) of all prophecy! Prophecy, as seen here, is the vital breath, inspired preaching, and interpretation of the divine will and purpose of God. The Sword of the Spirit is using prophecy to call those things that are not as though they are (see Rom.4:17). It is releasing the mind of God (intents and thoughts), as seen in Jeremiah 29:11-12 into the earth realm by the spoken Word and watching the Holy Spirit manifest the truth of that Word.

You do not have to be a prophet to prophesy; prophecy is a gift of the Holy Spirit.

> *Now about spiritual gifts, brothers, I do not want you to be ignorant....Now to each one the manifestation of the Spirit is given for the common good. To one there is given through the Spirit the message of wisdom, to another the message of knowledge by means of the same Spirit, to another faith by the same Spirit, to another gifts of healing by that one Spirit, to another miraculous powers, to another prophecy, to another distinguishing between spirits, to another speaking in different kinds of tongues, and to still another the interpretation of tongues. All these are the work of one and the same Spirit, and He gives them to each one, just as He determines* (1 Corinthians 12:1; 7-11 NIV).

Here God's Word tells us that by the function of His Holy Spirit, which we have been baptized into by Jesus, we will *prophesy*. Prophecy is the work of God in us, His Holy Spirit giving us the mind of God so that we will speak it forth on earth and watch Holy Spirit manifest God's plan. Moreover, God tells us in His Word that we are to desire the gift of prophecy because prophecy is the divine will and purpose of God's will—His mind for what He wants in our lives.

> *Eagerly pursue and seek to acquire [this] love [make it your aim, your great quest]; and earnestly desire and cultivate the spiritual endowments (gifts), especially that you may prophesy (interpret the divine will and purpose in inspired preaching and teaching* (1 Corinthians 14:1 AMP).

It is prophecy that calls things that are not as though they are! Jesus is the Spirit of prophecy, the spoken Word! Therefore, we are to call things that are not as though they are. What does this look like? God is a diverse God, and we do not need to put Him in a box, because He can use whatever He wants to speak His plans and purposes into the earth. Therefore, it is important to seek God and ask Holy Spirit what God wants us to do in speaking the Word of God forth into the earth.

From my personal experienced I make it a habit by the leading of God's Holy Spirit to maintain an intimate time with God each morning, reading the Bible, worshiping, and meditating on the Lord. I usually wake up between 4 and 5 A.M. to seek God and His plans and purposes for my life and those whom He lays on my heart. Moreover, all the teachings I get are during these times when I spend intimate time with God, and by His Holy Spirit in me, He starts downloading revelations into my mind about His Word.

As God starts giving me these revelations, I am able to comprehend and understand His will (mind) for my life and others and speak them out into the earth in the form of prayer or declarations. The prayer and declarations are the Sword of the Spirit, Word of God (Jesus) being released into the air, and God watches over His Word to perform it. *"Then said the Lord to me, You have seen well, for I am alert and active, watching over My word to perform it"* (Jer. 1:12 AMP). That is the same Holy Spirit who was hovering over the earth in Genesis 1:1-2 to wait for God to speak the Word to perform it.

Likewise, when we speak the Word of God through prayer or declarations, His Holy Spirit is watching over that Word to perform it in the earth. As I stated earlier, I had been in bondage to drinking when God's Holy Spirit came upon me. Prior to that time, however, I had been seeking God with all of my heart. I knew that I had no power in and of myself to get free from that bondage. It was only by God's Holy Spirit in my life that I received the power of His Word manifested in my life to be free from alcohol. This is a demonstration of Second Corinthians 3:17-18, which is the Scripture for the Glory to Glory Sisterhood.

> *Now the Lord is the Spirit, and where the Spirit of the Lord is, there is liberty (emancipation from bondage, freedom). And all of us, as with unveiled face, [because we] continued to behold [in the Word of God] as in a mirror the glory of the Lord, are constantly being transfigured into His very own image in ever increasing splendor and from one degree of glory to another; [for this comes] from the Lord [Who is] the Spirit* (2 Corinthians 3:17-18 AMP).

It is the testimony of Jesus in our lives, the spirit of prophecy (see Rev. 19:10) that is the Word of God that the Holy Spirit watches over to perform in our lives. Therefore, the Sword of the Spirit is Jesus (prophecy) through God's Word (Bible), being wielded in the earth to cut through the atmosphere and bring forth God's Word into the earth.

As Princess Warriors, we carry the Sword of the Spirit and use it when Holy Spirit calls upon us to bring forth God's Word, Jesus, into the earth. I do this all the time in my Christian walk with God. First, I do it in my alone time with God when I am up early in the morning in the Word. Somewhere, during my time with God, I can feel a shift in the atmosphere, and I know that Holy Spirit is there hovering and waiting for me to speak the Word of God (His divine will—Jesus) into the earth so that Holy Spirit can manifest it. It may take hours, days, months, or years for it to come forth in the natural, but I know with confidence when I've spoken it in that time it is already done in the supernatural. It is by faith that I know this.

Now faith is the assurance (the confirmation, the title deed) of the things [we] hope for, being the proof of things [we] do not see and the conviction of their reality [faith perceiving as real fact what is not revealed to the senses] (Hebrews 11:1 AMP).

Faith is the title deed, the guarantee that what I have spoken in using the Sword of the Spirit will come forth.

Before I wrote *The Glory to Glory Sisterhood series,* God had given me His mind on the entire book series. I believed by faith that what I was comprehending was the mind of God to bring forth the books, and I started speaking that God wanted me to write a book. God's Word says that there are actions to faith.

But someone will say [to you then], You [say you] have faith, and I have [good] works. Now you show me your [alleged] faith apart from any [good] works [if you can], and

I by [good] works [of obedience] will show you my faith (James 2:18 AMP).

There is obedience with faith, and I demonstrated that faith when I sat down and began simply by writing a table of contents for the book. I had taken six months off from law school between my second and third year to by faith write the book in six months. As I stepped out in faith to take the time off and focus only on writing the book, eventually after that six months I had what I thought was one book.

However, after submitting the book to a publisher, they contacted me to let me know that the manuscript was too big to be one book, but rather was four books! I was overwhelmed because what I thought was one book and by faith was obedient to write was not one, but four books! This book you are reading is actually the second book of that one writing I did for six months! That is faith! That is the Sword of the Spirit being used on earth to bring forth the mind of God, which was to bring forth *The Glory to Glory Sisterhood series* on earth. Similarly, this can be seen as well when I received all three of my degrees, a bachelors and masters in social work and a juris doctorate (law degree). I spoke each one of those degrees into being before I received my diplomas.

In addition, with everything that has come forth into my life by the glory of God, I have been attentive to His mind (plans and purposes, divine will) by hearing God's voice with His Holy Spirit inside of me and prophesying (using the spoken Word, Jesus) what I heard God telling me, into being in the natural. As I said, I am writing a book for God, declaring Jeremiah 29:11-13, Romans 8:28-30, Ephesians 3:20, and many more verses in the natural. What happened in the spiritual realm is that I was speaking Jesus, whom everything is made through, into the earth in my life, and before I knew it, I was an author and had several degrees. That is *power!*

Princess Warrior, what does God want you to prophesy and speak into the earth by His spoken Word (Jesus)? Speak it and watch God's Holy Spirit watch over that Word to perform it! Do you want your son to get off drugs? Prophesy like Ezekiel to the dry bones and prophesy that your son is off of drugs and serving God (see Ezek.37). Do you want to see your financial situation change? Prophesy God's Word that you are the lender and not the borrower, that you are the head and not the tail, that everything you put your hand to prospers in Jesus' name (see Deut. 28:1-13).

Let me add here, as discussed earlier about the name of Jesus, that I always use the Sword of the Spirit with the name of Jesus. For example, when I minister to others and make declarations over others, I will use the Sword of the Spirit in this manner: "In Jesus' name, I declare that you have the mind of Christ, that you are the righteousness of Christ Jesus, and that you are seated with Christ in heavenly places." Moreover, when I do deliverance on others while ministering, I call God's Word into their lives as follows: "I come against you spirit of fear, and I command you to loose my sister and go to the Abyss in Jesus' name. I call Your Word God into my sister that says You have not given her a spirit of fear, but You have given my sister power, love, and a sound mind in Jesus' name."

I listen to God's Holy Spirit to bring to my mind what God's plans are for that sister's life, and I speak His mind by using the Word and my authority in Jesus Christ. When I have ministered in this capacity, I see strongholds broken instantly and women delivered and set free. Many times I have women contact me and say the words I used changed their lives. I tell them that when you meet the Word, Jesus, He changes your life every time. If people are not changed after I've spoken the Word of God to them, I realize that I might have been in my flesh. However, sometimes we plant a seed when we bring the Word of God to them, and it takes a while for the seed to come forth and bear fruit. I have seen this in people whom God has had me praying for for years regarding their salvation. However, I know the anointed Word of God is going to bear fruit someday.

Princess Warriors, you keep prophesying the Word of God into your lives and the lives of those around you, and watch the Holy Spirit bring forth God's plans and purposes! Jeremiah 29:11-13! Glory!!

TESTIMONY ON THE POWER OF PROPHECY

As I edit the Princess Warriors book years later for the publication I have a testimony to add that recently occurred days ago, September 9, 2011 while on a missions trip here in the Philippines. I was invited to come do crusades in the early part of 2011 here in the Philippines in the month of September. I came over with my friend Amy Kay, who is a vessel of Honor God has me mentoring and sending her forth in the call of God on her life with the equipping of Holy Spirit power in her Call! As we left Manila Philippines and came to the Island of Samar in the Philippines we landed in Tacloban Philippines at 7:30pm. For those who are not familiar with the Philippines there is a strong muslim contingency in the nation that is trying to make a substate for themselves here in the Philippines. Moreover, there have been kidnappings of Americans and a few years ago a kidnapping of a missionary couple where the woman was drug through the jungle for a year being tormented and her husband was murdered in the midst of this tragedy. With that knowledge we knew that we would have to have intercessors covering us in prayers and make sure that we heard God on every step we were to take in proceeding forth to bring the Gospel in the Philippines.

When we arrived in Tacloban Philippines at 7:30pm we got a taxi to drive us to Cartarman Philippines which was a six hour drive. All along the way it was to my discovery that the six hour drive consisted of passing homes non-stop with people lining the street. I had never seen anything like it and discovered that this part of the Philippines was a third world country. It broke my heart to see the destitution of so many lives in one area of the nation. In the midst of the journey to Cartarman the taxi driver stopped the van an hour before Calybog. When he stopped he stated that there was something wrong with the car and that he would have to fix it. Well, one hour went by and before we knew it another hour. We were exhausted and had not slept in over 28 hours and would doze on and off in the middle of the street in this small town on the Island of Samar. As we continued to be stuck in the middle of the street while the driver was working on the car, four hours had already passed by and in the midst of the four hours there were many people all over the street. This is between 9pm and 1am by this time. Then around 2am in the morning all of sudden some of the people began looking in the van; we had the windows cracked open in order to get some air. The taxi driver continued to stay under the car trying to fix the problem. His wife was assisting him as he needed her to and continued to go back and forth to the driver seat to assist holding the light for him while he fixed the engine (the engine is under the passenger seat and the seat was raised up to allow the taxi driver's wife to shine a light for him to see.) By this time I was looking through the cracks of one of the windows and saw two young men walking by us and locked eyes with the two men. They were muslim and recognized that we were Caucasian females from the states in the van. All of a sudden in the spirit realm I felt knives going all in my back and I saw the demon spirit jumping on top of the van and knew that something was about to happen. The taxi driver's wife also saw that something was amiss and began to hear their conversations and jumped out of the driver's seat, locking the door and came around to our side of the van, where the van door was open and said "close the door! Close the door!" She knew that the mob was coming toward us. Next, I felt that dark spirit all over in the van and continually attacking me in the spirit realm. I was in the back seat while Amy Kay and Meshelle Cox were in the seat in front of me. I looked behind me through the window and before I knew it an entire mob was coming and surrounding the van. I was fighting in the spirit realm the devil that was on me and I tell you that I have never seen such a dark spirit in my life in anyone's eyes as I did those two men. As I was fighting that spirit pleading the blood of Jesus I then began to inquire of the Lord at the same time ("Press") to receive His strategies for the situation because I could see in a vision them overtaking the van and pulling us out to kill us. Holy Spirit said action had to be taken quickly. Holy Spirit said post on Facebook that you need prayer warriors covering you all right now! So I posted it and many people said that at that time they had been instructed to pray for us and felt that something was wrong. Then I pressed in and continued to ask Holy Spirit what to do and He said BEGIN TO PROPHESY!! I opened my mouth and Holy Spirit said "For surely you My daughters will live and not die and you will speak of the witness of My power, My faithfulness and My goodness in your life. I will bring you forth for you have overcome this demonic spirit that has risen up against you and has tried to overcome you but I tell you truly you have already overcome because greater is He that is in you than He that is in the world! I will show you My glory, My light and My life and bring all of Who I Am forth to you in this hour and you will see My glory!" We felt a shift in the atmosphere! It was like an atomic bomb of God's light had entered the area! We looked up and then all of a sudden the streets were empty! The darkness did not overcome the light (see John 1:5). Holy Spirit told me to take out my Altoids and use them as the bread of communion, the body of Christ Jesus so we took the mints in remembrance of what Jesus did for us in laying down His life. Then Holy Spirit said start humming the song "I Love You Lord" and such a sweet presence of God entered the van! It was His glory! Then within a short time, around 3am the taxi driver got in the van and it started up!! We were so overcome with God's goodness and His faithfulness. Holy Spirit wanted me to share this so that you can see the power of Prophecy, the Testimony of Jesus! It pushes out the darkness in the midst of what looks like a life and death situation! Therefore prophesy!

14

The Fire of God

The fire of God is a necessary part in walking out God's justification and sanctification in our lives. Here Princess Warriors will discover how the fire of God in their lives brings them closer to being in the image of Christ Jesus.

Many times when I go places to preach or am in the earth bringing God's Word in grocery stores, shopping centers, gas stations, restaurants, and the like, I hear people say that we have "God's fire" inside of us. That is what I live for in life! Burning for God and bringing the truth of the Gospel, Good News, into the earth! Many times I tell others I did not leave a lifestyle of bondage to be bored. If being a torch for God was not fun, believe you me, I would not be doing things for God! People want to think that God is sitting in Heaven with intentions to make us feel like we are slaves or are being tortured. However, that is not God!

My God is a supernatural God full of power and grace, ready to bring forth the most glorious things in our lives if we only let Him. I have been drunk from alcohol numerous times and done things I was not proud of only to seek for a "feeling or emotion" that would be ecstasy to my being. However, after being filled with God's Holy Spirit, I know there is no substance on this earth that can touch what I feel continually by being captivated in joy forevermore. However, I do have many times in life when things are not pleasant in my Christian walk, but that does not hinder me. I am not after the "feeling," but instead I am after God, and the feeling is a byproduct of my relationship with Him.

I know many believers who go from conference to conference to get a feeling from God's Holy Spirit. When people are only seeking the feeling of God's Holy Spirit and not Him, they are using God as a substance as well and are becoming addicted to the feeling. They are not seeking God; instead they are seeking the high that comes from being in God's presence. I love being in God's presence more than anything on this earth. However, we are to seek God and not the emotion. When we are emotionally driven, then we remain immature and can be manipulated by the attacks of the enemy, which are the crucifying of our flesh, with a risk of turning away from God. That is why we are baptized in fire! The fire helps to purify us whereby we become transformed into the image of Christ Jesus as we go from glory to glory.

Baptized in *Fire*

*...But He Who is coming after me is mightier than I, whose sandals I am not worthy or fit to take off or carry; **He will baptize you with the Holy Spirit and with fire.** His winnowing fan (shovel, fork) is in His hand, and He will thoroughly clear out and clean His threshing floor and gather and*

store His wheat in His barn, but the chaff He will burn up with fire that cannot be put out (Matthew 3:11-12 AMP).

As John the Baptist states, Jesus will baptize us with the Holy Spirit and with fire! When we are baptized with the Holy Spirit, it also includes a baptism of fire. This fire is an immersion into the fire of God, so to speak, that purges us from iniquitous roots and strongholds in our lives. When I asked for the baptism of God's fire, what I was in essence asking for, was for God to release a breath of His presence that would explode all yokes in my life. This is not a pleasant process, but is a crucifixion of the flesh.

Similarly to Jesus walking through a crucifixion process, we have to walk through that process, as well.

Therefore, brethren, we are debtors—not to the flesh, to live according to the flesh. For if you live according to the flesh you will die; but if by the Spirit you put to death the deeds of the body, you will live. For as many as are led by the Spirit of God, these are sons of God (Romans 8:12-14).

In this process of crucifying the flesh, which gets to many iniquitous roots inside of us, there is a fire process, a furnace of affliction that God takes us through. The whole purpose of going through the furnace is that all of the iniquitous roots that are in our souls will come up to the surface. Seeing those roots, we allow God to remove them from us. Therefore, through this process God's glory increases in our lives.

A Scripture that best demonstrates this process is Isaiah 4:2-6; God also showed me Song of Solomon 8:6-7. First let's look at Isaiah, and then we will come back to Song of Solomon.

In that day the Branch of the Lord shall be beautiful and glorious, and the fruit of the land shall be excellent and lovely to those of Israel who have escaped. And he who is left in Zion and remains in Jerusalem will be called holy, everyone who is recorded for life in Jerusalem and for eternal life, **After the Lord has washed away the [moral] filth of the daughters of Zion [pride, vanity, haughtiness] and has purged the bloodstains of Jerusalem from the midst of it by the spirit and blast of judgment and by the spirit and blast of burning and sifting.** *And the Lord will create over the whole site, over every dwelling place of Mount Zion and over her assemblies, a cloud and smoke by day and the shining of a flaming fire by night; for over all the glory shall be a canopy (a defense of divine love and protection). And there shall be a pavilion for shade in the daytime from the heat, and for a place of refuge and a shelter from storm and from rain* (Isaiah 4:2-6 AMP).

Here in Isaiah, when the prophet prophesies after the Lord has washed away the filth and has purged the bloodstains of Jerusalem by the Spirit and blast of judgment, he is speaking on a literal level. However, Scripture has many layers and dimensions to it. There is a literal translation of the Scripture, which means that God will literally do a work in His people, His nation Israel. Moreover, this Scripture has a prophetic implication, whereby God is prophesying about Jesus coming as one who will purge the bloodstains of Jerusalem with His own blood and meet the judgment of the law by coming to fulfill the law, thus fulfilling the judgment.

Do not think that I came to destroy the Law or the Prophets. I did not come to destroy but to fulfill. For assuredly, I say to you, till heaven and earth pass away, one jot or one tittle will by no means pass from the law till all is fulfilled (Matthew 5:17-18).

However, we can go deeper and get a personal application of this Scripture, too. This Scripture personally speaks of God bringing forth His work in our lives through the blood of Jesus fulfilling the judgment on all of our sins and paying our debt that we could not pay, which is the spirit of judgment met by the blood of Jesus. The washing away of our filth is symbolic of our sins being washed away.

> *For you will be His witness to all men of what you have seen and heard. And now why are you waiting? Arise and be baptized, and wash away your sins, calling on the name of the Lord* (Acts 22:15-16).

Likewise, our baptism of water testifies of turning away from sin and being cleansed by the blood of Jesus, the blood that paid the price for our sin.

When we go further into the Scripture, we see the words *"blast of burning and sifting."* In the New King James Version, it says, *"the spirit of burning"* instead of *"blast of burning."* The Holy Spirit showed me this spirit of burning or blast of burning was a prophetic implication and demonstration of the baptism of fire that Jesus came to baptize us in. This spirit of burning is seen in God's Word when God brought Israel out of the "iron furnace."

> *But the Lord has taken you and brought you forth out of the* **iron furnace***, out of Egypt, to be to Him a people of His own possession, as you are this day* (Deuteronomy 4:20 AMP).

*For they are Your people and Your heritage, which You brought out of Egypt, from the midst of the **iron furnace*** (1 Kings 8:51 AMP).

The "iron furnace" here is the spirit of burning or blast of burning that God's Word speaks about. The purpose of this furnace is to bring about a purification, which is demonstrated further in Isaiah. *"Behold, I have refined you, but not as silver; I have tried and chosen you in the **furnace of affliction"*** (Isa. 48:10 AMP). Therefore, there is a transformation process that comes forth, bringing the image of Christ Jesus in us through this spirit of blasting or spirit of burning. The refinement is one that brings out the impurities of a substance in order to get a purer form of the substance.

In regard to iron, the purification process for that is one of blasting, which is demonstrative of Isaiah 4:3, the "spirit of blasting." In the teaching "Spine of Steel" that God gave me in 2009, He showed me how iron was made into steel. Before iron was turned into steel, it was easier to break and could not be used to make big buildings. The more pure the steel, the stronger it is, and it can be used for airplanes, sky rises, military weapons, and the like. It is the purest form of steel, which comes from iron, which is used to make the strongest things in the world. Likewise, as we allow God to bring us through the iron furnace, we are allowing Him to take us through the spirit of blasting to purify us.

In turning iron into steel, there is a process known as Basic Oxygen Steelmaking.[1] What the Lord showed me was that the process for making steel was demonstrative of how we go through the purification process. Pig iron is placed in a blast furnace to go through the process of oxidation. In this process, the present iron is put in a ladle for pretreatment stage, where many impurities are removed through a process of sending chemical agents inside of the iron so that impurities come to the surface and are raked off. Finally, there is the process of blasting the iron with oxygen, in which 99 percent oxygen is blown faster than Mach 1 on the iron through a water cooled lance. It ignites all the carbon, whereby it becomes a gas and is burned off the iron, which has become steel. In this process, pig iron, which was once so fragile due to the high carbon content, has had the impurities burned off in order to strengthen the iron, changing its chemical compound through a blasting process that makes it steel.

REVELATION

When looking at this process prophetically, as Romans 1:20 discusses, we see the invisible qualities or attributes of God through the visible realm. Therefore, this process of refining pig iron and bringing it through the furnace demonstrates how God brings us from iniquitous roots and bondages into freedom— being strong in the Lord and the power of His might! When Jesus delivered the man who was demon possessed, he cast the demons out of him and sent them into a herd of pigs (see Luke 8:28-33). Therefore, pigs can represent things that are unclean in us, iniquitous roots that came either through our ancestor's sins or our sins.

The pig iron is placed in a ladle where chemicals are added and impurities are brought to the surface. When I look at this, I saw the baptism unto repentance! When we first come to Christ, Holy Spirit has to convict our hearts and show us that we are sinners in need of a Savior. Then after the chemicals are added initially, the first level of impurities are scooped off. When we first come to Jesus, we confess our sins and ask for forgiveness and then receive salvation. I picture our remnants of the world being scooped off of us by Holy Spirit, and we become born of the Kingdom of God!

Then as we continue our Christian walk, we go through fiery trials, which are the furnace of iron, the spirit of blasting! It is in this process that a lance—Sword of the Spirit (see Heb. 4:12)—is placed in the container, blasting 99 percent oxygen at Mach 1 speed. To me, Mach 1 represents the deity, the Godhead, and 99 percent represents the nine gifts and nine fruits of God's Holy Spirit. When we give ourselves completely over to God, through Jesus, Holy Spirit allows us to come forth in fiery trials, bringing the Sword of the Spirit into our hearts to divide between our motives and intents. Through this process, God transforms our minds by increasing measure into the mind of Christ, and the nine fruits of the Holy Spirit and the Gifts of the Holy Spirit operate within our very being. That's the revelation I receive from this visible demonstration of making steel.

When we come to God, we are full of impurities, which are iniquitous roots and strongholds, and we are full of living in the flesh. As we go through the fire of God, the baptism of fire, the impurities are removed from us, and as a result we become stronger in the process. The 99 percent oxygen that is blown on the iron to blast it is likened unto God's Holy Spirit bringing forth the breath of God to breathe on us. Therefore, the spirit of blasting/spirit of burning gets rid of those impurities and moreover brings the Word of God that is in us, the iron to a point that it has now become like that of steel. It is the Word that is like fire *shut up in our bones!*

> *And the Lord will create over the whole site, over every dwelling place of Mount Zion and over her assemblies, a cloud and smoke by day and the shining of a flaming fire by night; for over all the glory shall be a canopy (a defense of divine love*

and protection). And there shall be a pavilion for shade in the daytime from the heat, and for a place of refuge and a shelter from storm and from rain (Isaiah 4:5-6 AMP).

The whole reason for the spirit of blasting/spirit of burning is to bring about God's glory in our lives. After the spirit of blasting/burning, Isaiah then states that God will create a cloud of smoke by day and the shining of flaming fire by night to be a canopy of protection for the glory. The spirit of blasting is a preparation to bring us into a greater glory in God. It is similar to Second Corinthians 3:18, where we go from glory to glory.

Moreover, as the Holy Spirit showed me in the teaching on "Spine of Steel," what once became the very trial or tribulation that brought about the spirit of blasting then becomes the device whereby God's Word in us has made us like steel. God tells Jeremiah the prophet that He will forge Jeremiah like steel.

> *"Stand at attention while I prepare you for your work. I'm making you as impregnable as a castle, Immovable as a **steel post**, solid as a concrete **block wall.** You're a one-man defense system against this culture, Against Judah's kings and princes, against the priests and local leaders. They'll fight you, but they won't even scratch you. I'll back you up every inch of the way." God's Decree* (Jeremiah 1:18 MSG).

God's Word in Jeremiah was that he was making Jeremiah "immovable as a steel post." The steel here is representative of Jeremiah coming forth with God's Word so strong that it would make him like steel.

> *If I say, I will not make mention of [the Lord] or speak any more in His name, in my mind and heart it is as if there were a burning fire shut up in my bones. And I am*

weary of enduring and holding it in; I cannot [contain it any longer] (Jeremiah 20:9 AMP).

Fiery Seal upon My Heart

There is a particular Scripture that is a life verse for me, Song of Solomon 8:6-7.

Set me like a seal upon your heart, like a seal upon your arm; for love is as strong as death, Jealousy is as hard and cruel as Sheol (the place of the dead). Its flashes are flashes of fire, a most vehement flame [the very flame of the Lord]! Many waters cannot quench love, neither can floods drown it. If a man would offer all the goods of his house for love, he would be utterly scorned and despised (Song of Solomon 8:6-7 AMP).

God has had me pray this prayer over and over for years and showed me that this particular Scripture was a fiery seal to that of Isaiah 4:3, the spirit of burning, likened to the baptism of fire. The seal upon our hearts here is the very flame, a most vehement flame of love for the Lord. It is such a passionate love for King Jesus that we are willing to go through anything, any sifting and the spirit of blasting/burning, for Him.

When I became so passionate for the Lord in 2003 I told God that I wanted Him to bring down all my idols, give me prudence, and make me humble. Immediately after that prayer, my husband and I lost everything, our home, and my car, and we became utterly dependent on God for everything after that point. It is a place we remain to this day because through the process of the spirit of blasting/spirit of burning that we encountered during that time, our love for God deepened and became stronger.

Moreover, my love for the Word, Jesus, was purified to such a degree that the sifting made the Word inside of me as fire shut up in my bones! A God confidence came forth in me that only the trials and tribulations produced in my life. They produced a deeper faith in me, a miracle-working, God-confident faith that no devil and no person can take away from me.

Consider it wholly joyful, my brethren, whenever you are enveloped in or encounter trials of any sort or fall into various temptations. Be assured and understand that the trial and proving of your faith bring out endurance and steadfastness and patience. But let endurance and steadfastness and patience have full play and do a thorough work, so that you may be [people] perfectly and fully developed [with no defects], lacking in nothing (James 1:2-4 AMP).

Therefore Princess Warriors, receive the baptism of fire from King Jesus, to come forth in the Word of God with His words being as fire shut up in your bones.

The fire brings us to a place where His Word is made like that of steel inside of us so that the trials that we have gone through fortify us deeper in our faith in God. Being baptized in the fire of God changes us so that we are firebrands for the Lord Jesus Christ, spreading a passionate fire for Him across the earth.

In my personal life, I have experienced this when I go minister at different places. For example, at one women's conference I ministered at, there was a group of 80 women packed in a tiny room for the workshop I was doing that day. Out of that workshop, God's Holy Spirit used me as a firebrand to ignite the women there. One of the women in that workshop, Theresa, was ignited by the fire of God, and it was as if in a moment her entire world had changed. She forever was changed for the Lord Jesus and could never go back. It was as though she became aware of an entirely different dimension of God that she never knew existed, and she was never the same. From there she went back to her home and spread the fire of God to her entire church and city, winning many people to the Lord Jesus Christ. That is only one incident I know of from that meeting, and I am confident there are many more testimonies. As firebrands for God, we light other firebrands across the earth for God's glory.

Many times when people come across my path, all they say is, "You have the fire of God in you." It is that fire, the fiery seal upon my heart, a love for King Jesus that only Father God can flood through my being with His Holy Spirit, and it has forever changed me and continues to change others.

TESTIMONY OF THE BAPTISM OF FIRE

We go from glory to glory (see 2 Cor. 3:18) in our walk in the Lord and even in the baptism of fire we go from glory to glory. Therefore, Holy Spirit wanted me to share one of my experiences of being baptized by His fire. One Sunday morning I was in God Quest, my Sunday school room and Mike Harden was teaching that morning on the fire of God. He had an audio he wanted us to listen to with Lindell Cooley singing and Leonard Ravenhill preaching. He played that audio and while it was playing I felt my bones begin to vibrate and shake all throughout my body. Then I felt heat and fire go all through my bones and began to weep uncontrollably. I became weak and could barely lift my head. I came under such conviction by God's Holy Spirit and begin repenting of many things in my life. Then when the class was over I felt as though I had been a fish caught and filleted, laid open and gutted out. It was like a fiery flushing out of my entire being, of all sin nature that had been in my life. I could not walk and we had to go down the steps to the worship service. As I got up and continued to weep, Rich had to assist me to transfer into the worship service. I leaned on him the entire walk with him wrapping his arms around me and sobbing uncontrollably, repenting even to him as I went down the steps. Then he sat me on our pew we usually sit in during service while he went to the restroom. I could not lift my head and all I could do is throw my head over the pew and weep uncontrollably repenting the entire time. This baptism of fire by Holy Spirit was a purifying cleansing fire that I will never forget! It was so deep and so intense with Holy Spirit fire.

Endnote

1. http://www.steel.org/en/Making%20Steel/How%20Its%20 Made/Processes/Processes%20Info/The%20Basic%20Oxygen%20Steelmaking%20Process.aspx

chapter

15

The Victor's Crown

The Victor's Crown is the last symbol for Princess Warriors. In 2007, I had an encounter with God in which He forged a warrior mentality in my heart to win souls for His Kingdom. In my personal life, I have had souls God has given me to contend over for them to come out of darkness and into God's marvelous light.

As Princess Warriors, we are to minister to God first like that of the Zadok priesthood in Ezekiel 44, similarly as a warrior or soldier serves the king of their country first. It is out of that relationship, in serving their king that in turn they go to battle and carry out the orders given them by the king. As Princess Warriors, we will encounter many personal levels of warfare for ourselves, our families, our churches, our communities, our states, our nations, and other nations. Spiritual warfare in that regard is a natural byproduct of life. However, there is a greater call whereby we war for souls for our King. When we come into this level of spiritual warfare, we are setting the captives free!

The Spirit of the Lord God is upon me, because the Lord has anointed and qualified me to preach the Gospel of good tidings to the meek, the poor, and afflicted; He has sent me to bind up and heal the brokenhearted, to proclaim liberty to the [physical and spiritual] captives and the opening of the prison and of the eyes to those who are bound (Isaiah 61:1 AMP).

AN ENCOUNTER I'LL NEVER FORGET

The encounter I had with the Lord several years ago changed my life forever in how I view spiritual warfare and going after lost souls for God. In this encounter, God showed me how He would bring a move of His love through His Holy Spirit on the earth that would forever change how we go after souls.

The next Great Awakening that we will see move across the earth is what the Lord termed, "The Radiant Love Anointing." On July 14, 2007, the Spirit of God told me to start praying for the Radiant Love Anointing. I engaged the Lord regarding this move of God, and when I asked Him what the Radiant Love Anointing was, on July 18, 2007, He replied that it would be the Next Great Awakening. God wants His people to pray for His Radiant Love Anointing.

WHAT IS A GREAT AWAKENING?

The Great Awakening refers to several periods of dramatic religious revival. They have also been described as periodic revolutions.

Something that is awakened is that which was sleeping. Therefore, we can see in the scripture below Paul states "wake up o sleeper...and Christ will Shine on You." There-fore, a Great Awakening is a waking up from slumber those who are asleep in Christ to see through their spiritual lenses the truth of God in order that they might walk in the au-thority granted to them by Jesus and in the fullness of the Glory of God.[1]

There are four generally accepted Great Awakenings in U.S. history: The first Great Awakening occurred in 1730's and went to 1750 with people such as Jonathan Edwards and George Whit-field that were not the ordinary preachers who back in those days would read sermons but rather they wanted to be vessels used to engage the emotions of the audience. This brought a protestant movement awakening the church from dry sermons merely read to them as rhetoric without any engagement. This brought a fiery release of God into the people during that time. This movement went across British America and Protestant Europe to revitalize the church.

The second Great Awakening began in Cane Ridge, Ken-tucky in the 1800's and went up until 1870. This move of God supported the growth of the Methodist and Baptist churches. Upstate New York had many great fiery revivals so much, that it was known as the "Burned-Over District." Moreover, the Advent movement birthed in the midst of this in the 1830's and 1840's that was one bringing forth the message of the second coming of Christ Jesus. The entire second Great Awakening was known as a Restoration Movement overall focusing the church on the desire for a pure form of Christianity.

The third Great Awakening began in the late 1800's and went to the early 1900's bringing the church into the forefront as a "Social Gospel Movement" where the church was bringing the gospel into social outreach where missionary programs were put into place to address social issues.

The fourth Great Awakening began around 1960's into the 1970's and focused upon the individual having a personal relationship with Jesus. In this move non-traditional churches and parachurch organizations began to arise. Also, many identify this movement The Jesus Movement due to the emphasis on the personal relationship of a Christian with Christ Jesus.

WHAT IS THE RADIANT LOVE ANOINTING?

The Radiant Love Anointing is a move of God that consists both of His Light and His Love. Jesus said that He is the Light of the world (see John 12:46), and He has made us sons and daughters of light.

For you were once darkness, but now you are light in the Lord. Live as children of light (for the fruit of the light consists in all goodness, righteousness and truth) and find out what pleases the Lord. Have nothing to do with the fruitless deeds of darkness, but rather expose them. For it is shameful even to mention what the disobedient do in secret. But everything exposed by the light becomes visible—and everything that is illuminated becomes a light. This is why it is said: "Wake up, O sleeper, rise from the dead, and Christ will shine on you" (Ephesians 5:8-14 NIV).

Radiant is defined as emitting rays of light; shining; bright; a point or object from which rays proceed.[2]

When God first formed the earth, *"God said, 'Let there be Light'; and there was light"* (Gen. 1:3). Knowing that God is a full circle God (He brings us to full circle), we can know that He is coming all the way back to Genesis 1:3. Jesus said that He is the light of the world:

*I have come as a **Light** into the **world**, so that whoever believes in Me [whoever cleaves to and trusts in and relies on Me] may not continue to live in darkness* (John 12:46 AMP).

And the Light shines on in the darkness, for the darkness has never overpowered it [put it out or absorbed it or appropriated it, and is unreceptive to it] (John 1:5 AMP).

In addition, God says that He is love. *"He that **loveth** not knoweth not **God**; for **God is love**"* (1 John 4:8 KJV). Therefore, love speaks of Who God Is. When I asked the Lord for confirmation on this Radiant Love Anointing, the Spirit of God brought me to a specific Scripture, which He showed me to be His Radiant Love Anointing.

Read the prelude verses to the Radiant Love Anointing. When you get to the words in bold, that is the specific Scripture that has both *radiant* and *love* together. Remember that the main Scripture passage has a *then*. What that means is that all the stuff that happens in verses 1-4 will happen right before verse 5. *Then* is used to show what happens and why. The Radiant Love Anointing happens *because of* verses 1-4.

Arise, shine, for your light has come, and the glory of the LORD rises upon you.

See, darkness covers the earth and thick darkness is over the peoples, but the LORD rises upon you and His glory appears over you.

Nations will come to your light, and kings to the brightness of your dawn.

Lift up your eyes and look about you: All assemble and come to you; your sons come from afar, and your daughters are carried on the arm.

*Then you will look and be **radiant**, your **heart will throb and swell with joy** [love]; the wealth on the seas will be brought to you, to you the riches of the nations will come* (Isaiah 60:1-5 NIV).

I've been praying these verses of the Radiant Love Anointing at the Holy Spirit's prompting. I would encourage you to do the same.

WHAT DO WE DO WITH THE RADIANT LOVE ANOINTING?

The Spirit of God told me that we are to go into the dark places to bring His light and His love when this anointing comes upon us. He proved this in a revelation He gave me while I was asking for the Radiant Love Anointing. On July 16, 2007, when I was in intercession, the Lord placed upon my head a laurel crown, which I had never seen. When I looked up information regarding this crown, I found out that it was the *victor's crown.* I found this crown in the Bible in Revelation 3:11: *"I am coming soon. Hold on to what you have, so that no one will take your crown"* (NIV). This crown is referred to as the victor's crown and actually is stated as such in the New Jerusalem Bible. At the same time that I received the crown, the Spirit of God said, "Open the two-leaved gates."

Later when I was reading Isaiah, I found the "two-leaved gates."

Thus saith the LORD to His anointed, to Cyrus, whose right hand I have holden, to subdue nations before him;

*and I will loose the loins of kings, to **open before him the
two leaved gates; and the gates shall not be shut;** I will
go before thee, and make the crooked places straight: I will
break in pieces the gates of brass, and cut in sunder the bars
of iron: And I will give thee the treasures of darkness, and
hidden riches of secret places, that thou mayest know that
I, the LORD, which call thee by thy name, am the God of
Israel.* (Isaiah 45:1-3 KJV).

During that same week that the Spirit of God gave me the
victor's crown and said to open up the two-leaved gates, He told
me to watch Tomb Raider with Laura Croft. I watched it and discovered that she was a trained person who knew how to protect
herself from the enemy and was told by her father to protect the
light, which the bad guys were trying to acquire. Laura was going
to protect the light from getting into the enemy's hands.

I watched the awesome fight scene where she is hanging from
the ceiling doing all kinds of jumps. Then these bad guys break
into her place. She ends up fighting them in a way that made me
want to leap off of my chair. After I watched this, the Spirit of
God said, "Robin, what does Laura Croft mean?" I searched and
found out that Laura meant "victor" and Croft meant "skilled."
Then the Spirit of God opened my eyes to what was going on
underneath the drama of the movie.

Laura, who was a skilled victor, was raiding tombs (dark
places). A raider, according to Dictionary.com, is "a commando,
ranger, or the like, specially trained to participate in military
raids." Laura would go into the dark places and raid them. We are
to go into the darkness and violently take it for the Kingdom of
God and know that we walk in victory.

What we are to do with the Radiant Love Anointing is to
know that the gates will be opened up for us to take souls that

are perishing and going to hell out of the fire in which they are burning. God is going before us to make our paths straight and to cut down every obstacle that comes up against us. Moreover, He is going to give us the *"treasures of darkness and hidden riches of secret places."* God Almighty is going to bring us incredible victory over the enemy in the earth. We must hold onto our victor's crown as in Revelation 3:11 and not let *anyone* take it from us!

PRINCESS WARRIORS WHO WIN SOULS FOR GOD

The Victor's Crown for the Princess Warriors symbol stands for us going into the dark places to get treasures—lost souls—for God! We are a fearless group of women who do not shrink back from hell, but rather plunge forward and pull souls out of the flaming fire by the power of God's Holy Spirit, which gives us a boldness and fearlessness to do so. When all is said and done on this earth and we go to Father God, I want to hear, *"Well done My good and faithful servant"*.

It is this passion, this love for the Lord flooding into my being that gives me a passion and love for souls. Ask God to give you a love for souls, and watch what He will do in and through you. God is looking for laborers in the harvest! The harvest is plentiful, but the laborers are few. As Princess Warriors, we are committed to being laborers in God's harvest.

Endnotes

1. http://en.wikipedia.org/wiki/Great_Awakening

2. http://dictionary.reference.com/browse/radiant

16

Princess Warriors Ignited

Princess Warriors was given to me by Holy Spirit when I began to write the book series for *The Glory to Glory Sisterhood* in 2004. I was in the middle of law school, and during my second year of law school, Holy Spirit asked me to take six months off to write a book for God. I was sitting down going through my day in the spring of 2004 when I felt as though God had tapped me on the shoulder and said, "Robin do you remember years ago when you thought that I could never get any glory out of you getting black balled from being in a sorority and the little sister of a fraternity in 1887?" I responded "Yes Lord." Then God said, "I want you to bring my Sorority in where no woman is blackballed and every woman is accepted in the beloved." I was overwhelmed and grateful at the same time.

As I sat down to write the one book during that six months, my entire focus was on completing the task God asked me to complete. The entire six months, all I did was write what I thought would be one book and a chapter in the book was titled "Princess Warriors," which Holy Spirit gave me at that time. I continued that six months to finish the project, and I cannot even begin to express the exhaustion, warfare, doubt, questions from others, and much more that I encountered during that short time. I was not an ordained minister or a preacher. I simply loved my Jesus from pulling me out of the dark pit that I was once in. When the I came to the end of those six months in 2004 and came into the year 2005, I sent the book off to a publisher.

But when I heard back from the publisher, he said "Robin, this is going to be too big of a book for women to read." I was thinking to myself, *how crazy is that.* He told me that with the word count I had at that time the book would be close to 1,200 pages! This information completely tilted my mind. Therefore, the publisher suggested I break the book down into four different books, which would then be a series. In breaking down the one book into four books, Holy Spirit gave me the title to each book, telling me when to start the next book and end it, as well. The first book of the series ended up being the original name of the book, which was *The Glory to Glory Sisterhood: God's Sorority.* When I started marking the beginning and the ending of the next book, Holy Spirit told me to call the next book *Princess Warriors,* which would include the fear of the Lord—so that God's daughters would always make God bigger than anything else—and spiritual warfare.

Shortly after the book was finished, my husband, Rich, and I moved out of our home and were in the process of being completely stripped by God. I waited till I heard Holy Spirit tell me what home we were to move into, and two weeks before we had to move out of our old home, Holy Spirit showed me this one house that for months had been for sale. Only this time the house was not for sale, but instead for rent. I knew it was the right home, and we arranged a meeting with the owner. When we met with the owner, within 24 minutes we had signed a contract to rent this home for the next year of our lives. The new home was on the street Warrior Drive! Our old home address was 541 Warrior Drive. We moved in during the second week of October, and out of obedience, two months later in December I held the first Princess Warriors meeting in that home. God told me that that address would be the address to birth in His ministry, Princess Warriors.

We started out with only a hand full of women, and now God has me going around across the Birmingham metro area setting up Princess Warriors meetings. How awesome is our God? Through all the trials and tribulations we went through, I had no clued that God would be bringing forth a ministry whereby His Holy Spirit changes the lives of women, taking us from glory to glory.

At every meeting for Princess Warriors, we have the Word of God for that month come forth in what God wants His Princesses to know. Then after the teaching on the Word, we enter into a time of worship. After worship, we Princesses break up into small groups where we demonstrate the symbols of Princess Warriors.

THE SWORD OF THE SPIRIT

We Princess Warriors use the Sword of the Spirit, the Word of God (Bible), and the gift of prophesy. One woman is placed in the middle to be ministered to by other women in the group. One woman will anoint the Princess Warrior in the middle, and we will come together and listen to Holy Spirit for that woman's life. As we hear Holy Spirit speaking, we bring forth God's Word of prophesy and exhortation to that woman. Then someone else gets in the middle, and the process continues until every woman is prayed for in the meeting.

It's as though all of us women are iron sharpening iron when we minister and prophesy to each other. Princess Warriors is an equipping ministry in the gifts of Holy Spirit; therefore, all of the women in the meeting minister because we are all a Royal Priesthood, a Holy Nation. I encourage women to get a Princess Warriors meeting started in their area, where they meet at least once a month and seek God for the Word He has for them and minister to each other using the gifts of Holy Spirit.

THE FIRE OF GOD

In addition, in the Princess Warriors meetings, God's fire comes in such great measure. As Holy Spirit moves among God's daughters, it's as though God has brought many firebrands together—women who are so hungry and passionate for God that as we come together in unity we become a bonfire for God!

As we have seen the fire of God come so strongly in our meetings, we have witnessed women being delivered from strongholds of the enemy, as well as God healing people and bringing great freedom that has not been experienced before.

MY PASSION

"Seek first the Kingdom of God" (see Matt. 6:33) has been my passion since 2001. It is from that passion that God has brought me into a place where He is taking me from one level of glory to another level of glory (see 2 Cor. 3:18). All I have wanted to know is Christ in me the hope of glory (see Phil.1:20) in such a greater measure that I am forever left undone in His liquid love. This liquid love of Christ, which is poured into me by God's Holy Spirit, has healed so many wounds that were deep within my soul from past hurts and injuries.

I came from such a place of bondage, drowning my hurt in alcohol and numbing it by seeking the approval of people everywhere I turned, only to be rejected over and over. Then God brought me out of that pit, beginning in 2001, bringing me into a new life in Him, and firmly establishing me in 2002. I was never the same. My love and passion for Jesus was much deeper than that of my youth, because I knew the depths of hell my soul was held captive in and the place from which Jesus delivered me, bringing me into God's marvelous light. Therefore, since He delivered me from such a pit of hell, it has been my life's mission to lay down my life for Jesus and serve Him as only a lover would know how.

A lover will seek for nothing in return, but just to serve and be near the one she loves. I absolutely love my husband, Rich, whom I thank God for! I could not imagine a better partner in life. My husband does not have to pay me or entice me to love him. I love Rich because of my absolute desire to simply be his companion, his mate. Likewise, a deeper love that only God has placed in me has propelled me to love Jesus as never before and placed within me a desire like none other to live as a laid down lover for my King. This brings me to the Song of Solomon that I mentioned earlier, under the symbol of fire. It is the fiery seal of the Song of Solomon that God places on our hearts that creates in us unction, a drive, a compelling to walk out the will of God in our lives.

Set me like a seal upon your heart, like a seal upon your arm; for love is as strong as death, jealousy is as hard and cruel as Sheol (the place of the dead). Its flashes are flashes of fire, a most vehement flame (the very flame of the lord)!

Many waters cannot quench love, neither can floods drown it. If a man would offer all the goods of his house for love, he would be utterly scorned and despised (Song of Solomon 8:6-7 AMP).

Only God can give us a love for King Jesus that is outside of ourselves and that will create in us such a passionate jealousy to serve Him that we will be able to withstand the parameters of hell that try to come against us. When we determine in ourselves to be Princess Warriors for God, the devil and all of his legions of fallen angels will be threatened by it because they do not only see a warrior in the army of God, but they see something much more threatening than that, a lover of Jesus, a lover of the cross, and the price that was paid there to bring freedom.

When I became free of the bondages of satan and his attacks with other devils, I was set free in a way that would forever put a seal upon my arm! The seal upon my arm from Song of Solomon gives me a revelation that I am a bondservant of the Most High God! I have been given and have received His seal. This seal on the arm only signifies the work that has been done in the heart. God put such a fiery love in me for King Jesus that only He could give me that. No matter what would come up the rest of my life, I would be able to go through it because of the love resident within. It is that kind of love satan hates because he knows that nothing will stop us from fulfilling our destiny, from bringing the Kingdom of Heaven forth into the earth.

As Princess Warriors, we bring the Kingdom of Heaven forth in a great measure into earth!

And from the days of John the Baptist until the present time, the kingdom of heaven has endured violent assault, and violent men seize it by force (as a precious prize – a share in the heavenly kingdom is sought with most ardent zeal and intense exertion) (Matthew 11:12 AMP).

When we become fiery lovers for King Jesus, we arise with such boldness within us that we are violent in bringing the Kingdom of Heaven forth. After I got on fire for God in 2002, I was filled with a jealousy unlike before. I was jealous for people to be set free from the bondages of the enemy. It grinded in my spirit woman to see someone in bondage to alcohol, low self-esteem, abuse, fear of man, and so forth. This zeal in me was God's nature of jealousy (which I go into great detail on in the next book, *At His Feet*) that all I wanted to do was protect the covenant of God in making manifest the Kingdom of Heaven everywhere I went.

MANIFESTING THE KINGDOM OF HEAVEN

When I was invited to minister in a rehab center, the woman initially invited me to "bring correction" to the women in that facility. However, Holy Spirit told me that the women had been flogged by the spirit of religion their whole life and that they were acting the only way they knew how, which was to bite each other spiritually by gossiping, judging, envying, and so forth. When I arrived, I asked God what He wanted me to say to the women, and He said to tell them, "I love them!" All of a sudden, I was filled from the top of my head to the bottom of my feet with the Song of Solomon 8:6-7 love for God's daughters in that room. That love became so infused in me that it spilt over onto those women in the gift of prophesy. Thus, when I prophesied over these women (used the Sword of the Spirit), instantly bondages fell off of them and the women even looked different than before.

As Princess Warriors, when we bring the Kingdom of Heaven forth, bondages on others will fall to the ground. Using the Sword of the Spirit and the fire of God, while walking in the overcomer's anointing as a victor, propels us as Princess Warriors to bring the Kingdom of Heaven forth. "God is looking for warriors, not wimps," the Holy Spirit told me years ago. Warriors will pay the price to bring victory to their king. It is Princess Warriors of God who will pay the price to bring victory to King Jesus!

17

Psalm 91 Protection

When the enemy comes in like a flood, he sends the assignment of python against you, cooperating with the spirit of Jezebel, which ends up opening up the door to Leviathan. Then you have to enter the stronghold of God.

I tell a dream I had in the section on "Pride" in *The Glory to God Sisterhood*. The dream, which I had in 2006, consisted of Mr. and Mrs. Pride. God was warning me that I was about to go through an attack of a brood of vipers, leading to such magnitude that it would be Leviathan attacking me. Leviathan is a brood of vipers that are cooperating with satan's plan to come against the anointing of Christ in you, the hope of *glory! Glory* is the copiousness of God; it is all of who God is—His Names, His Characters, His Attributes, His Fullness! Therefore, God wants this glory, Himself, to be manifested in you as it was made visible in His Son, Jesus Christ! Here is the dream:

For example, in 2006 I received a dream from the Lord where I was going to go through great persecution from other Christians. In the dream the people were very tall. I was walking around and heard them all clamoring to talk with a specific couple, Mr. and Mrs. Pride. Then we all went into a larger room to listen to a well known teacher of the Word of God. In this room I sat by another lady whom I had known years earlier somewhere else. This lady had been treated as an outcast by her church because her husband had cheated on her and left. While I was sitting by this lady, a partition came down between me and all of the tall people who were sitting by Mr. and Mrs. Pride, and I was no longer able to be a part of them. After that, a lady in the dream came up to me and said that I had two demons on me and I told her I did not. Then I walked away dejected in the dream for a long walk and eventually came back to tell her I did not have two demons on me. She apologized to me, said she knew and was sorry, and the dream was over.[1]

After I had the dream, I even repented for having the dream after I told my husband Rich, because he couldn't believe I had the dream either. However, within a matter of two weeks, the occurrences started happening as I had dreamt, and I had to endure two to three years of being rejected, persecuted, accused of doing the work of satan, and discredited. However, simultaneously, God worked in me like He did in Joseph, who was misunderstood by His brothers (see Gen 39). It was not about me; it was about the *seed!* The seed of *Christ in me the hope of glory!* God was turning this around to my good because I love Him and I am called according to His purpose!

In order to bring me higher, God allowed me to go through a greater *fire*—a fire within and fiery darts without! The fire of

God began to purge and consecrate me in greater measure for the *call!* Many are called and few are chosen (see Matt. 20:16). Not many are willing to go through the test of being hit by Leviathan to expose the pride that is present in others and even within ourselves in order to allow more room for God's glory to be poured into our lives! It is the very thing the enemy thinks he is going to crush us with, yet it becomes our launch pad, our acceleration, our elevation by God Himself! God promotes and elevates those who are low, who are humble and contrite.

When we get hit by Leviathan, to everyone else (those who are unknowingly in agreement with the enemy) the iniquity in their hearts and the lack of love for Christ sucks them in, in *their own pride,* to believing that they are *truly* doing the *work of God.* However, it is not God at all, but it is satan who has them deceived into believing that they are doing the work of God. Those in this web of deceit are given over so much to the delusion that they try to protect the system from the perceived danger or threat—the anointed vessel of God going through the attack.

They will even use the story of the righteous indignation that Jesus presented in the temple, when He went in with the whip among people given over to this deceit (see John 2:15) to justify their actions. They will say, "See, I told you she had Jezebel; I told you he had pride." In reality, it was the humility of Jesus that also was bold to get the whip and chase out the devil! Therefore, when righteous indignation rises up in a vessel of God to expose the system because the system has been hissing and biting, it actually looks like the vessel of God is in rebellion.

That is how satan works! He makes those who are deceived believe they are doing the work of God and causes them to point fingers at the vessel who has interrupted the system of pride, religion, mammon, control, and manipulation. When we are going through this type of attack where satan is using our brothers and sisters in Christ (I'm talking about the Church in general), we do not want to be a part of the Civil War Leviathan has raging and turn on each other. Instead, God's banner over us is *love* (see Song of Sol. 2:4). It is all about God's love because that is how faith operates! Faith operates by way of *love!* Therefore, if satan can get us to be offended with those attacking us, he can affect our love tank and stop the flow of the anointing. It is *all about God all the time*—every attack, every test, and every tribulation is about God, about Christ in us the hope of glory being manifested in the earth.

Therefore, the greater end is for God's Holy Spirit to pull us toward the position of love, the place of love. In that place we choose not to war, because if we do, it will mean that we will be fighting our own brother or own sister. Since they are consumed with it, any truth we might offer in love will actually make the situation worse. This is why we enter *God!* We enter Psalm 91! The first four verses describe the protection of entering the stronghold.

> *Whoever dwells in the shelter of the Most High will rest in the shadow of the Almighty. I will say of the LORD, "He is my refuge and my fortress, my God, in whom I trust." Surely He will save you from the fowler's snare and from the deadly pestilence. He will cover you with His feathers, and under His wings you will find refuge; His faithfulness will be your shield and rampart* (Psalm 91:1-4 NIV).

The next verses in Psalm 91, verses 5-8 describe the outcome of those who do not enter love (God), but instead continue to operate in pride.

> *You will not fear the terror of night, nor the arrow that flies by day, nor the pestilence that stalks in the darkness, nor the*

plague that destroys at midday. A thousand may fall at your side, ten thousand at your right hand, but it will not come near you. You will only observe with your eyes and see the punishment of the wicked (Psalm 91:5-8 NIV).

The last verses of Psalm 91 describe the victory of those who are in the stronghold of God.

Because you have made the Lord your refuge, and the Most High your dwelling place, There shall no evil befall you, nor any plague or calamity come near your tent. For He will give His angels [especial] charge over you to accompany and defend and preserve you in all your ways [of obedience and service]. They shall bear you up on their hands, lest you dash your foot against a stone. You shall tread upon the lion and adder; the young lion and the serpent shall you trample underfoot. Because he has set his love upon Me, therefore will I deliver him; I will set him on high, because he knows and understands My name [has a personal knowledge of My mercy, love, and kindness--trusts and relies on Me, knowing I will never forsake him, no, never]. He shall call upon Me, and I will answer him; I will be with him in trouble, I will deliver him and honor him. With long life will I satisfy him and show him My salvation." (Psalm 91:9-16 AMP).

We who enter the stronghold of God are protected from the fiery arrows of the enemy. We are set free from the oppressor and the destruction of the attack of Leviathan (it started out as Jezebel, which co-labored with python to bring about an attack of Leviathan so strong that we feel as though we are crushed). However, God knows how much we can bear, and He will not allow us to go past a point where we are crushed (see Luke 20:18). We have instead chosen to throw ourselves on the rock to be broken!

King David describes very well in Psalms 55–59 his attack of being hit by a brood of vipers and Leviathan and the way it operated through others. We will look at these verses and then come back to what God wants us to realize! We come back to *God*—to God's *glory!* **God's glory is love!** After the Psalms, read with me farther.

PSALM 55

Listen to my prayer, O God, and hide not Yourself from my supplication! Attend to me and answer me; I am restless and distraught in my complaint and must moan [And I am distracted] at the noise of the enemy, because of the oppression and threats of the wicked; for they would cast trouble upon me, and in wrath they persecute me. My heart is grievously pained within me, and the terrors of death have fallen upon me. Fear and trembling have come upon me; horror and fright have overwhelmed me. And I say, Oh, that I had wings like a dove! I would fly away and be at rest. Yes, I would wander far away, I would lodge in the wilderness. Selah [pause, and calmly think of that]! I would hasten to escape and to find a shelter from the stormy wind and tempest. Destroy [their schemes], O Lord, confuse their tongues, for I have seen violence and strife in the city. Day and night they go about on its walls; iniquity and mischief are in its midst. Violence and ruin are within it; fraud and guile do not depart from its streets and marketplaces. For it is not an enemy who reproaches and taunts me—then I might bear it; nor is it one who has hated me who insolently vaunts himself against me—then I might hide from him. But it was you, a man my equal, my companion and my familiar friend. We had sweet fellowship together and used to walk to the house of God in company. Let desolations and death come suddenly upon *them; let them go down alive to Sheol (the place of the dead), for evils are in their habitations, in their hearts, and their inmost part. As for me, I will call upon God, and the Lord will save me. Evening and morning and at noon will I utter my complaint and moan and sigh, and He will hear my voice. He has redeemed my life in peace from the battle that was against me [so that none came near me], for they were many who strove with me. God will hear and humble them, even He Who abides of old—Selah [pause, and calmly think of that]!—because in them there has been no change [of heart], and they do not fear, revere, and worship God. [My companion] has put forth his hands against those who were at peace with him; he has broken and profaned his agreement [of friendship and loyalty]. The words of his mouth were smoother than cream or butter, but war was in his heart; his words were softer than oil, yet they were drawn swords. Cast your burden on the Lord [releasing the weight of it] and He will sustain you; He will never allow the [consistently] righteous to be moved (made to slip, fall, or fail). But You, O God, will bring down the wicked into the pit of destruction; men of blood and treachery shall not live out half their days. But I will trust in, lean on, and confidently rely on You* (AMP).*

PSALM 56

Be merciful and gracious to me, O God, for man would trample me or devour me; all the day long the adversary oppresses me. They that lie in wait for me would swallow me up or trample me all day long, for they are many who fight against me, O Most High! What time I am afraid, I will have confidence in and put my trust and reliance in You. By [the help of] God I will praise His word; on God I lean, rely, and confidently put my trust; I will not fear. What can man, who is flesh, do to me? All day long they twist my words and trouble my affairs; all their thoughts are against me for evil and my hurt. They gather themselves together, they hide themselves, they watch my steps, even as they have [expectantly] waited for my life. They think to escape with iniquity, and shall they? In Your indignation bring down the peoples, O God. You number and record my wanderings; put my tears into Your bottle—are they not in Your book? Then shall my enemies turn back in the day that I cry out; this I know, for God is for me. In God, Whose word I praise, in the Lord, Whose word I praise, In God have I put my trust and confident reliance; I will not be afraid. What can man do to me? Your vows are upon me, O God; I will render praise to You and give You thank offerings. For You have delivered my life from death, yes, and my feet from falling, that I may walk before God in the light of life and of the living (AMP).

Psalm 57

Be merciful and gracious to me, O God, be merciful and gracious to me, for my soul takes refuge and finds shelter and confidence in You; yes, in the shadow of Your wings will I take refuge and be confident until calamities and destructive storms are passed. I will cry to God Most High, Who performs on my behalf and rewards me [Who brings to pass His purposes for me and surely completes them]! He will send from heaven and save me from the slanders and reproaches of him who would trample me down or swallow me up, and He will put him to shame. Selah [pause, and calmly think of that]! God will send forth His mercy and loving-kindness and His truth and faithfulness. My life is among lions; I must lie among those who are aflame— the sons of men whose teeth are spears and arrows, their tongues sharp swords. Be exalted, O God, above the heavens! Let Your glory be over all the earth! They set a net for my steps; my very life was bowed down. They dug a pit in my way; into the midst of it they themselves have fallen. Selah [pause, and calmly think of that]! My heart is fixed, O God, my heart is steadfast and confident! I will sing and make melody. Awake, my glory (my inner self); awake, harp and lyre! I will awake right early [I will awaken the dawn]! I will praise and give thanks to You, O Lord, among the peoples; I will sing praises to You among the nations. For Your mercy and loving-kindness are great, reaching to the heavens, and Your truth and faithfulness to the clouds. Be exalted, O God, above the heavens; let Your glory be over all the earth (AMP).

PSALM 58

Do you indeed in silence speak righteousness, O you mighty ones? [Or is the righteousness, rightness, and justice you should speak quite dumb?] Do you judge fairly and uprightly, O you sons of men? No, in your heart you devise wickedness; you deal out in the land the violence of your hands. The ungodly are perverse and estranged from the womb; they go astray as soon as they are born, speaking lies. Their poison is like the venom of a serpent; they are like the deaf adder or asp that stops its ear, Which listens not to the voice of charmers or of the enchanter never casting spells so cunningly. Break their teeth, O God, in their mouths; break out the fangs of the young lions, O Lord. Let them melt away as water which runs on apace; when he aims his arrows, let them be as if they were headless or split apart. Let them be as a snail dissolving slime as it passes on or as a festering sore which wastes away, like [the child to which] a woman gives untimely birth that has not seen the sun. Before your pots can feel the thorns [that are placed under them for fuel], He will take them away as with a whirlwind, the green and the burning ones alike. The [unyieldingly] righteous shall rejoice when he sees the vengeance; he will bathe his feet in the blood of the wicked. Men will say, Surely there is a reward for the [uncompromisingly] righteous; surely there is a God Who judges on the earth (AMP).

PSALM 59

Deliver me from my enemies, O my God; defend and protect me from those who rise up against me. Deliver me from and lift me above those who work evil and save me from bloodthirsty men. For, behold, they lie in wait for my life; fierce and mighty men are banding together against me, not for my transgression nor for any sin of mine, O Lord. They run and prepare themselves, though there is no fault in me; rouse Yourself [O Lord] to meet and help me, and see! You, O Lord God of hosts, the God of Israel, arise to visit all the nations; spare none and be not merciful to any who treacherously plot evil. Selah [pause, and calmly think of that]! They return at evening, they howl and snarl like dogs, and go [prowling] about the city. Behold, they belch out [insults] with their mouths; swords [of sarcasm, ridicule, slander, and lies] are in their lips, for who, they think, hears us? But You, O Lord, will laugh at them [in scorn]; You will hold all the nations in derision. O my Strength, I will watch and give heed to You and sing praises; for God is my Defense (my Protector and High Tower). My God in His mercy and steadfast love will meet me; God will let me look [triumphantly] on my enemies (those who lie in wait for me). Slay them not, lest my people forget; scatter them by Your power and make them wander to and fro, and bring them down, O Lord our Shield! For the sin of their mouths *and the words of their lips, let them even be trapped and taken in their pride, and for the cursing and lying which they utter. Consume them in wrath, consume them so that they shall be no more; and let them know unto the ends of the earth that God rules over Jacob (Israel). Selah [pause, and calmly think of that]! And at evening let them return; let them howl and snarl like dogs, and go prowling about the city. Let them wander up and down for food and tarry all night if they are not satisfied (not getting their fill). But I will sing of Your mighty strength and power; yes, I will sing aloud of Your mercy and loving-kindness in the morning; for You have been to me a defense (a fortress and a high tower) and a refuge in the day of my distress. Unto You, O my Strength, I will sing praises; for God is my Defense, my Fortress, and High Tower, the God Who shows me mercy and steadfast love* (AMP).

It is in the place of being misunderstood, the place where the anointing of Christ in us is being rejected, persecuted, and despised that we are promoted to the place of glory. This is what we were always meant to find in Christianity (see Gal. 2:20). It is no longer I that live, but Christ lives in me! We come to a place of realization that Christ fought the battle with *love!* Christ is the stronghold!

Isaiah 59 describes appropriately how we go through this attack of great persecution, this pit of vipers, and it shows us that God is Lord of the battle. The vipers are lured into their own trap, and we come out in victory! The ultimate end is because of *love* because of the *covenant!* God brings us forth from Psalm 91 protection once we have passed the test of entering the stronghold of God in the midst of the attack and not being part of the civil war satan wants to bring about in the Church. We come into Psalm 92:10 anointing where *God has exalted* *our horn like a wild ox and given us the **new anointing**. Glory to God! It Is the very attack that brings us into an increased anointing—a new anointing!*

ISAIAH 59

Behold, the Lord's hand is not shortened at all, that it cannot save, nor His ear dull with deafness, that it cannot hear. But your iniquities have made a separation between you and your God, and your sins have hidden His face from you, so that He will not hear. For your hands are defiled with blood and your fingers with iniquity; your lips have spoken lies, your tongue mutters wickedness. None sues or calls in righteousness [but for the sake of doing injury to others—to take some undue advantage]; no one goes to law honestly and pleads [his case] in truth; they trust in emptiness, worthlessness and futility, and speaking lies! They conceive mischief and bring forth evil! They hatch adders' eggs and weave the spider's web; he who eats of their eggs dies, and [from an egg] which is crushed a viper breaks out [for their nature is ruinous, deadly, evil]. Their webs will not serve as clothing, nor will they cover themselves with what they make; their works are works of iniquity, and the act of violence is in their hands. Their feet run to evil, and they make haste to shed innocent blood. Their thoughts are thoughts of iniquity; desolation and destruction are in their paths and highways. The way of peace they know not, and there is no justice or right in their goings. They have made them into crooked paths; whoever goes in them does not know peace. Therefore are justice and right far from us, and righteousness and salvation do not overtake us. We expectantly wait for light, but [only] see darkness; for brightness, but we walk in obscurity and gloom. We grope for the wall like the blind, yes,

*we grope like those who have no eyes. We stumble at noon-
day as in the twilight; in dark places and among those
who are full of life and vigor, we are as dead men. We
all groan and growl like bears and moan plaintively like
doves. We look for justice, but there is none; for salvation,
but it is far from us. For our transgressions are multiplied
before You [O Lord], and our sins testify against us; for
our transgressions are with us, and as for our iniquities,
we know and recognize them [as]: Rebelling against and
denying the Lord, turning away from following our God,
speaking oppression and revolt, conceiving in and mut-
tering and moaning from the heart words of falsehood.
Justice is turned away backward, and righteousness (uprightness and right standing with God) stands far off;
for truth has fallen in the street (the city's forum), and
uprightness cannot enter [the courts of justice]. Yes, truth
is lacking, and he who departs from evil makes himself
a prey. And the Lord saw it, and it displeased Him that
there was no justice. And He saw that there was no man
and wondered that there was no intercessor [no one to in-
tervene on behalf of truth and right]; therefore His own
arm brought Him victory, and His own righteousness
[having the Spirit without measure] sustained Him.*

*For [the Lord] put on righteousness as a breastplate or coat
of mail, and salvation as a helmet upon His head; He put
on garments of vengeance for clothing and was clad with
zeal [and furious divine jealousy] as a cloak. According as
their deeds deserve, so will He repay wrath to His adversaries, recompense to His enemies; on the foreign islands and
coastlands He will make compensation. So [as the result
of the Messiah's intervention] they shall [reverently] fear
the name of the Lord from the west, and His glory from
the rising of the sun. When the enemy shall come in like a*

flood, the Spirit of the Lord will lift up a standard against him and put him to flight [for He will come like a rushing stream which the breath of the Lord drives]. He shall come as a Redeemer to Zion and to those in Jacob (Israel) who turn from transgression, says the Lord. As for Me, this is My covenant or league with them, says the Lord: My Spirit, Who is upon you [and Who writes the law of God inwardly on the heart], and My words which I have put in your mouth shall not depart out of your mouth, or out of the mouths of your [true, spiritual] children, or out of the mouths of your children's children, says the Lord, from henceforth and forever (AMP).

Immediately following Isaiah 59 is Isaiah 60:1! The attack that satan meant for our destruction and harm is the attack that brings in God's glory! Immediately after an attack of this magnitude, with Leviathan now gone, we enter into Isaiah 60:1:

Arise [from the depression and prostration in which circumstances have kept you—rise to a new life]! Shine (be radiant with the glory of the Lord), for your light has come, and the glory of the Lord has risen upon you (AMP).

Welcome to promotion, to more glory, to more of God's goodness!

Another dream that I had recently demonstrated a series of events that were to happen, which have already begun to play out. However, the end of the dream was this: I stood in front of a mirror after a series of persecuting events took place. When I stood in front of the mirror, a friend of mine was there with me who resembled the Holy Spirit and a new anointing, that of the tribe of Dan. When I walked to the mirror and I looked into the mirror, it was a manifestation of Second Corinthians 3:18—as we look with unveiled faces into a mirror, we are being transformed into the image of Christ Jesus from glory to glory! Therefore, when I looked into the mirror, the Holy Spirit said, "Receive the fullness of My power!" Then I felt the power of God infuse me, leaving me wrecked! Moreover, God told me that this particular friend of mine represented the anointing of the Tribe of Dan. I looked up the promise spoken over the Tribe of Dan and here it is:

> *Dan shall judge his people as one of the tribes of Israel. Dan shall be a serpent by the way, a horned snake in the path, that bites at the horse's heels, so that his rider falls backward. I wait for Your salvation, O Lord* (Genesis 49:16-18 AMP).

> *Dan will provide justice for his people as one of the tribes of Israel. Dan will be a snake by the roadside, a viper along the path, that bites the horse's heels so that its rider tumbles backward. I look for your deliverance, LORD* (Genesis 49:16-18 NIV).

Dan was anointed as judge of Israel, judge of God's people. When we pass this test, God can trust us to judge correctly, not by our eyes, but with righteous judgments, and we can operate in a greater anointing for deliverance and the prophetic! Moreover, it says of Dan that he shall be like a serpent by the way, a horned snake in the path. Here I am reminded of Jesus when He said in Matthew 10:16,

> *Behold, I am sending you out like sheep in the midst of wolves; be wary and wise as serpents, and be innocent (harmless, guileless, and without falsity) as doves* (AMP).

The root word of *serpent* here means to "diligently observe." Dan diligently observes with justice and righteousness and provides God's justice! The enemy wants to stop the flow of God's power! It is those who have been through the test—have been hit on every end by the attack of python turned into Leviathan and entered into the stronghold of God, Psalm 91—who are able to overcome. When we enter into *love,* God Himself takes the battle on to bring victory, to bring us forth into the image of Christ Jesus from glory to glory!

Endnote

1. Robin Kirby-Gatto, *The Glory to God Sisterhood: God's Sorority* (Shippensburg, PA: Destiny Image, 2010), 89.

18

Overcoming Jezebel

I feel impressed at this time to include a teaching on the spirit of Jezebel and how to thwart the attack of Jezebel. Ask Holy Spirit to give you discernment in recognizing this spirit's attack against you, your family, your ministry, and your church. This is one spirit I absolutely hate because it nearly took my life, marriage, ministry, and destiny. Therefore, when it comes to the spirit of Jezebel, I come forth like a mighty warrior and tear the throne of Jezebel down when Holy Spirit tells me to come against others in the Body of Christ who are under its attack.

DON'T EAT AT JEZEBEL'S TABLE

After many days, the word of the Lord came to Elijah in the third year, saying, Go, show yourself to Ahab, and I will send rain upon the earth. So Elijah went to show himself to Ahab. Now the famine was severe in Samaria. And Ahab called Obadiah, who was the governor of his house. (Now Obadiah feared the Lord greatly; **For when Jezebel cut off the prophets of the Lord, Obadiah took a hundred prophets and hid them by fifties in a cave and fed them with bread and water.***) And Ahab said to Obadiah, Go into the land to all the fountains of water and to all the brooks; perhaps we may find grass to keep the horses and mules alive, that we lose none of the beasts. So they divided the land between them to pass through it. Ahab went one way and Obadiah went another way, each by himself. As Obadiah was on the way, behold, Elijah met him. He recognized him and fell on his face and said, Are you my lord Elijah? He answered him, It is I. Go tell your lord, Behold, Elijah is here. And he said, What sin have I committed, that you would deliver your servant into the hands of Ahab to be slain? As the Lord your God lives, there is no nation or kingdom where my lord has not sent to seek you. And when they said, He is not here, he took an oath from the kingdom or nation that they had not found you. And now you say, Go tell your lord, Behold, Elijah is here. And as soon as I have gone out from you, the Spirit of the Lord will carry you I know not where; so when I come and tell Ahab and he cannot find you, he will kill me. But I your servant have feared and revered the Lord from my youth.* **Was it not told my lord what I did when Jezebel slew the prophets of the Lord, how I hid a hundred men of the Lord's prophets by fifties in a cave and fed them with bread and water?** *And now you say, Go tell your lord, Behold, Elijah is here; and he will kill me. Elijah said, As the Lord of hosts lives, before Whom I stand, I will surely show myself to Ahab today. So Obadiah went to meet Ahab and told him, and Ahab went to meet Elijah. When Ahab saw Elijah, Ahab said to him, Are you he who troubles Israel? Elijah replied,*

I have not troubled Israel, but you have, and your father's house, by forsaking the commandments of the Lord and by following the Baals. **Therefore send and gather to me all Israel at Mount Carmel, and the 450 prophets of Baal and the 400 prophets of [the goddess] Asherah, who eat at [Queen] Jezebel's table** (1 Kings 18:1-19 AMP).

Here Jezebel had slain the prophets of God. The spirit of Jezebel hates the prophetic and is always after the prophetic *voice* of God in order to stop the Word of God from coming forth. Jezebel had persuaded Ahab to serve her gods and knew the power and the authority of Elijah's God, the true God. It was because of the threat of God's prophets, who would prophesy the Word of God, that Jezebel was given orders from the gods she served to kill the prophets of God. Notice here that Jezebel had a *table,* a place where she fed the prophets of Baal and Asherah, the gods whom she served. Therefore, Elijah had Ahab send for the prophets that served Baal and Asherah who ate at Jezebel's table to come to Mount Caramel.

God showed me that the Jezebel spirit has a table, representative of influence, where this spirit feeds others, most of whom might even operate in the prophetic area. However, the main influence of Jezebel is to feed people the food of the devil, not the true food of the Word of God. As Jesus said to satan: *"But He replied, 'It has been written, Man shall not live and be upheld and sustained by bread alone, but by every word that comes forth from the mouth of God'"* (Matt. 4:4 AMP).

The spirit of Jezebel knows how to woo others to its table. What it will do in order to get you to sit at the table of Jezebel is feed you with flattery! Whenever, the spirit of Jezebel is trying to gain another person in its camp, it will do so by feeding you with delicacies to entice you to sit at the table of Jezebel.

Eat not the bread of him who has a hard, grudging, and envious eye, neither desire his dainty foods; For as he thinks in his heart, so is he. As one who reckons, he says to you, eat and drink, yet his heart is not with you [but is grudging the cost] (Proverbs 23:5-7 AMP).

Here in Proverbs there are dainty foods that are used for enticing those who are not guarded to sit at the table of the unrighteous—of the hard, grudging, and envious one. Jezebel will lure you to her (the spirit, not the person) table by giving you "dainty foods" in the form of flattery. Usually, it will happen by people telling you how awesome you are and recognizing you.

Many people who have been wounded in their lives are easily enticed to the table of Jezebel. If they have not healed from their wounds, they still have a root or tear the enemy has sown in them that Jezebel can pull on in order to persuade them to sit at her table. This is a *false acceptance.* Usually, people who have experienced rejection or abandonment issues will find this spirit very "nice or good." They will believe that the person it is operating through is the most accepting or nicest person they have ever met. However, the niceness is a false niceness. It is not genuine, and it's only motive is to lure them to the table of Jezebel. Therefore, Jezebel first gets people by preparing dainties and flatteries and bringing them to a table where others have been lulled to sleep and flattered to gather them at her table.

Elijah knowing of Jezebel's deceived prophets, called for those prophets to come to Mount Caramel.

When all the people saw it, they fell on their faces and they said, The Lord, He is God! The Lord, He is God! And Elijah said, Seize the prophets of Baal; let not one escape. They seized them, and Elijah brought them down to the brook Kishon, and [as God's law required] slew them there (1 Kings 18:39-40 AMP).

Elijah followed the instructions of the Lord to open up the eyes of those who had been deceived by Jezebel's prophets and worshipped Baal. The people Elijah went to were people of Israel. The people who were chosen to serve God had been persuaded to serve a devil, a false god. Elijah was there to show them who God truly was and to stop them from being double-minded, going between two opinions of who was the true God. Once Elijah completed what God had set him to do, the people's eyes were opened and they realized that they had served a false God. They repented, stating that the true God is God! Then Elijah slew every prophet of Baal, as required by God's law.

Jezebel was after the true prophetic voice because it led people to repentance from worshipping idols. As long as Jezebel could kill the prophets, the message of the true God would not go forth to open the eyes of the people so they could see their deception.

When people are enticed by this spirit, they truly believe that the person that this spirit is operating through is of God. Don't get me wrong; the person could be saved. Most likely if the person is operating through a ministry for Jesus, this person probably is saved, but fell into serving another god without realizing it. How do people serve another god when they are saved? Israel did the same thing when they came out of Egypt. They believed, when Moses went up to the mountain to meet with God and they were at the bottom of the mountain, that the golden calf was God (see Ex. 32:3-5). It is not difficult to be deceived in this way.

We either serve God and His will, or we serve our own will (carnal nature), or we can also serve the devil's will. The devil has a plan; it is to pull as many as possible away from God and to pull them toward himself. As long as we are not doing the will of God and obeying Him, the devil has a way to wiggle his way in our lives and get us to serve him. This is what Jezebel did. Jezebel had persuaded others to sit at her table and eat her foods, her plans and purposes.

The spirit of Jezebel is always looking for those who have been wounded and rejected to entice them to sit at her table so she can persuade them to believe that her god is the true god. Jezebel tries to make people feel accepted and see how good and "nice" she is so that they will believe Jezebel is truly worshipping the true God. However, she is not worshipping the true God; she is worshipping the devil. However, the followers of Jezebel believe that they are really worshipping God; they are deceived.

Holy Spirit also showed me how Jezebel cloaks itself in order to not be seen. The way the spirit cloaks itself is through "spirituality" and "intellectualism." Therefore, someone given over to a jezebel spirit is very spiritual but they have combined with that intellectualism and it is not of God but of the world. Therefore, when the person talks it starts bringing confusion to your mind and your head feels as though there is something like a vice grip squeezing it and bringing confusion. Then as the person keeps talking you cannot make sense of what they are saying and it comes across like "wha wha wha wha wha" is all I can say to explain it. Similar to Charlie Brown's teacher in the cartoon Charlie Brown. Therefore, when that happens to you that should be an indicator that Jezebel is operating.

JEZEBEL'S MESSAGE

Ahab told Jezebel all that Elijah had done and how he had slain all the prophets [of Baal] with the sword. Then Jezebel sent a messenger to Elijah, saying, So let the gods do to me, and more also, if I make not your life as the life of one of them by this time tomorrow. Then he was afraid and arose and went for his life and came to Beersheba of Judah [over eighty miles, and out of Jezebel's realm] and left his servant there (1 Kings 19:1-3 AMP).

Jezebel's message was what terrified Elijah. Jezebel did not walk up to Elijah to scare or intimidate him, but it was the message she sent through *another* to Elijah that scared him and made him fear for his life. The spirit of Jezebel that is operating through mainly one person does not use that main person to tell another person things that would make that person afraid. No! That's a waste of Jezebel's time. Usually the Jezebel spirit has already persuaded people at her table that she is all good, that she is of the true God, and they are deceived. So it is the messengers, those who do Jezebel's work, who confront the prophetic voices and try to dishearten them.

I'll tell it like it is. If you have been persuaded to not be hooked into Jezebel's system, then you buck the system because you are a threat to the false god being exposed. Thus Jezebel will send messages of *death* to you, your ministry, your family, and your marriage in order to keep the deceptive blanket over people so they will not wake up to the deception. Jezebel does not want a repeat of what happened with those in the nation of Israel who prostrated themselves before the true God, recognizing that Elijah's God was the true God. They determined to serve the God of Elijah, not the false god of Jezebel.

Therefore, Jezebel will send her little minions to others to try to intimidate them. How do you know if you're passing on the message of Jezebel? (It is possible to unwittingly do it without really knowing it.) Ask yourself *what the fruit of your message is.* Is the message life-giving, encouraging, and uplifting? Does it draw people toward Jesus and the will of God? If the answer is yes, then the message is not of Jezebel because the fruit is godly fruit. However, if the message is to intimidate, confuse, and cause fear, inadequacy, and control (uh, let me say it again—*control*), then the message is most likely from the spirit of Jezebel. Jezebel tries to keep her kingdom by intimidating others, controlling others through making them feel like they are stupid, inadequate, un-qualified, and inferior.

It sounds like what many people do when they think they know better how to run someone else's life. This spirit does not waste time going straight to the person because the spirit has too many worker bees, too many servants. She will instead have all of the people eating at her table convinced that she is doing the work of the true God, and it is up to all of her servants to go let the "real" deceived person know that what that person is doing is not of God. She tells them that it is up to Jezebel and her servants to *make things right!*

People who are deceived think they are serving the true God and God's will, but they are not; it is satan's plan, not God's plan. Usually it will operate through people's immaturity—in the places where they are not conformed into the image of Christ Jesus—to come against a person. The people will truly believed they are the ones who are enlightened and that they have to protect the group from the person. They start attacking the person by intimidating that person and those attached to that person.

For instance, when someone doesn't do what the spirit of Je-zebel wants, the messengers of Jezebel will start going to the per-son who is not deceived and who is getting out of the *system* (out of the control of Jezebel), and they will start making that person feel ungodly. They will try to convince them, "You do not hear

God. You are making bad decisions. You cannot make right decisions. You need to be protected from yourself, and we definitely need to protect the rest of the group from you." **When you see something like this, run for your life from that group of people! It is not God!**

However, if God has told you not to leave and you have the strength to remain along with a few others who are not deceived, then all I can tell you to do, from personal experience, is to press in harder to God and to know that you truly hear Him. When the spirit of Jezebel has finally been broken off of that group, true repentance will come, and they will realize that they did not serve the will of the true God.

Holy Spirit showed me that the spirit of Jezebel will come much like an octopus and try to puppet people by putting three tentacles in people's spiritual spines. As things are in the natural, they are in the spirit. We have a spiritual body, too. We are body, soul, and spirit. God has given me many dreams about Jezebel and shown me how Jezebel looks like an octopus, much like in the movie *The Little Mermaid*. The whole purpose of the octopus in *The Little Mermaid* was to take away the little mermaids *voice!* The spirit of Jezebel hates the prophetic voice and tries to squeeze the voice of God out of people. Therefore, many times it operates along with the Python spirit, which is another teaching.

From personal experience, I can say that when I got away from a Jezebel spirit, I literally felt my back open from my neck to the bottom of my spine, and I felt like three huge octopus tentacles had come out of my spine and like my back was sown back together. Immediately, I felt the life, the breath of God, enter me, and I realized that the Jezebel spirit had been sucking on my anointing, the anointing of God in me, and I felt like all life was being sucked out of me. That spirit was looking good by using and sucking my anointing in order to appear as though it was anointed.

Holy Spirit showed me that it takes three of these tentacles to puppet us or make us servants of the spirit of Jezebel. God showed me that it was threefold because a *threefold cord is not quickly broken* (see Eccles. 4:12). The spirit of Jezebel will flatter us to gather us to her table to put one tentacle in us. Later, when we start serving her a little bit, she will put another tentacle in us. Her goal is to put the third tentacle in us so we will become her servants. It is that cord that we have to break with the power of Holy Spirit.

While I was being controlled by Jezebel, I many times felt confused or wonder if I really heard God. I believed I truly heard God, and I truly did when He told me His will for my life. However, the Jezebel spirit will try and make us think we don't hear God and we are making poor decisions and that we cannot make decisions without telling Jezebel or getting Jezebel's input. I will continue this line of thought later.

BECOMING A THREAT TO JEZEBEL (1 KINGS 21)

The Jezebel spirit looks to usurp authority and is drawn to find people who are not operating in their authority in order to take control. I have experienced many attacks in this area in many parts of my life and especially in ministry. When we step out in the call of God on our lives, Jezebel is going to try and weave in and out of our ministry, business, and destiny so that she can look for an opportune time to take the seated position of authority in our lives, ministries, businesses, and so forth. She wants to rule that place.

The Jezebel spirit does not want to end our ministries or businesses as long as she is in a place of authority; then she can bring in her "table" to begin the reproduction of her system and begin feeding more people with her food to keep them asleep to the call of God on their lives. As long as we remain in a place with small authority or small success, we are not a threat. It is when we are awakened to the *greatness* of *God* inside of us that we become a threat to the Jezebel spirit.

Three years ago, Holy Spirit told me that I was not *"dangerous enough for the Jezebel spirit."* I said, "What are you talking about, Holy Spirit? What do you mean 'dangerous enough.'" One day later, when my husband and I went to the beach, I took Frances Frangipane's small book on the Jezebel Spirit. I remember seeing that implication in something I had heard about being dangerous enough for the Jezebel spirit. It was as though God was saying, "I want you to become so filled with the fullness of My Holy Spirit inside of you and be compelled with the love of Christ and My name Jealous that you will make war against the spirit of Jezebel." I knew I was in training camp to be hit time and time again until I awakened to the greatness of God, of Jesus Christ in me, to such a measure that I was a walking threat to the spirit of Jezebel.

The Jezebel spirit attacks those who do not do what she desires and what her servants' desire. It has been my experience, and is identified in the Word, that if someone does not do what the Jezebel spirit wants, a pressure beyond all extent is applied to that person to manipulate and control that person into do what Jezebel wants—even unto the point of *death* (see John 10:10). Whenever we see a Jezebel spirit operating, the premise behind it is death and death abundantly.

In First Kings 18, Jezebel killed 150 of God's prophets. Interestingly enough, 100 signifies "the fullness of" and 50 signifies "Pentecost" and "harvest." Therefore, Holy Spirit is speaking about the very thing Jezebel is after. She is after the harvest of God, and she wants to keep us from entering into the *fullness of the harvest! Fullness* means "the entire completeness, portion, and destiny of a matter." This is why Jezebel is after the prophetic voice; it is the prophetic voice that speaks life and life abundantly (see John 10:10). The life in John 10:10 is a God kind of life, *zoe.* It is the God kind of life where there is fullness of healing, joy, gladness, and so forth.

The Jezebel spirit recognizes those who are pushing forth toward the zoe kind of life, the God kind of life. Revelation 19:10 states that the testimony of Jesus is the spirit of prophecy. Therefore, the very basis of prophecy testifies of Jesus. Holy Spirit showed me in the spiritual realm what occurs when someone is getting a prophetic word from the Lord. In the natural, it sounds like, "God is saying that you are coming into a season of restoration and that what the enemy took from you in the last eight years...." And so forth. However, in the spiritual realm, what is actually happening is the transmission of the name of Jesus is coming forth into that person's life so the prophetic word in the spirit realm actually sounds like this "Jesus, Jesus, Jesus, Jesus, Jesus, Jesus, Jesus!" The spirit of prophecy testifies of Jesus! Jesus came to bring life and life abundantly and to *destroy* the works of the devil, which we will get into with Jezebel.

Therefore, since the prophetic voice brings life and life abundantly, it is a target for the assignment of the Jezebel spirit. People who have a prophetic mantle on them, even when they are not walking in the will of God, will find attack after attack coming against them and keeping them in a position and state of constant death. They are losing their minds, their jobs, their families, their marriages, and their destinies. It is death, death, death all around them. However, when people are awakened by Holy Spirit to the seed of Jesus Christ, the hope of glory within them, and they are sober to the attack of the enemy, they will come forth by the Spirit of the Lord and be free of much bondage.

Thus, the people who have become free in the Lord Jesus awaken to their destiny, the greatness of God inside of them. This causes them to become an actual threat to the spirit of Jezebel. Jezebel has taken the high places for her gods, Baal and Asherah, and when anything comes against those high places, it is a threat to the spirit of Jezebel. Therefore, when people are awakened to the prophetic voice of God, the greatness and destiny of God, the testimony of Jesus within their spiritual DNA, those people or ministries become a target for the Jezebel spirit.

We can see with Naboth in First Kings 21 that he was awakened to his inheritance, his destiny, and would not relent at moving from his calling.

Now Naboth the Jezreelite had a vineyard in Jezreel, close beside the palace of Ahab king of Samaria; and after these things, Ahab said to Naboth, **Give me your vineyard,** *that I may have it for a garden of herbs, because it is near my house. I will give you a better vineyard for it or, if you prefer, I will give you its worth in money.* **Naboth said to Ahab, The Lord forbid that I should give the inheritance of my fathers to you. And Ahab [already depressed by the Lord's message to him] came into his house [more] resentful and sullen because of what Naboth the Jezreelite had said to him; for he had said, I will not give you the inheritance of my fathers. And he lay down on his bed, turned away his face, and would eat no food. But Jezebel his wife came and said**

***to him, Why is your spirit so troubled that you eat no
food?*** (1 Kings 21:1-5 AMP)

Here Ahab, Jezebel's husband, who was King of Israel, was
used to getting what he wanted, and when he could not, he became sullen. However, the thing that he wanted was Naboth's
inheritance, Naboth's destiny, Naboth's call of greatness! Ahab
pretty much threw a temper tantrum because he could not get
what he wanted. This is symbolic of Jezebel's servants or those
who are manipulated and controlled by Jezebel because they
have an immaturity in walking in the fruits of the Spirit (see Gal.
5:22) and are used to walking in the fruits of the flesh. The flesh
controls them, and when they cannot get what they want, they
come to Jezebel to wine and complain.

However, the interesting thing here is that Ahab's immaturity
caused him to turn away from eating at Jezebel's table. It was his
absence from eating the food, what she was used to feeding him,
that caught her attention. Jezebel likes to know what everyone is
doing and to have complete control. Therefore, when a person is
not present for any reason at her table, she will come forth and
inquire of their absence to see if it is because of breaking out of
the system or their own fleshly appetites. If it is of their fleshly
appetites, like Ahab pouting and being sullen because he didn't
get what his flesh wanted, Jezebel will come in and manipulate
to bring forth to her servants or those who are under her control.
Thus, they will continue to look at her as though she is great and
not realize their own rebellion. Instead, like Ahab here, they will
believe that Jezebel hears God and is doing the will of God, even
at the expense of killing another and bringing about death and
death abundantly.

Many books have great in-depth teachings about the Ahab
spirit that is a bedding ground for the spirit of Jezebel to operate

on. Also, Holy Spirit showed me that it is in the areas in our lives where the carnal nature, the flesh, is ruling that the spirit of Jezebel operates. Therefore, when the Jezebel spirit comes into a ministry or business in order to usurp and take authority, this spirit is looking for the areas in which the carnal nature, the flesh, is still ruling. I will add here that I have had to overcome the spirit of Jezebel in as many men as I have women. Therefore, this spirit is not prominent to women, from my experience, because this spirit has attacked me greatly through men, too.

Going from Authority to Authority

The spirit of Jezebel brings us into a greater dimension of ruling and reigning with Christ Jesus because it is important, like Jacob, that we wrestle for our blessing. Therefore, the spirit of Jezebel knows our weaknesses, such as how poorly we think about ourselves because we grew up in abusive homes, were in abusive relationships, were shamed, were treated like we did not matter, and so forth. The areas in which the woundedness has not healed and we have not allowed our flesh to die are the areas where Jezebel will try to wiggle in so that she can put a hook in you, a tentacle.

> *And he said to her, Because I spoke to Naboth the Jezreelite and said to him, Give me your vineyard for money; or if you prefer, I will give you another vineyard for it. And he answered, I will not give you my vineyard.* ***Jezebel his wife said to him, Do you not govern Israel? Arise, eat food, and let your heart be happy. I will give you the vineyard of Naboth the Jezreelite*** (1 Kings 21:6-7 AMP).

Jezebel here answers Ahab that she will take care of the whole issue by giving King Ahab what his flesh wants, and later she tells him to "eat food." There we see the food again. Jezebel constantly wants to pull people to her table, where she creates a false sense of fellowship. People who are eating at her table are getting what they want because she is getting it for them through all of her manipulation tactics, through the other messengers she gets to carry out her plans and purposes. In addition, Jezebel states, "Let your heart be happy." This is where the false sense of fellowship appears with those in a Jezebel group, those sucked into her web of deceit and lulled to sleep. The fact that Jezebel was getting her servants; those who are deceived, what they "want," what their flesh screams out for, tickles and pleases the flesh. They are happy in the fact that their flesh is pleased.

In the Book of Revelation, this is demonstrated clearly:

But I have this against you: that you tolerate the woman Jezebel, who calls herself a prophetess [claiming to be inspired], and who is teaching and leading astray my servants and beguiling them into practicing sexual vice and eating food sacrificed to idols (Revelation 2:20 AMP).

Jezebel's whole purpose is to lead astray the servants of God, to beguile them into practicing sexual vice and *eating food sacrificed to idols.* Jezebel wants to keep us at her table no matter how she can do that. It actually gives her strength when we come to her table because she is feeding our carnal self by getting us the things our *flesh desires.*

How is it that we can eat food sacrificed to idols? When we go to Jezebel's table and eat with her, her food is sacrificed to idols, to Baal and Asherah. Therefore, being in fellowship with her happens when we eat at her table. (Remember here to keep the person separated from the spirit because the ultimate desire is for the person who is used by Jezebel to be set free. However, it is a process because the Jezebel spirit is allowed to operate to the depth of the wounds that are in the person's soul. Therefore, there has to be a process of deliverance and healing.) She knows how to keep us in her web. The only way to get out of her web is to be crucified with *Christ Jesus!*

THE GREATNESS OF GOD DRAWS JEZEBEL

It was the greatness of Naboth's destiny that drew the attack of Jezebel against his life. Naboth talked about not giving up his inheritance when Ahab tried to persist at getting the land of Naboth. Land here is representative of promises, likened to the Promised Land. In addition, inheritance here is likened to the inheritance that God has for His people.

When we wake up to the greatness of God in us, Christ in us that is when we become a threat to Jezebel. It is somewhat like the movie, *The Matrix*. Once we start increasing in the greatness of Christ in us, the Anointing, the spirit of Jezebel sucks on the life of God in us. The more of the life of God we have in us, the more it sucks it out. When Neo was in the pod in the Matrix, he was asleep to destiny. While he was asleep, the whole time the machine had suctions in his body, all down his spine and in other parts of his body where it was sucking the life out of him in order to get its power, its ability to operate. Likewise, Jezebel will use our carnal nature that is not transformed into Christ to keep us in her web of deceit in the pod where she is sucking on the anointing. She tries to keep us little.

When I was coming forth into the call of God on my life and my husband and I were stepping out in ministry, the Jezebel spirit tried to operate through others to keep me "little." There was a constant wrestling in the spirit; Jezebel would come to me and say, "little Robin," trying to keep me little, keep me in a low position. God awakened me to this strategy and showed me that the spirit of Jezebel was trying to keep me pressed down. It was then that I woke up and wrestled in the spirit saying, "No! I am not what you say. *I am what God says!* I have a destiny of greatness, not what you say!" I did this spiritually for three to four years and finally got a breakthrough, and because of overcoming that spirit several times, the authority of Christ in me has increased.

When people wake up to this type of greatness, that's when Jezebel will start her normal attack of sending messengers of *death*, much like what happened to Elijah. Her strategies are the same—to send messages of death to put you in fear.

> *So she wrote letters in Ahab's name and sealed them with his seal and sent them to the elders and nobles who dwelt with Naboth in his city. And in the letters she said, Proclaim a fast and set Naboth up high among the people.* ***And set two men, base fellows, before him, and let them bear witness against him, saying, You cursed and renounced God and the king. Then carry him out and stone him to death.*** *And the men of his city, the elders and the nobles who dwelt there, did as Jezebel had directed in the letters sent them. They proclaimed a fast and set Naboth on high among the people.* ***Two base fellows came in and sat opposite him and they charged Naboth before the people, saying, Naboth cursed and renounced God and the king. Then he was carried out of the city and stoned to death*** (1 Kings 21:8-13 AMP).

Here Jezebel sent messengers again. Remember Jezebel has plenty of servants so she is not going to do something herself; her job is to keep her web of deceit with her servants, not to actually use her time carrying out the attack. Therefore, the messengers of death kill Naboth. When we wake up to the greatness of God in us, the spirit of Jezebel is going to send her servants to constantly speak death to our destiny, to our inheritance, so that we will agree with her and not wrestle with her and put her in her place. We have to understand that this spirit wants us dead; it does not like us, so we should have no mercy with the spirit! Have mercy with the person it's operating through, but not the spirit.

> *Then they sent to Jezebel, saying, Naboth has been stoned and is dead.* **Then Jezebel said to Ahab, Arise, take possession of the vineyard of Naboth the Jezreelite which he refused to sell you, for Naboth is not alive, but dead.** *When Ahab heard that, he arose to go down to the vineyard of Naboth the Jezreelite to take possession of it* (1 Kings 21:14-16 AMP).

Once Jezebel gets her messengers to do the dirty work, she will come to us as though she is the one carrying out all of the details and efforts for the Lord. She doesn't let us know that she just sucked on other people's anointing of Christ in them to deceive them and trick them into carrying out her dirty work, even though they truly believed they were carrying out the Word of the Lord. She keeps all of her worker bees in fellowship with her, but not with each other. Jezebel gets jealous and suspicious when her worker bees begin having fellowship outside of her presence. Therefore, she keeps a division in the camp among the worker bees to keep them in her web of deceit and under her spell to carry out her work.

When King Ahab got the news, all he heard was that Naboth was dead. He didn't know that Jezebel had her messengers kill him. So to Ahab, it looked like it was God who killed Naboth. It looks like God brought on the destruction, which is not truth, but a lie from the enemy. That is why it is so hard to see the reality of the true God at work when people are in a Jezebel group or under that spirit's control. The Jezebel spirit goes to great lengths in order to make people think they are doing the will of God when they are doing the will of satan.

THE STRATEGIES OF JEZEBEL

Holy Spirit showed me the tactics Jezebel uses in attacking others in order to continue her ruling and reigning. Jezebel had taken a position of queen in the natural when she married King Ahab. Likewise, in the spirit, the spirit of Jezebel is a queen, one who rules in the demonic realm. Let me first preface this by saying that everyone has some type of control tendency or leaning in their fallen nature, their sin nature. Therefore, not every control issue is of Jezebel. Remember, we are born into this fallen world with iniquitous roots and our flesh, both of which we have to overcome.

What I am referring to here is the actual spirit of Jezebel who's entire intent is to take dominion over others in order to rob them of their destiny, add to her own camp, and bring about death by causing others to worship other idols and commit acts in which she leads many people astray from the living God (see Rev. 2:20). The deceit comes in when it truly looks as though she is serving the living God, but she truly is not because she is in rebellion to God's plans and purposes. Rather she is having others serve her, and she is serving Baal and Asherah.

Moreover, this spirit manipulates others so that when she is operating, she has them utterly convinced that she is serving the living God. She operates and controls others out of their own woundedness so that they truly think she is a hero of sorts. Usually, the Jezebel spirit will try and rise to a place of authority if she can in order to usurp authority. We will get into her tactics in a minute. Remember, when I say *her*, I am referring to the spirit of Jezebel, but she can operate through both males and females. Again we are to separate the spirit of Jezebel from the person through whom she is operating. The person through whom the spirit is operating has allowed her to do so as a result of that person's own woundedness from a series of injuries received in life from abuse, rejection, abandonment, and shame. Therefore, it is necessary to pray for the person through whom it is operating. Here, we are going to be talking about overthrowing the spirit, not the person.

God hates this spirit and He clearly demonstrates in His Word that He does not tolerate this spirit:

> *I know your record and what you are doing, your love and faith and service and patient endurance, and that your recent works are more numerous and greater than your first ones. But **I have this against you: that you tolerate the woman Jezebel**, who calls herself a prophetess [claiming to be inspired], and who is teaching and leading astray my servants and beguiling them into practicing sexual vice and eating food sacrificed to idols* (Revelation 2:19-20 AMP).

God does not tolerate the spirit of Jezebel, and it is necessary for us to see and understand that we are in a holy war, the war that satan has brought upon this earth when he fell from Heaven. Satan hates God and longs to take as many souls as possible with him to hell before the final judgment day. Therefore, the ultimate goal of the spirit of Jezebel is to bring about spiritual death to others. If the spirit cannot bring about spiritual death, then the ultimate goal is to stop people's destinies and to bring death to their marriages, families, and so forth. The goal of the Jezebel spirit is to destroy, to bring about death. This happens as a result of her enticing people not to do the will of the Father.

> *Enter through the narrow gate; for wide is the gate and spacious and broad is the way that leads away to destruction, and many are those who are entering through it. But the gate is narrow (contracted by pressure) and the way is*

straitened and compressed that leads away to life, and few are those who find it. **Beware of false prophets, who come to you dressed as sheep, but inside they are devouring wolves. You will fully recognize them by their fruits.** *Do people pick grapes from thorns, or figs from thistles? Even so, every healthy (sound) tree bears good fruit [worthy of admiration], but the sickly (decaying, worthless) tree bears bad (worthless) fruit.* **A good (healthy) tree cannot bear bad (worthless) fruit, nor can a bad (diseased) tree bear excellent fruit [worthy of admiration]. Every tree that does not bear good fruit is cut down and cast into the fire** (Matthew 7:13-19 AMP).

Here, Jesus is saying that we are to be sober so that we are not deceived by false prophets. The false prophets are those who sit at Jezebel's table, the ones who carry out the will of her gods, Baal and Asherah. She feeds the false prophets and uses many of them to prophesy lies and speak the messages of her gods. Jezebel's prophets speak death, not life.

In this passage, Jesus showed us the way to determine if people are doing the will of God and serving Him—examining their fruit to see what they produce. They appear to be sheep, of God, but they are wolves, not of God. Similarly, the Israelites were deceived because they truly believed they were worshipping God in the desert when they made the molten calf, but they were not (see Ex. 32:3-5). Moreover, it is not impossible, if we could ask the Israelites during Ahab's time if they believed they were worshiping the true God, that some would have said yes. They truly believed they were worshiping the real God, but in reality they were worshiping the devil.

Therefore, the way to stay sober and to know who is of God is to examine people's fruit. The fruit is the production of people's life, ministry, and service. It demonstrates who they are worshipping. The fruit of the spirit is identified in Galatians 5:

> *But the fruit of the [Holy] Spirit [the work which His presence within accomplishes] is love, joy (gladness), peace, patience (an even temper, forbearance), kindness, goodness (benevolence), faithfulness, Gentleness (meekness, humility), self-control (self-restraint, continence). Against such things there is no law [that can bring a charge]. And those who belong to Christ Jesus (the Messiah) have crucified the flesh (the godless human nature) with its passions and appetites and desires* (Galatians 5:22-24 AMP).

The fruit of the Holy Spirit, of God, is love, joy, peace, patience, kindness, goodness, faithfulness, gentleness, and self-control. These fruit of the Spirit is present when someone is pursuing God's will, serving the Lord Jesus Christ, and being led by the Holy Spirit.

However, a Jezebel spirit does not bear the fruit of the Spirit; rather the Jezebel spirit bears the fruit of the flesh.

> *Now the doings (practices) of the flesh are clear (obvious): they are immorality, impurity, indecency, Idolatry, sorcery, enmity, strife, jealousy, anger (ill temper), selfishness, divisions (dissensions), party spirit (factions, sects with peculiar opinions, heresies), Envy, drunkenness, carousing, and the like. I warn you beforehand, just as I did previously, that those who do such things shall not inherit the kingdom of God* (Galatians 5:19-21 AMP).

The fruit of the flesh is carried out when the Jezebel spirit is present. There is jealousy, strife, anger, enmity, selfishness, divisions, and so forth. Therefore, in order to first overthrow the

Jezebel spirit, we have to look at the fruit to identify if the person or group operating in this spirit is carrying out works of the flesh or works of the Spirit.

> *Therefore, you will fully know them by their fruits.* **Not everyone who says to Me, Lord, Lord, will enter the kingdom of heaven, but he who does the will of My Father Who is in heaven.** *Many will say to Me on that day, Lord, Lord, have we not prophesied in Your name and driven out demons in Your name and done many mighty works in Your name?* (Matthew 7:20-22 AMP)

Even many who thought they were doing the will of God will see on the Day of Judgment that they were in fact not doing His will at all. Even though they prophesied in the name of Jesus and the cast out demons in the name of Jesus, as well as doing mighty works, they were not doing the work of the Lord at all. Rather, they were doing their own will or the will of the devil, which can be carried out by the Jezebel spirit.

Therefore, it is possible to be in a Christian group, even a prayer group, and believe you are doing the will of the Father and later find out that you were not doing His will at all, but serving your own or the devil's will. The way to know is by examining the fruit of that person or the group. Do they have contentions among each other or other Christians; is there selfishness or strife in the group?

Understanding the Operations of Jezebel

I have been attacked many times over by the spirit of Jezebel that operates in willing vessels it chooses in order to rob me of my own destiny, marriage, family, and health. When I was attacked by this spirit, it would operate mainly through three methods. These methods were revealed to me when I watched a video with

Jason Westerfield[1] on the witchcraft spirit and how witchcraft operates. Jezebel operates on witchcraft because it is rebellion, not doing the will of God. Therefore, the Jezebel spirit will operate three ways: *1) intimidation, 2) putting you on the defense and 3) self-pity.* She moves in these ways in order to do whatever she can to keep you in her web of deceit and control you. When she is controlling you, then she can make you serve her and her demonic plans rather than God's plans.

Therefore, when we are being attacked by a Jezebel spirit, she most likely is going to wait to bring an all out assault until after she has already flattered us and made us feel accepted, as though she totally understands you. Later, you will find that she begins to attack you by causing you to be *intimidated,* using fear to cause you to submit, which often causes a spiritual paralysis. I have felt this often when I encounter someone with a heavy Jezebel spirit because this person ends up coming on really strong and acting as though this person is the expert and the only one who truly knows how to do things.

For example, for years I have served in ministry, serving others and pressing into a deeper relationship with Jesus. I felt as though I had given my last blood almost to serve as I did, sacrificing my family, marriage, and time with God. When I informed the lady whom I had been serving in ministry that I was unable to do something she asked me to do, immediately she started snapping at me and telling me I could not receive correction and I was in rebellion. Holy Spirit showed me that she was controlling me and I was hearing God and that it was time for me to step away from the work that I had been doing for this person. This person then spread news to others saying I was in rebellion and I would not serve her as I had been asked to. The woman I had been serving was trying to intimidate me into serving.

Other times, I have had people come against me in ministry, trying to control me and intimidate me as though I was doing the work of the devil and they were doing the work of God. In each circumstance, the situation tried to make me feel inadequate, to make me give up on my call, to pull me from my husband and family, and to rob me of serving the will of God for my life. I had to press in and not be intimidated or afraid of others.

Next, the spirit of Jezebel will try to put you on the defense. If you are not intimidated by the spirit of Jezebel, she will often try another approach within the same conversation or engagement. When she sees that you are not intimidated, she will try and put you on the defense so that you feel as though you are at a great inquisition, having to give answers or justify your position. *Do not answer* people when they are operating in contentions or strife. It is of the devil; it is a control that is operating by making you feel as though you have to defend yourself.

Many times this would happen when I knew that God had told me to do something, and when I was not intimidated by Jezebel these people would play 21 questions and make me feel as though I owed them answers. However, I did not owe them answers at all. If you begin answering their questions, the Jezebel spirit has accomplished what she set out to, which is to keep you engaged with her in an argument or debate.

Holy Spirit showed me many times over how Jezebel has done this to me. Even in our ministry 22 IS 22 (Isaiah 22:22 Company), there was a season when I was being attacked by Jezebel at every front, from the north, south, east, and west. At the north end, people were telling me that I was not ministering correctly, and moreover, that I was a woman and in rebellion because my husband should be teaching and leading the meetings. My husband, Rich, set them straight. However, they continued the attack and even tried to bring me up to a hearing of sorts at a church that was not even my church, and the pastor there was not even my pastor and was not involved in any measure with our ministry. It was crazy. Holy Spirit showed me the trap and said, "Do not go to the church and answer their questions as to why you and your husband do the ministry work of the Lord the way you do." On the South front I had other people calling me and coming against me and my husband because we do not have television in our home and haven't for years. They tried to put me on the defense and come against me in many measures, saying I was a horrible mother. I finally had to see that I was to only answer to God, to confer with husband and God.

Finally, if that doesn't work, the spirit will operate in self-pity and the victim mentality, getting you to feel sorry for her. When you begin to come in and say, "Oh, I'm sorry," she will then bite you and pull you back into the cycle of intimidation, defense, and self-pity. Those are the three tactics of Jezebel. Later we will discuss dismantling her throne and the victory you receive. However, for the first part of overthrowing her, you have to know her strategies and come against falling into her web of deceit and attack.

DISMANTLING JEZEBEL'S THRONE

God's ultimate goal is for the people who are operating in the Jezebel spirit to repent from their works and return to the Lord. In Revelation 2:21 the Word states, *"I gave her time to repent, but she has no desire to repent of her immorality [symbolic of idolatry] and refuses to do so"* (AMP). Therefore, our prayer should be that God open the eyes of the person or group of people who are operating in the Jezebel spirit. God demonstrates that He will bring judgment to the people yielded to this spirit, such as anguish. Moreover, the people who are serving this spirit will experience pressing distress and severe affliction until they repent of the conduct or doings of Jezebel's affairs and work.

Take note: I will throw her on a bed [of anguish], and those who commit adultery with her [her paramours] I will bring down to pressing distress and severe affliction, unless they turn away their minds from conduct [such as] hers and repent of their doings. And I will strike her children (her proper followers) dead [thoroughly exterminating them]. And all the assemblies (churches) shall recognize and understand that I am He Who searches minds (the thoughts, feelings, and purposes) and the [inmost] hearts, and I will give to each of you [the reward for what you have done] as your work deserves (Revelation 2:22-23 AMP).

I believe in being overly cautious because, in spiritual matters, as it relates to repenting, it does not hurt to be overly cautious. Therefore, I repent to the Lord if there has been anything in my life that has led to any works or affairs of Jezebel that I unknowingly or knowingly have perpetuated. Pray this prayer:

Father God I repent for any works I knowingly or unknowingly have committed in my actions and heart that have perpetuated the work of the spirit of Jezebel in my life. I ask You, Holy Spirit, to search my heart and expose to the light any ways in me that are connected with the spirit of Jezebel. I thank You, Jesus, for Your Blood that redeems me from sin and iniquity, and I appropriate Your Blood to completely annihilate the iniquitous root in me that has provided a hook for Jezebel to utilize me. I ask for forgiveness, God, where I have had any unforgiveness in my heart toward anyone and repent for that unforgiveness in Jesus' name. I ask You, Holy Spirit, to expose to the light any wounds I have in my soul that are present and in need of healing that have been used as a hook for the spirit of Jezebel. I repent for not coming to You, God, for complete healing of my soul, and right now I ask You, my Great Physician, to bring the Sword of the Spirit into my heart and go to the places of woundedness to bring Your divine and complete healing in Jesus' name. Amen.

Praying the prayer above is the first step to overthrowing the throne of Jezebel in your life.

Next, God brings us up in a warrior anointing to come forth and annihilate this spirit. This is not for the faint-hearted, because once we start coming against the spirit of Jezebel, she will take opportunities to hit us on every end imaginable to stop our progression in overcoming her. We are to show the love of God, and it is the love of God that turns people to repentance (see Hos. 11:4). But when it comes to the spirit of Jezebel, we are to be confrontational.

For example, when I came from having the tentacles of Jezebel pulled out of my spiritual spine, as I discussed earlier, I realized that the very life of God had been sucked out of me and by no means did I ever want that to occur again. Moreover, this spirit had nearly destroyed my marriage and my family because the person through whom she operated began to puppet me and would on occasion make me think poorly of my husband and would absorb most of my time so that I was being pulled from spending time with my family. The crazy thing is that it was to do spiritual activities.

I cannot repeat it enough; this spirit looks spiritual and as though she is doing the work of God, but if she has a prayer meeting, and God has told you to spend time with your family instead of attending the prayer meeting, then she will tell you that you are in rebellion because you are not doing the will of God. The prayer above that you just prayed gives Holy Spirit permission to expose with the light areas in which you might be doing spiritual matters, but once the truth is exposed, you might realize that Holy Spirit wants you spending more time with your family to pour into them and love them as God desires.

When the spirit of Jezebel is not puppeting you and you have broken out of her system, then the attack is totally different; she wants to destroy and annihilate you, your present victory, and your destiny. When I broke out of the system of the spirit of Jezebel and saw the deceit, then the attack turned into me being discredited and called Jezebel myself. Many people acted as though I was carrying out the plans of the devil, and people called me angrily, acting like I was supposed to follow through with certain activities I had in the past in caring for others physically and doing particular ministry activities that I had stopped.

Once you get out of the system, there is a violent wrestling that you have to do with a two-sided coin. You have to have love on one side, to love those with in whom this spirit operates to control them. It is imperative to pray for the person/group and to bless them in the midst of the attack. God is using this opportunity that satan's attack has brought against you by the spirit of Jezebel to test the love of God, the mercy of God, within you. There is always a mercy test before promotion, and believe me, we are getting to that part. Therefore, this testing of your faith, which is more precious than gold, will bring about an increased measure of God's mercy within you to make you that Romans 9:23 vessel of mercy on which He can pour more of His glory.

And [what if] He thus purposes to make known and show the wealth of His glory in [dealing with] the vessels (objects) of His mercy which He has prepared beforehand for glory (Romans 9:23 AMP).

The other side of the coin is to become a valiant warrior to violently seize the Kingdom of Heaven by force by annihilating every assignment of the spirit of Jezebel through prayers and declarations. The prayer strategy is to press into God so that you can know His strategy, His plan for coming against the assignment of Jezebel, and the appointed time to overthrow her throne. When you get ready to dismantle Jezebel's throne in a person's life, many times the person is being attacked by the spirit of Jezebel. Therefore, you have to pray in the anointing and not in your flesh. You can sit here and say words such as "In Jesus name, I dismantle the throne of Jezebel...." However, if you do not have the anointing at that moment to do that very thing, then you are doing it in the flesh. Therefore, the prayer part of warring is pressing into God to get His Word, His strategies, His plans for dismantling Jezebel's throne in your life and in the lives of others. *Glory!* Woo! I'm getting fired up!

God has an anointing He wants to give His people for being valiant warriors to come against the spirit of Jezebel. Holy Spirit has come upon me at times to pray this mantle on many people—the mantle of Jehu, who was a warrior king who went to Jezebel's home to confront the demonic force and destroy her. Remember, we are talking about the spirit. Therefore, when we overthrow Jezebel's thrown, we are overthrowing the spirit of Jezebel.

And Elisha the prophet called one of the sons of the prophets and said to him, Gird up your loins, take this flask of oil in your hand, and go to Ramoth-gilead. **When you arrive, look there for Jehu son of Jehoshaphat son of Nimshi; and go in and have him arise from among his brethren and lead him to an inner chamber. Then take the cruse of** *oil and pour it on his head and say, **Thus says the Lord: I have anointed you king over Israel. Then open the door and flee; do not tarry.** So the young man, the young prophet, went to Ramoth-gilead. And when he came, the captains of the army were sitting outside; and he said, I have a message for you, O captain. Jehu said, To which of us? And he said, To you, O captain. And Jehu arose, and they went into the house. And the prophet poured the oil on Jehu's head and said to him, Thus says the Lord, the God of Israel: **I have anointed you king over the people of the Lord, even over Israel. You shall strike down the house of Ahab your master, that I may avenge the blood of My servants the prophets and of all the servants of the Lord [who have died] at the hands of Jezebel.** For the whole house of Ahab shall perish, and I will cut off from Ahab every male, bond or free, in Israel. I will make the house of Ahab like the house of Jeroboam son of Nebat and like the house of Baasha son of Ahijah **And the dogs shall eat Jezebel in the portion of Jezreel, and none shall bury her. And he opened the door and fled** (2 Kings 9:1-10 AMP).*

Jehu was anointed by one of the young prophets, who had been instructed by Elisha, to be the King over Israel. Kings in God's Word signify ruling and reigning, so when the young prophet anointed Jehu, he anointed him to take his position of rightful authority, rightful ruling and reigning to bring down Jezebel herself. It's this anointing we receive from Holy Spirit by being in Christ Jesus. Thus, we arise in our rightful position of authority as a Royal Priesthood, the portion of royalty being that of a king or queen where we have the anointing to destroy the spirit of Jezebel.

When Jehu came out to the servants of his master, one said to him, Is all well? Why did this mad fellow come to you?

And he said to them, You know that class of man and what he would say. And they said, That is false; tell us now. And he said, Thus and thus he spoke to me, saying, Thus says the Lord: I have anointed you king over Israel. **Then they hastily took every man his garment and put it [for a cushion] under Jehu on the top of the [outside] stairs, and blew with trumpets, saying, Jehu is king!** *So Jehu son of Jehoshaphat, the son of Nimshi, conspired against Joram [to dethrone and slay him]. Now Joram was holding Ramoth-gilead, he and all Israel, against Hazael king of Syria, But King Joram had returned to be healed in Jezreel of the wounds which the Syrians had given him when he fought with Hazael king of Syria. And Jehu said, If this is your mind, let no one make his escape from the city [Ramoth-gilead] to go and tell it in Jezreel [the capital]* (2 Kings 9:11-15 AMP).

When you arise in this anointing, your anointing through Christ Jesus, and are in proper authority to annihilate this spirit, it is not only evident to you, but to others who are around you that the authority of God has increased in you. You have to understand that God is a purposeful God, and He would not simply allow you to go through so much warfare and attack of the enemy, not putting more on you than you can bear, with it being in vain! No God has a purpose! The purpose is for you to come forth into the authority that is already at work within you, the power of God Himself arising in you to come against the enemy!

Therefore, when you have been attacked by Jezebel, that is when your authority *glory* is increasing! It is not merely evident to you, but others can also recognize the authority of Christ in you increasing. They see that you walk in a greater anointing, a greater authority to come against the works of the devil, especially the spirit of Jezebel, not only for your life, but for the lives of others!

When I overcame the attack of Jezebel against my own life, something happened and a switch flipped inside of me; all of a sudden the warrior that I had been had changed. I became infused with a fiery anointing and a zeal of God, the anointing of God's name Jealous, the purpose of which is to protect covenant, to *make war* against the enemies of God! I no longer did spiritual warfare in a defensive posture! No! I began to *make war,* to get on the offense with the devil and to go to the devil's camp, Jezebel's camp to make war against that spirit! I was not scared anymore of devils. **I knew who my God is, and my God is bigger than any devil!** Moreover, I knew who I was in Jesus Christ!

During the attacks of Jezebel on my life, I had gotten into a deep dark pit, and the only people who could fit in that pit were me and Jesus. I could see my husband at the top of the pit saying, "Robin, you are going to make it." However, Rich, my husband, could not be in the pit with me because it was a work that God was bringing forth in me to know who I am in Christ Jesus and to shift all of my identity to Christ instead of who I thought I was because of my past and present circumstances.

And all I can say is that the devil was stupid enough through the attack of Jezebel, to drop one more straw on me from the east side (you will know what east side means as you continue reading). When the Jezebel spirit came against me on the east side, Holy Spirit infused me with my identity in Jesus Christ as not only the Lamb, but also the Lion of the Tribe of Judah, and I was changed. I was different. The part of Jesus Christ that is the Warrior King came forth in me, and I came out of that pit like Superman! Jehu did the same thing after he was anointed as king.

So Jehu rode in a chariot and went to Jezreel, for Joram lay there. And Ahaziah king of Judah had come down to see Joram. A watchman on the tower in Jezreel spied the company of Jehu as he came, and said, I see a company. And Joram said, Send a horseman to meet them and have him ask, Do you come in peace? So one on horseback went to meet him and said, Thus says the king: Is it peace? And Jehu said, What have you to do with peace? Rein in behind me. And the watchman reported, The messenger came to them, but he does not return. Then Joram sent out a second man on horseback, who came to them and said, Thus says the king: Is it peace? Jehu replied, What have you to do with peace? Ride behind me. And the watchman reported, He came to them, but does not return; also the driving is like the driving of Jehu son of Nimshi, for he drives furiously (2 Kings 9:16-20 AMP).

King Jehu was focused and did not turn to the left or to the right when the horsemen came to Jehu. He did not become distracted; he did not have time to talk, but all he could do was tell them to "fall in!" That is what the Jehu anointing, the anointing of a warrior, does to you when it comes upon you. It brings you up as a mighty warrior to keep your focus and to call forth the troops of God to fall in behind you. Moreover, here the Word talks about Jehu's "driving," his going forth. Jehu had a reputation that the watchman knew his driving, and the watchman reported that Jehu was driving "furiously." When this warrior anointing comes upon you, you will drive with a focus, with a fury from the Lord that satan and his minions will recognize, especially Jezebel. It is that anointing that comes upon you by Holy Spirit that causes you to *arise* and see your enemies scattered!

Moreover, the field in which the enemy met Jehu was the field of Naboth, the person whom Jezebel had stoned and gave his land to King Ahab. When God anoints you with this anointing, you will be able to come forth like a mighty warrior in the anointing of God's name Jealous. The purpose of this name is to bring forth the scorn of God against those who have touched the apple of God's eye. Holy Spirit showed me that God's name Jealous (see Exod. 34:14) has a purpose, to "protect covenant." (I get into detail with this dimension of God in my third book, *At His Feet.*)

That dimension of God to protect covenant causes two things, it causes a protection mode of God to come forth to cover His people when He senses that the covenant is going to be threatened, when His people are harmed. Also, it causes God to bring forth scorn against our enemies. God's name Jealous is in this warrior anointing; therefore, the fruit of this anointing is to come forth in the acceptable year of the Lord, the *Day of Vengeance* of our God (see Isa. 61:2) for God's people. Therefore, Jehu met the enemy head-on in a place where God was taking vengeance on Naboth's death by Jezebel. God even brought to Jehu's remembrance how He would avenge Naboth and his sons in verse 26:

> *Joram said, Make ready. When his chariot was made ready, Joram king of Israel and Ahaziah king of Judah went out, each in his chariot.* ***Thus they went out to meet Jehu and met him in the field of Naboth the Jezreelite. When Joram saw Jehu, he said, Is it peace, Jehu? And he answered, How can peace exist as long as the fornications of your mother Jezebel and her witchcrafts are so many? Then Joram reined about and fled, and he said to Ahaziah, Treachery, Ahaziah! But Jehu drew his bow with his full strength and shot Joram between***

his shoulders; and the arrow went out through his heart, and he sank down in his chariot. Then said Jehu to Bidkar his captain, Take [Joram] up and cast him in the plot of Naboth the Jezreelite's field; for remember how, when I and you rode together after Ahab his father, the Lord uttered this prophecy against him: As surely as I saw yesterday the blood of Naboth and the blood of his sons, says the Lord, I will repay you on this plot of ground, says the Lord. Now therefore, take and cast Joram into the plot of ground [of Naboth], as the word of the Lord said. When Ahaziah king of Judah saw this, he fled by the way of the garden house. Jehu followed him and said, Smite him also in the chariot. And they did so at the ascent to Gur, which is by Ibleam. And [Ahaziah] fled to Megiddo and died there. His servants took him in a chariot to Jerusalem, and buried him in his sepulcher with his fathers in the City of David. In the eleventh year of Joram son of Ahab, Ahaziah's reign over Judah began (2 Kings 9:21-29 AMP).

When Jehu was on his way to carry out the final execution of Jezebel, he carried forth God's vengeance on behalf of Naboth. We likewise, can carry out the vengeance of God, being led by Holy Spirit, when we start calling back what the canker worm and locusts have eaten in the midst of the attack of Jezebel in the lives of those to whom Holy Spirit leads us.

Now when Jehu came to Jezreel, Jezebel heard of it, and she painted her eyes and beautified her head and looked out of [an upper] window. And as Jehu entered in at the gate, she said, [Have you come in] peace, you Zimri, who slew his master? Jehu lifted up his face to the window and said, Who is on my side? Who? And two or three eunuchs looked out at him. And he said, Throw her down! So they threw her down, and some of her blood splattered on the wall and on the horses, and he drove over her. When he came in, he ate and drank, and said, See now to this cursed woman and bury her, for she is a king's daughter. They went to bury her, but they found nothing left of her except the skull, feet, and palms of her hands. They came again and told Jehu. He said, This is the word of the Lord which He spoke by His servant Elijah the Tishbite, In the portion of Jezreel shall dogs eat the flesh of Jezebel. The corpse of Jezebel shall be like dung upon the face of the field in the portion of Jezreel, so that they shall not say, This is Jezebel (2 Kings 9:30-37 AMP).

Here Jezebel was trying to flatter one last time before she was annihilated. She heard of what Jehu did, and she fixed herself up, trying to become pleasing and appealing to the warrior Jehu. Moreover, she called Jehu, Zimri, which means "praise worthy." The root word in Hebrew is a musical instrument, so she was actually praising Jehu for annihilating the King of Judah, one through whom she manipulated and operated. When you are getting ready to overthrow Jezebel's thrown, she will have flattery and try to distract you from your course of action.

Finally, Jehu arrived, came forth in the anointing of a warrior king, and had Jezebel's eunuchs throw her down, fulfilling the prophetic word of the Lord that the dogs would eat the flesh of Jezebel. In this area, Holy Spirit showed me that once you come forth in the warrior anointing and confront the spirit of Jezebel, she has *no power!* Moreover, those who have been serving her are the ones who throw her down! That is symbolic! Jehu came forth in a warrior anointing and asked who was on his side. Those who had been under the spell, under the rule of Jezebel, when the warrior anointing arrived, turned against her. When that anointing comes upon you by Holy Spirit, it awakens those who have been in a spiritual slumber! The anointing destroys the yoke of bondage! Then Jehu said *"Throw her down!"* This has many levels of meaning. Jehu has those who were her servants throw her down, and Jehu also spoke an apostolic word, as one being sent to throw her down.

Here is the declaration part of coming against Jezebel and dismantling her throne. After praying as Holy Spirit leads you, when you get the green light by Holy Spirit, declare in that apostolic anointing from the Lord that comes upon you that you dismantle and throw the spirit of Jezebel off of her throne, the place where she had been ruling and reigning! Remember Jezebel is a queen and the whole purpose of that spirit is to rule and reign in every area she can. Therefore, you have to dismantle her throne as you are led by Holy Spirit in that particular area.

God has me do this for others who have been attacked by Jezebel and for ministries that have been attacked by Jezebel. As I press in to pray for others, Holy Spirit will come upon me like He did Jehu, when he was anointed by the young prophet, to come forth like that of a wild ox and receive the new anointing (see Ps. 92:10) to declare:

I take the Sword of the Spirit, and I pull you down, Jezebel. I dismantle your throne in this ministry in Jesus' name! I call forth the utter annihilation of your seed, Jezebel, of all that you have sown in this ministry and in the lives of those attached to this ministry in Jesus' name! I call in the blood of Jesus to infuse every area where the seed of Jezebel has been destroyed and to redeem the time, break the curse, and fulfill the promise of God for this ministry in Jesus' name! I speak life to this ministry and prophesy that this ministry will live and not die in Jesus' Name! I call in the fiery breath of God to infuse this ministry and the people attached to the ministry and declare that they will fulfill the call of God on their lives in Jesus' name! I call forth the throne of Jesus Christ to be established in this ministry and declare that of the increase of God's government and of His peace there will be no end, upon the throne of David and over His kingdom, to establish and uphold it with righteousness and justice from the latter time forth, and the zeal of the Lord will perform it in Jesus' name! (see Isa. 9:7).

Glory! One last thing—when God wants to promote you from one level of glory to another, from one place of authority to another, guess what is most likely going to happen? That's right—an attack from the spirit of Jezebel against your life. Holy Spirit showed me that God keeps His promises and His Word, and when God wants to increase your ministry and your authority in Christ Jesus, at times you will have an opportunity to overcome the spirit of Jezebel, which we see in Revelation 2:

But to the rest of you in Thyatira, who do not hold this teaching, who have not explored and known the depths of Satan, as they say—I tell you that I do not lay upon you any other [fresh] burden: Only hold fast to what you have until I come. **And he who overcomes (is victorious) and who obeys My commands to the [very] end [doing the works that please Me], I will give him authority and power over the nations; And he shall rule them with a sceptre (rod) of iron, as when earthen pots are broken in pieces, and [his power over them shall be] like that which I Myself have received from My Father; And I will give him the Morning Star. He who is able to hear, let him listen to and heed what the [Holy] Spirit says to the assemblies (churches)** (Revelation 2:24-29 AMP).

Here, to those who hold fast to the Word of the Lord in overcoming Jezebel, God promises that He will give *"authority and power over the nations"* and that they will *"rule them with a scepter rod of iron, as when earthen pots are broken in pieces"* and the power they receive shall be like that which Jesus received from God! Moreover, He will give them the Morning Star! This anointing is to increase their authority not only in Heaven, but *on earth now!*

God wants to increase your spiritual authority; the authority that Jesus received from God is available for you *now* on this earth when you overcome the spirit of Jezebel! You will receive the Morning Star, a revelation of Jesus infused in you that will *shine like the stars and win many to righteousness!* When God wants to grow your ministry, you must get ready to overcome this spirit. He keeps His promises, which are yes and amen, and He wants to give you His promises! So when God wants to give you an increased measure of spiritual authority, most likely you will have a Jezebel spirit that you will have to overcome so that He will bring you up into an increased measure of authority. And the whole purpose is that Christ in you the hope of glory is not only realized, but actualized in the winning of many to righteousness to Jesus!

God, I pray that everyone reading this teaching will be anointed with the same anointing of Jesus Christ—the Lion of the Tribe of Judah, who is returning on a white horse, with His robe dipped in blood, who wages war in righteousness, whose name is the Word of God—and will carry out Your battle plan in Jesus' name! That same warrior anointing, warrior mantle, that rested on Jehu, I call it forth by Holy Spirit upon your sons and daughters in Jesus' name! God I declare that they will *arise* in the *power* of *Your might* and that their enemies will be scattered by

Christ in them, the hope of glory! I declare that they are entering another level of glory, another level of authority, another level of knowing and understanding Christ in them, the hope of glory in Jesus' name! I apply the blood of Jesus over them and ask Holy Spirit that You would seal the Word of God. And, God, I ask that over Your Word in their lives there will be a 100-fold return *now* in *Jesus' name!*

Woo hoo!!!!

Endnote:

1. http://www.youtube.com/watch?v=1nn7tKjpd60

About Robin Kirby-Gatto

Robin Kirby-Gatto is the author of *The Glory to Glory Sisterhood series* by the unction of the Holy Spirit. She drives to get the GGS series out to the female gender in order to bring down strongholds among women corporately and individually and bring godly unity. Some strongholds that exist are competition, rejection, jealousy, fear, and much more. The first book, *God's Sorority*, deals with how GGS was created by God to invade the earth realm beginning in the year 2007, along with what sister's are to do and not do toward each other, as well as seeing Jesus as the lover of their souls.

The series has now been picked up by Destiny Image and the revised first book, *Glory to Glory Sisterhood; God's Sorority* was released on July 1, 2010. It is revised to include much more, including offense and the glory of God. The book brings readers into a purging of ungodly behaviors that might hinder the advancement of the Kingdom of God and then brings them through the Redeemer, Jesus Christ, and the Glory of God meant for His daughters. Robin is promoting the book in partnerships. If you want further information, contact her at 205-862-6152.

The second book, *Princess Warriors*, deals with the fear of the Lord and spiritual warfare. *Princess Warriors* equips women to battle for their lives, families, destinies, churches, communities, and nations. The third book, *At His Feet*, deals with strongholds set up by satan to keep women in bondage. *At His Feet* addresses forgiveness, rejection, jealousy, and unhealthy devices that have set up residence in women's minds. *At His Feet* brings full deliverance to women who are dealing with strongholds and bondage. The last book, *Destiny*, releases women into their destiny and empowers the female gender to become a big sister in God's Sorority, whereby the reader becomes a reproducer of the seed of Jesus Christ, bringing Heaven down to earth.

Robin has a bachelors and masters degree in Social Work and her Juris Doctorate. She has been married to her wonderful husband, Rich Gatto, since 2001 and has two wonderful sons, Christopher and Matthew Kirby.

Robin has a ministry God's Fire Wall in which she equips people for the Prophetic Mantle upon their life and brings the Fire of God (http://Godsfirewall.com). She and her husband have a prophetic ministry for young people called 22 IS 22 (Isaiah 22:22 Company), which equips young people with the prophetic mantle to take dominion over the earth by opening doors for the Kingdom of Heaven that no person can shut and shutting doors to the kingdom of darkness that no person can open. In addition, she has her own ministry, Princess Warriors, where she receives the war strategy from the throne of God for each season and trains women to rise up and become mighty warriors.

Currently, Robin is ordained under Advocate Ministries in Irondale, Alabama.

Robin ministers under the unction of the Holy Spirit and operates in many of the gifts of the Spirit. Her office as teacher is coupled with her prophetic anointing and the fire of God. She receives from the throne the coming move of God and speaks it into the lives of those with whom she comes in contact. Her desire is not only to minister to people in the Church, but to also be Christ outside of the Church. She does power evangelism while shopping, pumping gas, walking in the park, and accomplishing other daily activities. One of her favorite sayings is, "The enemy has a plan, but God has an appointment, which will disrupt the enemy's plan." Robin loves to see God bring freedom to everyone!

GOD'S FIRE WALL
http://Godsfirewall.com

GLORY TO GLORY SISTERHOOD
http://glorytoglorysisterhood.com

PRINCESS WARRIORS
22 IS 22 (Isaiah 22:22 Company)
http://22is22.com

Other Books by Robin Kirby-Gatto

At His Feet

Destiny

IN THE RIGHT HANDS, THIS BOOK WILL CHANGE LIVES!

Most of the people who need this message will not be looking for this book. To change their lives, you need to put a copy of this book in their hands.

> *But others (seeds) fell into good ground, and brought forth fruit, some a hundred-fold, some sixty-fold, some thirty-fold* (Matthew 13:8).

Our ministry is constantly seeking methods to find the good ground, the people who need this anointed message to change their lives. Will you help us reach these people?

> *Remember this—a farmer who plants only a few seeds will get a small crop. But the one who plants generously will get a generous crop* (2 Corinthians 9:6).

EXTEND THIS MINISTRY BY SOWING
3 BOOKS, 5 BOOKS, 10 BOOKS, OR MORE TODAY,
AND BECOME A LIFE CHANGER!

Thank you,

Don Nori Sr., Founder
Destiny Image
Since 1982